SIR JAMES MACKINTOSH
The Whig Cicero

1 Sir James Mackintosh sketched in old age (artist unknown).

SIR JAMES MACKINTOSH
The Whig Cicero

Patrick O'Leary

'The Holy Spirit hath said that the man who loves conversation will not prosper
on earth'
'from the notes to visitors to the Abbey of La Trappe, quoted in
The London Magazine 1821 February'

ABERDEEN UNIVERSITY PRESS

First published 1989
Aberdeen University Press
A member of the Pergamon Group

© Patrick O'Leary 1989

The Publisher acknowledges subsidy from the Scottish Art Council towards the publication of this volume.

British Library Cataloguing in Publication Data

O'Leary, Patrick
Sir James Mackintosh: the Whig Cicero
1. Scotland. Law. Mackintosh. Sir, James,
1765–1832
I. Title
344.11'0092'4

ISBN 0 08 034531 X

PRINTED IN GREAT BRITAIN
THE UNIVERSITY PRESS
ABERDEEN

Contents

List of Illustrations

Acknowledgements

Thanksgiving and Forewarning

It was while working on an earlier book, *Regency Editor: Life of John Scott,* that I first became interested in his friend, Sir James Mackintosh. Once again it has been my good fortune to encounter much kindness in collecting material for this biography of one of the best loved—and worst hated—men of his time (1765–1832).

First and foremost I wish to thank the Honourable Dr Margaret Buxton and her family, who welcomed me to their home and allowed me free access to their Mackintosh manuscripts, and also provided some illustrations. Lord Bridges and the Hon Anne Farrer kindly provided further material.

I am specially indebted to Mr Hensleigh Wedgwood who allowed me to share the fruits of his own research and airmailed across the Atlantic copies of two rare portraits. It was a further advantage to have read the book of which he is co-author with his wife Barbara, *The Wedgwood Circle,* a real-life Forsyte Saga which will surely one day become a television classic. Another family descendant, Mrs Margaret Boxall, allowed me to make use of the scrapbook assembled by Sir James's granddaughter, Julia (Snow) Wedgwood.

Other manuscript material quoted in this book includes: letters in the Blair Adam Papers (by permission of Mr Keith Adam); Lord Woodhouselee letter (by permission of Colonel Angus Cameron); Mackintosh letters to Sir William Scott and notes for a lecture (Yale University Library); Longman Archive material held at the University of Reading, by permission of the company; letter to Earl Moira (The Huntington Library); extracts from the Brougham papers and the Goldsmid Letterbook (University College Library); extracts from the Fraser-Mackintosh Collection (printed with the approval of the Keeper of the Records of Scotland, ref GD128/48); extracts from the Farr manuscripts (by courtesy of Edinburgh City Libraries); Mackintosh letters (National Library of Scotland); extracts from Crown-copyright records in the Public Record Office (HO 42/46, 42/22 and 23, 30/22, and WO 12/5105) appear by permission of the Controllers of Her Majesty's Stationery Office.

John Murray (Publishers) allowed me to quote from Byron's Letters and Journals ed Leslie A Marchand, and Creevey's Life and Times, ed John Gore.

A work of this kind taxes the resources of many libraries (and the patience of their staffs). In addition to those already named above, I owe much to the British Library in its various branches at Bloomsbury, Colindale and the India Office collections; I have also drawn extensively on the Wedgwood papers owned by the Wedgwood Museum Trust and deposited at the University of Keele; the British Library of Political and Economic Science allowed me to see manuscripts, as did Cambridge University Library and the Bodleian Library. Among those who sent me valuable material or information were: Dyfed County Library, Highland Record Office, Harry Ransom Humanities Research Centre, University of Durham Department of Paleography and Diplomatic, Hereford Record Office, Lincoln's Inn Library, the Royal Medical Society, and Avon County Reference Library.

Others who kindly answered my queries or opened their doors to me included: the libraries of Aberdeen University, the Athenaeum, Canning House, Christ Church, Oxford, London's Guildhall, Dr Williams, Buckinghamshire County Library, the Wellcome Institute for the History of Medicine, Dove Cottage, University of Glasgow, Hughenden Manor, Oriel College and New College, Oxford, Birkbeck College (University of London); the record offices of Devon, Bristol, Greater London, Hampshire, Derbyshire, Gwent, and Surrey. Additional libraries consulted were: Boston Public, North Yorkshire, the National Library of Wales, Charleston County Library (South Carolina), the Library of Congress, Ealing Central, the Newberry, New York Public, South Caroliniana (at the University there), William L Clements, Westminster Public, and of course two personal favourites, the London Library and Highgate Literary and Scientific Institution.

Many other bodies were helpful: Brooks's, the Travellers Club, and the Oriental, Keats House in Hampstead, Inverness District Council, Sun Alliance Insurance Group, Coutts & Co, Times Newspapers Archives, the Royal Society, the Royal Society of Literature, the National Portrait Gallery of Scotland. So were individuals: Mr Robert McGillivray, co-editor of the Clan Chattan Journal, Mr E E F Smith of Clapham Antiquarian Society, Reverend Father C Copleston, Mr James D Scarlett, Mr E George, and Lord Abinger.

If anyone has been overlooked I hope they will believe that my regret is as sincere as their own, and that such omission is a failure of memory and method, not of manners. Any other mistakes in this work are also mine alone.

Some warnings on editing: for the sake of clarity and to avoid the sickening (*sic*), in transcribing Mackintosh family manuscripts I have silently corrected obvious slips of the pen and of grammar, and have occasionally modernised and regularised spelling. I have not tampered with the sense. After some thought, I have not attempted to follow Sir James's style of capitalising every second or third noun in his letters and journals. It seemed only to make him harder to read without adding anything in compensation. Like many Georgians he used the dash as an all-purpose mark of punctuation. I have, where appropriate, substituted full-stops, semi-colons, and commas, since it would hardly be right to invest his prose with the nervous energy of Byron.

Finally, a note on the lack of running annotation. I write primarily with the general reader in mind, and it seems unfair that he or she should have to suffer the distraction and expense of pages spattered with little numbers and a lengthy appendix of tiny letters and numbers. If anyone would like chapter and verse for any quotation or statement in this book, they can write to me and I will do my best to provide them. I cannot of course promise access to material which, as I write, is still in private hands.

Chapter One

Prodigy from Loch Ness

James Mackintosh was born on 24 October 1765 in a mansion since transformed into Aldourie Castle on the south bank of Loch Ness, some seven miles from Inverness. 'No Highland gentleman need want a goodly-spread family tree', as Thomas De Quincey declared, and the boy had an imposing pedigree. In middle age he prepared a genealogical survey which began: '1. MacDuff Thane of Fife . . . 1057 defeat and death of usurper MacBeth.'

His family were of the Kyllachy branch of Mackintoshes and part of the Highland confederacy, the Clan Chattan. They were also linked by blood or marriage to Frasers, Grants, Mackenzies, Mackays, Campbells, Stuarts, and other famous names. Nevertheless the baby was poor; his father, John, was easy-going and as the younger son of a younger son had no easy fortune and no prospects beyond his army lieutenant's pay. The broken leg he suffered when hit by a musket ball in the Seven Years War in Germany left him with a limp which made it difficult to gain promotion.

The mid eighteenth century was a time of particular hardship for the Highlanders. Many men who survived the bloody battles which ended attempts to restore the Stuart dynasty in 1715 and 1745–6 went to America, either sentenced to transportation as rebels, or driven there by poverty.

Among them was James Mackintosh's maternal grandfather Alexander MacGillivray, who became a merchant in South Carolina. He married Ann Fraser, and their daughter Marjory, the mother of James was described by De Quincey as a native of that place, then a colony. But when her son drafted an inscription on her memorial he said she was 'born at Dalziel, near Inverness' in 1739.

Although Aldourie had once been part of extensive lands owned by the Mackintoshes of Kyllachy, Marjory was only a guest there when James, her first child, was born. The cottage called Clune where she lived with her mother and sisters on the estate had been damaged by fire, and they were given refuge in the mansion by a relative, William Fraser. The boy's father, Lieutenant John, had been posted a few months   before to the 68th Regiment of Foot stationed on the West Indian island of Antigua.

Consequently the boy's early years were guided by his mother and grandmother, with additional spoiling from two aunts. James wrote 30 years later of life in the cottage, which still stands although it has been enlarged on the outskirts of the village of Dores, looking down on Loch Ness. He recollected

> the prospect from the window of our little parlour, of the lake with its uninterrupted expanse of twenty-four miles, and its walls of perpendicular wooded rock; the road that leads down to the village, all its windings, all the smallest objects on each side of it; the little path where we walked down the burn, and the turf seat where we rested, are more present to my fancy than any other objects in nature.
>
> My mother was not happy. My father, a subaltern and younger brother, found his pay not too much for his own expenses, and all the kindness of her family did not deliver her mind from the painful feelings of dependence. This perhaps, contributed to the extreme affection which she felt for me . . . There is nothing which so much lightens the burden of receiving benefits as the pleasure of conferring them.
>
> I alone depended upon her. She loved me with that fondness which we are naturally disposed to cherish for the companion of our poverty. The only infant in a family of several women, they rivalled each other in kindness and indulgence towards me, and I think I can at this day discover in my character many of the effects of this early education.

Lieutenant John's regiment remained on Antigua for six years. But he was not entirely separated from his wife for the couple had two more children whose births were recorded in the parish of Dores, John born 15 March 1769, and Anne on 9 November 1771. It seems the little family were too busy with their own affairs to notice when an oddly-assorted couple passed through the village in 1773—Dr Johnson and Boswell on their way from Inverness to the Western Isles. Mackintosh never met the Doctor, although proud to be elected late in life to The Club which he founded; Boswell he knew only in decline.

In spite of his father's absence, the boy was interested in his exploits. One of the first pieces of writing that lodged in his memory was an account of the Seven Years War in *The Scots Magazine*, lent to him by local Minister John Grant. His love of learning was apparent, and in 1775 James went to school at Fortrose on the Black Isle, overlooking the Moray Firth. He owed this to a bachelor uncle, Captain Angus Mackintosh, who paid the bills for his first two years there.

He was groomed as a gentleman as well as scholar, for among the items charged were five shillings for 'cock's fight dues', and 18 shillings 'for three months fees at the dancing school, minuet, country dances and horn-pipe etc' with additional expense for taking a partner to a ball. During his five years at school he lodged in Fortrose, spending holidays with relatives. In a memoir of his early life, Mackintosh wrote:

> An usher of the school, one Duncan, who boarded in the same house with me, was suspected of some heretical opinions. The boarding mistress, who was very pious and orthodox, rebuked him with great sharpness; and I remember her reporting her own speech to her husband, and the other boarders, with an air of no little exultation . . .
>
> My boarding mistress, the schoolmaster, and the parson, were orthodox Calvinists. I became a warm advocate for free will, and before I was fourteen I was probably the boldest heretic in the county.

This first master, William Smith, was strict but competent. On his death, Mackintosh wrote, 'he was succeeded by the usher, a man of the name of Stalker, of great honesty and good nature, but far too indulgent to me to be useful . . . He employed me in teaching what very little I knew to the younger boys. I went and came, read and lounged, as I pleased.' As his mother had difficulty in paying the fees, he may have been under pressure to assist in the school. His continued education rested mainly on incessant reading, and a remarkable memory. The Clune cottage contained some books, including Pope and Swift, and in spite of his father's protests that studious ways were unmanly he often spent all day with a book and picnic lunch out in the hills. At night he would read in bed by candlelight, to the alarm of a Mackintosh uncle with whom he stayed who feared his house might be burned down.

From an early age he was eager to display his knowledge, leading one old lady to remark 'he was a spontaneous child'. On another occasion a professor from Aberdeen staying with a relative of the Mackintoshes, Sir Alexander Mackenzie of Coul, mentioned that while rambling round Fortrose he met a boy whose conversation and appearance impressed him. Sir Alexander told him 'everybody knows that boy—that Jamie Mackintosh'.

At thirteen the prodigy proclaimed himself a Whig, and a Whig he remained. The American War of Independence was the main political issue of the 1770s, and a clergyman at Fortrose described how Mackintosh persuaded his schoolfellows to give up part of their playtime to join him in debates. These were based on reports in *The Aberdeen Journal* of speeches in the House of Commons by Lord North, prime minister, and the opposition orators, Charles James Fox and Edmund Burke. According to the clergyman, the Reverend John Wood, James liked to harangue his audience in the character of Fox or Burke, but if no one replied he would change roles, becoming Lord North and refute his own

Whig arguments. Seeing both sides of a question was good training for a future judge but of doubtful value to a politician.

Meanwhile his family were the victims of various misfortunes. Lieutenant John's regiment returned from Antigua, but was redeployed in Ireland. At the cottage about 1776 one of the MacGillivrays had an argument with a neighbour, young Fraser of Foyers, and struck him over the head with a bottle. Fraser escaped through a window but died later; his assailant took refuge in America.

James's benefactor, Captain Angus, also crossed the Atlantic, but in honourable circumstances. For some time he farmed the family estate of Kyllachy, renting it from his aunt Elizabeth, widow of Alexander Mackintosh, a cloth merchant in London's Lombard Street. Judging from letters to agents in charge of his Scottish affairs, Alexander was businesslike to the point of brusqueness. After unexpectedly inheriting the land he succeeded in restoring the family fortunes to some extent. Kyllachy, 'The Place of Grouse Cocks', overlooks the River Findhorn, south of Tomatin in Inverness-shire. It still possesses wild beauty well-suited to the clan badge which shows a Cairngorms cat-a-mountain with the motto, 'Touch not the cat but (without) a glove.'

Although Captain Angus had lost his right eye in the German campaigns he was no more inclined than John to settle down. He wrote to Colonel Sir Robert Murray Keith, under whom he served, complaining of his 'life of dreary retirement, confined to the plough', and volunteered for the American war. There he died of fatigue and exposure, at Beaufort, near Port Royal, in 1779.

Another relative, General Lachlan Mackintosh of Georgia, fought with distinction on the other side in the war. The captain's second brother, James Mackintosh, who was a trader among the Chickasaw Indians in South Carolina, also died. The American war had already cost the life of Brigadier-General Simon Fraser, brother of the fond grandmother of young James. He was shot near Saratoga in 1777; General John Burgoyne attended the funeral of the man he called his gallant friend. The Fortrose schoolboy had begun to compose verse, and he wrote an elegy on his great-uncle.

A bigger blow was about to fall. On his return from the West Indies, Lieutenant John tried to win promotion and an active posting against a background of mounting money problems. Letters from his wife at Clune, as he moved from London to Ireland and back to England, showed their plight. One dated 21 February 1778 in which Marjory addressed him as 'my beloved friend' and begged him to 'spare your money, every shilling of which is now a sum to us', declared: 'My mind is so taken up about you, day and night that I neither know what to do or say. Pray God my dearest friend may get a company of invalids in some comfortable place.' Another letter complained she had no money for James's board at the Fortrose school, and reproved his father for not writing to the boy, whom she wished to send to university at Aberdeen.

Her husband replied with a touch of exasperation, it was beyond his power to educate the two boys as she wished. The most he could hope was that James might go to India in a minor post in the East India Company, and John, when old enough, would go there as a soldier. Even these appointments would require the influence of 'Mrs Fraser'.

Writing from Dublin he exerted his charm on the distraught Marjory:

> Amiable and lovely as you always appeared to me since first we were acquainted you never could be dearer to my heart than you are at this instant . . . I am much at a loss at present which way to get home should I get leave but you may assure yourself in whatever manner it will be on the wings of love.

Finally, promotion was obtained, in 1779 John Mackintosh became a captain in the second battalion of the 73rd Regiment. But this was no company of invalids, the unit was about to embark for Minorca, then in British hands. His wife refused to cope any longer with debts, children and angry relatives. She travelled down to Plymouth and sailed with him.

Marjory Mackintosh did her best to ease the pain this separation caused her son in ways calculated to amuse a growing boy. She sent him an account of the great sea battle off Cape St Vincent in January 1780, fought at night in a storm, when Admiral Sir George Rodney defeated a Spanish fleet. The British warships were convoying troopships carring the 73rd Regiment and those on board had a good view of the action. James received one more letter from his mother—'in her last she sent me two Scotch bank-notes of one pound each, which seemed at that time an inexhaustible treasure'.

When the convoy reached Gibraltar, the Rock was under siege by Spaniards hoping to take advantage of Britain's preoccupation in America. In command was Governor George Augustus Eliott, who retained the battalion of the 73rd to reinforce his own troops instead of sending them on to Minorca. This probably saved Gibraltar, but Minorca fell. Bombardment from land and sea caused casualties, but the garrison suffered chiefly from poor food, scurvy and the discomfort of being quartered in ruined buildings, hardships which affected civilians as much as soldiers. The wife of Lieutenant-Colonel William Green, engineer in charge of defence works, kept a diary of the siege. On 17 June 1780 she wrote: 'Capt. Mackintosh's Lady (73rd) died suddenly this day.'

John Mackintosh was a widower, without capital and far from his three children. He even had to borrow money to meet the funeral expenses. His one resource was his commission, at that time a sizeable asset; a fellow officer had just sold his captaincy to a lieutenant for £2,400 and was to sail home. Captain John sent a humble memorial to Lord Amherst, army commander-in-chief, describing his 22 years as an officer, and stating he had

> continued to do duty without intermission further than was occasioned by an infirm state of health contracted from his service abroad. This your memorialist feels with concern he is no longer able to discharge, and his anxiety is heightened with the thoughts that his children in Scotland require his care, and might be left destitute by his death.
>
> To his own services your memorialist hopes he will derive some additional consideration from those of his brother, Captain Angus Mackintosh of the 71st Regiment, twenty years a faithful servant of his Majesty, and who lost his life in Georgia.

The petition ended with a request to sell his commission at the regulated price. It was not immediately accepted, and the captain remained on Gibraltar until the siege ended in 1783. At least he knew he had played a role in the outstanding victory of a war marked by British disasters.

The name John Mackintosh is now much honoured in Gibraltar. But the bust in the main piazza, which is named after him, commemorates a merchant and benefactor to the community who died there in 1940. His father was a native of Scotland.

Captain Mackintosh's eldest child had left school for university, travelling to Aberdeen by hired chaise in October 1780. There he attended King's College, following the example of his great-grandfather, Angus Mackintosh, more than a century earlier. He later wrote:

> I had brought with me to college a collection of my verses, which were so generally read that I gained the most undeserved name of 'the poet', by which I was known for two or three winters. My manuscripts were shown to the learned Dr Charles Burney, then finishing his term at Aberdeen.

The young poet was delighted when told the doctor said 'in his opinion, I should go on and might do well'.

He remained a studious reader. Only fifteen, he bought *Institutes of Natural and Revealed Religion* by Joseph Priestley, James Beattie's *Essay on Truth*—'which confirmed my disposition to metaphysical inquiries'—and Bishop Warburton's *The Divine Legation of Moses Demonstrated*—'which perhaps tainted my mind with a fondness for the twilight of historical hypothesis, but which certainly inspired me with that passion for investigating the history of opinions which has influenced my reading through life'.

During his second winter in Aberdeen (the boys spent summers at home), Mackintosh's tutor was Dr James Dunbar:

> Under his care I remained till I left college. He taught mathematics, natural and moral philosophy, in succession. His mathematical and physical knowledge was scanty, which may, perhaps have contributed to the scantiness of mine. In moral and political speculation, he rather declaimed, than communicated (as he ought) elementary instruction.

However, the young Whig forgave his mentor because he was liberal in politics and opposed the American war. When Lord North resigned in 1782 Dr Dunbar went up to his pupil in the street and declared: 'Well, Mr M, I congratulate you:—the Augean stable is cleansed.'

More to his taste were lectures on Latin literature given by Professor William Ogilvie; Mackintosh learned much of Cicero's works by heart, providing him with a store of quotations through life. But he did not disdain lighter fare. A favourite book was *The History of Miss Betsy Thoughtless* by Eliza Haywood whose novels were noted for thinly disguised portraits of her contemporaries earlier in the century and scandals associated withe them. It became a life-long foible of James to read trashy fiction as eagerly as more serious publications.

He continued to heighten his conversational powers by pitting his wits against anyone who would argue with him. His favourite antagonist at Aberdeen was Robert Hall, a student who later became a noted dissenting preacher at Cambridge. Mackintosh said of him:

> His society and conversation had a great influence on my mind. Our controversies were almost unceasing. We lived in the same house, and we were both very disputatious. He led me to the perusal of Jonathan Edwards' book on Free-Will . . . that most extraordinary man, who, in a methaphysical age or country, would certainly have been deemed as much the boast of America, as his great countryman, Franklin . . . During one winter, we met at five o'clock in the morning to read Greek, in the apartments of Mr Wynne, a nephew of Lord Newburgh, who had the good nature to rise at that unusual hour for the mere purpose of regaling us with coffee.

They were nicknamed Plato and Herodotus by less earnest students.

Such exertions did not dull the Highlander's spirits. One of his contemporaries, later to become the Reverend William Jack, principal of King's College, recalling him 'possessing in his own person all the qualifications of a gay Troubadour' noted for 'general courtesy, tasteful manners, a playful fancy, and an easy flow of elocution'. With qualities like these, the next stage in Mackintosh's life was predictable:

> About the year 1782 I fell violently in love with a very beautiful girl, Miss Scott, daughter of Mr Scott, of Inverness, about three years younger than myself. I wooed her in prose and rhyme, till she returned my passion. For three or four years this amour was the principal object of my thoughts; during one half-year almost the only occupation of my time. I became impatient for an early establishment in life, which should enable me to marry.

But family poverty clouded his otherwise happy career. In three years his expenses reached £154, a considerable sum 200 years ago. He was hurt by hints of extravagance by relatives paying the bills. In the absence of Captain John the management of his son's affairs was left to a kinsman, Bailie John Mackintosh. He did not find it easy.

In December 1782 James wrote to the bailie assuring him of 'my determined resolve to avoid running into debt with the most serious attention', but this was coupled with a request for money to pay for lessons and 'to purchase a gown, my old one being entirely worn out'. When the money did not arrive he wrote again: 'I cannot help being somewhat surprised at not having received any answer.' Mentioning he would be expected to tip college staff at Christmas, he added: 'To me it appears very extraordinary conduct first to send me here and then to refuse what is absolutely necessary for my subsistence.' This tone was not likely to appeal to Bailie Mackintosh who had cares of his own, having just remarried, and also bore some responsibility for young John and Anne.

The next letter from Aberdeen, dated 1 March 1783, was clearly in response to a rebuke. James wrote:

> I should be extremely sorry (considering the numberless favours which you have heaped upon me and upon my father's family) that you could believe me capable of entertaining any other sentiments towards you but those which were dictated by gratitude, by esteem and by respect. Other faults I may have committed but my heart tells me that I never will stoop to the meanness of falsehood or to the vileness of ingratitude. Believe me Sir if anything escaped from my pen inconsistent with what I owed to my best benefactor and my truest friend, it was the hasty effusion of an inconsiderate hour.

He admitted receiving a small sum of money from his father, already on his way home from Gibraltar, but the indulgent soldier had suggested spending this on books and clothes. When he reached England the captain was able to sell his commission. One of his sisters, Catharine, wrote from

Farr to congratulate him, but asked why he was delaying his return to Scotland; the reason became apparent after he had done so. Bailie John received a letter from London dated 19 November 1783 which began: 'Sir, I take the liberty of addressing myself to you as the friend and relative of my husband, Captain John Mackintosh, from whom I have received a letter of a most extraordinary tenor.'

This second Mrs Mackintosh said John parted from her at Newark, Nottinghamshire, in May, and told her it was not convenient to send her money, suggesting she borrow on his credit. Now he wanted to make the separation permanent. Her letter ended:

> If his friends think it more conducive to his interest and happiness that we should live separately matters being properly adjusted I shall not fail to acquiesce, at the same time let it be remembered that he is mine by all laws divine and human and that should it happen that we might pass our lives together I should do the best that neither his friends, his dear children nor himself repent of, S. Mackintosh.

Taxed with this, the gallant captain admitted: 'I am a married man, I hope to a good woman.' But he showed no wish to be reunited with Sarah Mackintosh, and she was content with a deed of separation and payment of £20 a year.

Rebukes from the bailie and love for Miss Scott led James to seek independence by becoming a professor in Aberdeen. It was not altogether a wild ambition, he had the gift not only of acquiring knowledge but of imparting it to others. He sought aid from Major James Mercer, who served with the Mackintosh brothers in Germany, and described John as 'one of the most lively, good-humoured gallant lads I ever knew', and Angus as 'a most accomplished gentleman'. On retirement Major Mercer settled in Aberdeen, writing poetry and moving in literary and academic circles.

He wrote to John:

> I can safely congratulate you upon such a son. He is indeed, a very extraordinary young man. In his literary studies he is highly accomplished, and what is equally surprising, and perhaps of equal importance in life, the propriety and elegance of his manners are such as to attract the notice of every person who is but for a moment in his company.

Nothing came of this attempt to make the university his career, and after receiving his degree on 30 March 1784, James left Aberdeen. His summing up on four years there: 'I finally quitted college with little regular and exact knowledge, but with considerable activity of mind and boundless literary ambition.'

He was now potentially a man of property. Captain John, the sole survivor of three brothers, was head of the Kyllachy family. But this was of little benefit to him since his aunt, sometimes known as Lady Kyllachy, still held a life-interest in most of the estate's revenues. Young Mackintosh would need to earn his living.

> My own inclination was towards the Scotch bar [he wrote], but my father's fortune was thought too small for me to venture on so uncertain a pursuit. To a relation from London, then in the Highlands, I expressed my wish to be a bookseller in the capital, conceiving that no paradise could surpass the life spent amongst books, and diversified by the society of men of genius . . . He astonished me by the information that a creditable bookseller, like any other considerable dealer, required a capital, which I had no means of commanding, and that he seldom was at leisure to peruse any book but his ledger.

It was decided he should study medicine, and in October he went to Edinburgh. Riding south he tumbled from his horse, and suffered a broken tooth which marred the attraction of his smile, and was later the target for an unkind gibe. James no longer wanted a home of his own, love for Miss Scott had cooled, and she eventually married an Inverness doctor, but he still envied the life of a professor. A year after reaching Edinburgh he put himself forward as successor to Adam Ferguson, who resigned as professor of natural philosophy at the city's university. Professor Ferguson treated the young man kindly, but the post went to Dugald Stewart, who became a revered figure among Scots intellectuals, not least Mackintosh himself.

He was not yet done with Highland ways. His chief, since known as The Mackintosh, retained the right to call out members of the Clan Chattan, although nobody any longer expected a Jacobite rising, or a battle over territory, as in the past between the Mackintoshes and the MacDonalds. In the autumn of 1785 Chief Aeneas asked young James to accompany him to the ancient rendezvous of Brae Lochaber. Captain Mackintosh was apparently still short of money, in spite of selling his commission and receiving some £43 in prize money, for he asked a friend to provide his son with a few pounds for the excursion. In later life James liked to recall this event, and the danger he ran of being engaged in a second Mulroy, a seventeenth century affray in which the MacDonalds routed his own clan.

But his arrival in Edinburgh opened a new world. At that time Oxford and Cambridge universities granted degrees only to students who paid at least lip service to the established Church of England, so nonconformists went to Scotland, making it a haven for anyone of a speculative turn of mind. Mackintosh enjoyed the hospitality of his mother's cousin and her husband, Ann and Alexander Fraser Tytler. Tytler, who later became a judge as Lord Woodhouselee, was a history professor, and at his home this young relative met many notable men, including Henry Mackenzie.

He lost no time in plunging into the medical world; it might have been better if he had hesitated. Controversy raged over theories put forward by John Brown who, having been secretary to Dr William Cullen, professor of practical medicine, decided to found a new system of healing. Some of his ideas were sounder than those of conventional teachers, he realised the fallacy of purging and bleeding patients already at a low ebb. Unfortunately his recipe for raising their spirits involved liberal doses of alcohol, especially when mixed with opium as laudanum. His prescriptions were more attractive to the young than the conservative wisdom of septuagenarian Dr Cullen.

> Within a few weeks after my arrival in Edinburgh, I became a Brunonian. [James wrote]. This extraordinary man . . . had the usual turbulence of an innovator, with all the pride of discovery, and the rage of disappointed ambition. Conscious of his great powers, and very willing to forget the faults which obstructed their success, he gladly imputed the poverty in which he constantly lived to the injustice of others, rather than to his own vices. His natural eloquence, stimulated by so many fierce passions, and delivered from all curb by an habitual or rather perpetual intoxication, was constantly employed in attacks on the systems and doctrines, which had been the most anciently and generally received among physicians, and especially against those teachers of medicine who were most distinguished at Edinburgh . . .
> I was speculative, lazy and factious, and predisposed to Brunonianism by all these circumstances . . . During a fever with which I was attacked, Mr Alexander, a very excellent young man, the son of a physician at Halifax, visited me. He was a zealous Brunonian. By his advice I swallowed a large quantity of wine, and by that prescription I either was, or seemed to be, suddenly and perfectly cured. I suddenly became a Brunonian . . . In three months after my arrival in Edinburgh, before I could have distinguished bark from James's powder, or a pleurisy from a dropsy, I discussed with the utmost fluency and confidence the most difficult questions in the science of medicine.

These discussions centered on the meetings of the Royal Medical Society, which Mackintosh attended first as a visitor. After listening for a time, he asked permission to speak, and so impressed his audience that he was immediately elected to the society. Among members were Thomas Addis Emmet, later arrested for political activities in Ireland, and Thomas Beddoes, whose career as a doctor was almost as eccentric as Brown's own. Debates were sometimes so heated that the society passed a rule forbidding duelling, on pain of expulsion.

Mackintosh became one of the four presidents elected annually. He received a similar honour from the Speculative Society, devoted to literature and science, where his first speech was against the slave trade. He made friends of several men who became eminent, including Charles Hope, judge, Malcolm Laing, historian, and Benjamin Constant de Rebecque, whose later career embraced literature, politics and Mme de Staël. Constant was already writing for newspapers, and liked to play cards until two or three in the morning.

Another boon companion at the Speculative was John Wilde 'full of information and knowledge, a most amusing speaker and delightful companion, and one of the most generous of men'. Wilde sounds like a willing lender; he became professor of civil law at the university and finally went mad. Discipline was not strict, and James was more regular in attendance at the societies than at lectures. As he put it, 'Accurate and applicable knowledge was deserted for speculations not susceptible of certainty, nor of any immediate reference to the purposes of life.' Even John Brown chided his disciple for spending too much time defending his opinions, instead of 'coming to his lectures to learn them'.

Bacchus and Venus held court at Edinburgh, as well as Dr Brown. John Fleming, a fellow student related of James:

> The literary fame which the superiority of his talents had acquired at Aberdeen, travelled before him to Edinburgh; and on his arrival, his acquaintance and company were eagerly courted by those students who aspired to equal eminence, or who embarked on similar pursuits. If Edinburgh afforded him more various facilities for improvement, it also held out opportunities of pleasure and dissipation, in which even the most cautious youth is often too prone to indulge.
>
> Young Mackintosh was not altogether proof against the frailties of his age, and he indulged pretty freely in all those enjoyments in which its ardour and impetuosity are wont to revel. The character, however, of his dissipation was very different from that of the generality of young men. Whatever might be the inconstancy of his other amours, the love of knowledge never once deserted him; for whether he sighed in the Idalian groves, or joined in the roar of the convivial board, he had constantly a book in his hand, and most commonly an ancient or a modern poet, upon whose sentiments or diction he frequently interposed some observations, and to which he endeavoured to direct the attention and remarks of others. He was thus unremittingly active in the exercise of his mind, and thus happily contrived to imbibe instruction with his wine.

A less discreet picture of this early life was drawn long after by Elizabeth Stuart, who became his sister-in-law. She said one of the student's Clune cottage aunts, worried by his failure to write to them, made the long journey to find out what was happening: 'Mary

MacGillivray came to Edinburgh and turned away a Mistress Mackintosh.' The culprit bore no grudge, for Elizabeth, who presumably heard the story from him added: 'In compliment to his aunt Sir James called his eldest daughter Mary.'

The habit of mixing drink with the pursuit of knowledge was carried back to the Highlands on his vacations. One of his Fraser uncles lived at Moniack, near Inverness. When Mrs Fraser could not find the key to the wine cupboard one day, she sent a servant in search of her nephew. He was found in a pool near the house, busy feeling his pulse to discover the difference made by plunging into the water. The key was in the pocket of his waistcoat by the pool.

Despite such wildness, at the end of his studies in autumn 1787 examiners showed no hesitation in making him a doctor. They were impressed by his thesis on the action of muscles, and readiness in answering questions. But obtaining degrees in the eighteenth century was more a formality than an ordeal.

Dr Mackintosh showed no urgency about putting his qualifications into practice. remaining in Edinburgh for weeks before returning home. There he considered going abroad, as so many of his relatives had done. Young men could make their fortunes in the service of the East India Company, and he sought the help of Hector Munro, MP for the town of Inverness, who himself prospered as an army officer on that subcontinent. On 26 February 1788 he wrote to Wilde at Edinburgh: 'The grand difference between my India plan and any British settlement is that the former supposes an appointment, the latter requires expenditure. The difference is unfortunately but of too much consequence to me.'

Both he and Wilde abhorred the narrow franchise in Scotland, which meant parliamentary representation depended on a handful of votes in each constituency. But he admitted good-humouredly that his hopes of enlisting the influence of Mr Munro rested on 'that iniquitous traffic of votes you mention . . . I shall be warmly recommended by his constituents'.

How far his father influenced his plans is not clear. A sad little note to him from the young man seems to date from this period, and is apparently the only letter between them to survive. Sent from Inverness it ran:

My dear Sir, I was sorry to have passed you unconsciously yesterday in my way home and would go up today if I knew where to find you as I am told you propose coming down to Farr the west road. If you would be so kind as let me know where I could meet you tomorrow or Saturday if you stay till then I will certainly take a ride to call on you, I am my Dear Sir, Yours very afftly, J . Mackintosh.

The captain did what he could for his other son, John, arranging for him to become an ensign in the army, a rank open to officers' sons at 14. The regiment to which he was attached, the 73rd in which his father served, had been disbanded, so he was entitled only to half-pay.

James now set out for London, bound it was thought for a medical career. But this was a life which rarely went according to plan.

Chapter Two

In Defence of Revolution

On his journey to London in the spring of 1788 Mackintosh was accompanied by Lewis Grant, eldest son of Sir James Grant of Grant, who became Lord-Lieutenant of Inverness-shire. With such a father, the young man, an acquaintance from the Speculative Society, might have been an influential friend, but before long he fell into deep melancholy. The chief benefit the doctor derived was a chance to study derangement closely. In the capital he lived with a cousin, John Fraser, a wine merchant in Clipstone Street, near Fitzroy Square. Nothing more was heard of taking a post in India, but James thought of going to St Petersburgh. Having met Dugald Stewart in London in June, he solicited from him a letter of introduction in which the good-natured professor recommended 'Dr Mackintosh, who proposes soon to go to Russia as a physician . . . and has the reputation of uncommon abilities in the line of his profession'.

This scheme proved transitory, he had never been whole-hearted in his devotion to medicine, and two events in 1788 loosened its ties. His professional mentor, Dr Brown, died after spending two years in London. As he was only fifty-two and left eight children unprovided for, his pupil must have felt doubts concerning the value of Brunonianism.

More significant was the death of Captain John, removing all parental control and raising his son to the status of James Mackintosh of Kyllachy. Status was virtually all the captain, who was buried in Petty Church, had to bequeath, for estate rents still went to great-aunt Elizabeth. However, she had generously helped pay the education expenses of her young relative, and as she was close to ninety those rents would soon be his.

Meanwhile James enjoyed the social pleasures London offered on the eve of a quarter of a century of turmoil and war. It is said 'he was sometimes accustomed to indulge in dancing until the approach of daylight'; those minuet lessons at school were not wasted. When a clergyman who lived nest door to Mr Fraser complained his studies were being disturbed by the noise, he was so charmed by the delinquent's conversation he went away pleased to have made his acquaintance.

Even a Highlander with expectations, who had long abandoned his resolve to avoid debt, needed some income. The insult applied to Hazlitt was that he declined into a journalist; more tactfully one of Mackintosh's biographers said he aspired to become a journalist. He could make money out of his wide reading, and help the Whig side of politics.

Towards the end of the eighteenth century newspapers were beginning to show some of the qualities which transformed them into powerful organs of opinion early in the next. But most of the London press still relied heavily on government bribes, aristocratic patronage, subserviance to advertisiers, and occasional blackmailing of those who wished to keep their names and deeds out of the papers. Ministers looked with contempt on journalists they controlled, and with suspicion on those they did not.

Among those struggling to keep afloat in these unsavoury waters were three Stuart brothers from Edinburgh, who were acquainted with John Fraser and his wife. Charles and Peter Stuart were both at times in the pay of politicians; their much younger brother Daniel was more shrewd than either. He treated journalism as a business, and if his methods were not always above suspicion, they enabled him to retain his independence and eventually become a landed gentleman.

It was not considered respectable to write for money, so contributors either left their articles unsigned or used pseudonyms. Although Mackintosh never acknowledged the connection, it seems likely, as Lucyle Werkmeister has suggested in books on the press of the period, he became associated with *The Star and Evening Advertiser*, edited by Peter Stuart, which first appeared in May 1788. Stuart boasted he had on its staff an authority on insanity. The paper was a strong supporter of the Prince of Wales, then the favourite of the Whigs; when the proprietors protested against their editor's bias, Peter started a rival paper with his brother Charles. This was also called *The Star*, a common trick in circulation wars of the day. This alternative *Star* was distinguished by articles on the leading issue, the ill-health of George III and its political implications.

His indisposition was treated as insanity, although doctors have since suggested a different diagnosis. It was a subject in which Mackintosh took a special interest, attending debates in the House of Commons. The battles he fought by proxy in the Fortrose classroom were now played out before his eyes.

If the King was unable to carry out his duties, there would have to be a regency and the obvious choice was his eldest son, the Prince of Wales. But while Prime Minister William Pitt and his colleagues argued Parliament should have the privilege of nominating the Regent and the right to limit his powers, the opposition, led by Charles James Fox, maintained the Prince should rule as of right. Both parties were fighting for their political lives, since the royal prerogative included power to nominate ministers and dissolve Parliament.

The Prince, following the traditions of the Hanoverian royal family, was at loggerheads with his father. It was assumed he would turn out the Tories and invite his Whig friends, such as Charles Grey, who had joined him in many a convivial evening, to take power. Mackintosh made his own contribution to the controversy with an article in a daily newspaper, *The Gazetteer*, on 11 December 1788. His article was reprinted as a pamphlet, *Arguments Concerning the Constitutional Right of Parliament to appoint a Regency*, claiming in the preface 'the privilege of an Englishman to enquire freely, and give his opinion on public affairs'. That opinion was resoundingly Foxite, and printed in italics:

> *From the moment that the incapacity of the Sovereign to govern is established by constitutional enquiry, from that moment, the Heir Apparent, lying under no disqualification, is, de jure, Regent of these Kingdoms, with all the powers of the prerogative undiminished.*

Allowing Lords and Commons to fetter a regent would, he maintained, be contrary to tradition by allowing two estates to assume the rights of the third. The pamphlet ended:

> May those who know him be permitted to congratulate their country that Heaven has provided the only adequate alleviation of the present calamity in the virtues of the Heir Apparent. Hitherto it has only been for a few to feel in what an irresistible manner he never fails to attach those who know him.

If the writer had been among the privileged few he might have felt less confident of the virtues of a prince who was already dissolute, and eventually deserted the friends anxious to serve him.

The publication did little at the time either for Mackintosh or for the Prince. It was only one of a spate of pamphlets on the subject, and in any case George III soon recovered. No regent was required for another twenty-two years.

At least the author had made contact with a better class of journalist than on *The Star*. James Perry, an Aberdonian, was editor of *The Gazetteer*, where he laid the foundations of a reputation for integrity which lasted to his death. Yet he had sociable habits likely to appeal to his new recruit. It was probably then that Mackintosh met Boswell. When work was done Perry, his future brother-in-law the scholarly but drunken Richard Porson, and Alexander Chalmers, another Scot, would sometimes meet the biographer of Johnson at the Turk's Head coffee house in the Strand. Even Boswell commented on the amount the newspapermen drank.

Perry, who described *The Gazetteer* as 'the Paper of the People', supported Fox'. His views were shared by John Debrett, part-owner of the newspaper and publisher of the *Regency* pamphlet. His premises in Piccadilly were the haunt of like-minded politicians, and sometimes referred to as Debrett's Divan.

Mackintosh's relationship with the Stuart brothers suddenly assumed a new dimension. They lived with two sisters, Catharine and Elizabeth, in Charlotte Street, Portland Place, and Catharine was friendly with John Fraser's wife. On 8 April 1789 James Mackintosh, bachelor, and Catharine Stuart, spinster, were married by licence at St Mary le Bone, in Marylebone High Street, a parish church since demolished. Although the *Memoirs of the Life of Sir James Mackintosh*, edited by his son, give the date as 18 February, church records say otherwise. Possibly this anticipation of marriage is connected with the fact that their first child, Mary, was born on 18 November of the same year. So quiet was the wedding the witnesses were two minor church officials, Thomas Bird and Barbara Roussett.

The marriage angered both families. In Inverness-shire it was seen as another example of fecklessness. The Stuarts had a double reason for displeasure; most of what little money the young couple possessed belonged to Catharine, and she kept house for her brothers. In addition, when she left, she took her young sister with her. However, it proved a happy partnership, for, as in his relationship with his mother, James found shared poverty a bond rather than a barrier.

He thought it prudent to leave London and at last make an attempt to make use of his medical qualifications. They retreated to Bath where his grandmother's brother, William Mackinen Fraser, who had graduated as a doctor at Edinburgh 12 years before his great-nephew, was in practice. But first he would need to draw on the financial skills of Bailie John Mackintosh.

Perhaps James had riotous evenings at the Turk's Head in mind when on 15 June 1789 he wrote to Mary MacGillivray at the Clune cottage:

> I now address my dear Aunt at the first moment of tranquillity that I have enjoyed for nine months and I have escaped from a life in which may Heaven preserve me from being again immersed. I have found Dr Fraser warmly and cordially disposed to serve me and he has presented prospects to my mind which if they have not elated have at least taught me not to despair. The object he has at present in view is a settlement at Salisbury within 40 miles from here where the principal physician is lately dead and where he can procure powerful recommendations. He thinks the expense of

living the first two years will be £200 that the third year will defray itself and that the ultimate object may be £1,200 or £1,500 a year. On the probability of success either there or at some other town where he has no doubt in a few months of advantageously placing me he strongly advises me to convert whatever shreds of property remain in Scotland into ready money and if the reversion be sufficient commit it on the adventure.

Probably aware that such a cavalier attitude to his family estate of Kyllachy would be frowned upon in the north, the young doctor asked Aunt Mary to plead his case with Bailie John, and added:

If the Salisbury plan did not succeed Dr Fraser advises me to take shipping from Southampton (without returning to London) for some village on the coast of France where £20 or £25 would support us for 4 or 5 months in which time he is almost certain of finding a new one for me. I would there finish a medical volume on insanity of which I have already written a part and the publication of which the Doctor approves as likely to be of service to me.

Since Dr Mackintosh and Mrs Mackintosh spent the autumn of 1789 on the Continent the Salisbury plan must have failed. Nor did they enjoy a quiet economical life devoted to his book, presumably a development of the articles in *The Star*. This was unfortunate, for he had views in advance of most practitioners of that day; he regarded insanity as an illness requiring treatment like any other, and not a crime calling for restraint. Although he visited Leyden, famous as a centre for medical scholarship, and Liege, they passed most of their time in Brussels, accompanied by his Edinburgh friend, Alexander. Apart from daughter Mary the principal products of the excursion seem to have been that Mackintosh acquired fluency in French, and first-hand knowledge of erupting revolution in Europe—the people of Liege rose against their prince-bishop in sympathy with neighbouring France which saw the fall of the Bastille.

Doctoring as a career was finally abandoned. Back in London he became foreign editor for a while of *The Oracle*, a daily newspaper belonging to John Bell. At first he was paid by the quantity of material from his pen, but when the proprietor discovered one week's contributions cost ten guineas he protested 'no paper can stand this', and put the writer on a fixed salary. Journalist Mackintosh also renewed his connection with James Perry, providing articles for *The Morning Chronicle*, of which he was now joint-owner and editor. Among contributions form James were letters signed 'The Ghost of Vandeput', and a character sketch of a man he admired, the Count de Mirabeau, the Jacobin who tried to lead France towards constitutional monarchy.

He did not confine himself to foreign politics. He became friendly with Thomas Brand, a religious nonconformist and advocate of parliamentary reform who added the surname Hollis to his own in acknowledgement of a handsome legacy from his friend Thomas Hollis. The Scotsman enjoyed the run of Brand Hollis's library, and frequent entertainment at his table. Another friend who influenced him was a man who extended his name in a similar manner, John Horne Tooke. Having heard Mackintosh speak at a debating society, Horne Tooke carried him and several others off to a champagne supper at his house in Dean Street, Soho. It was the kind of introduction the Highlander liked, and he often spoke warmly of such hospitality. for his part the host had a high opinion of Mackintosh and declared 'he was a very formidable adversary across a table'.

When Horne Tooke stood at the parliamentary election for the constituency of Westminster in June 1790, James canvassed for him, in spite of his boyhood hero Fox being among the three contestants. Fox won easily. Polls for the City of Westminster and the neighbouring County of Middlesex were keenly fought, for they had a much larger and more representative franchise than other parts of the country. There voting was often little more than formal, a small electorate doing as the local landowner directed.

This affair was yet another black mark in the eyes of relatives. An unknown correspondent, possibly wine merchant Fraser, reported to the Highlands: 'Instead of attending to his business, *my gentleman* was parading the streets with Horne Tooke's colours in his hat.' James had the chance to repair his image when he visited Dores that same summer to show off his wife and child to grandmother MacGillivray and his aunts, and to settle his Kyllachy affairs. Although great-aunt Elizabeth had finally died the estate was much encumbered, not least by his own borrowing in advance of his inheritance.

He also sought the advice of his Tytler cousin, now advocate-general for Scotland, about the will of Uncle James, who died among the Chickasaw Indians. He wanted to leave his money to his brothers and sisters, or their children but, as his nephew put it the executor, Daniel Ward of West Florida, 'ungenerously keeps possession of the whole estate', amounting to nearly £1,000. Tytler, pocketing his fee of two guineas, advised that without proper probate of the will nothing could be done.

Perhaps the ease with which two guineas could be earned precipitated the next change in a chequered career. Poor Bailie John was about to receive the blow which convinced him he could no longer support his relative's way of life. James reverted to an earlier ambition, he registered at Lincoln's Inn in London to qualify as a barrister, and he wanted his uncle to raise money to finance his studies and meet other commitments. John Mackintosh gave up administering Kyllachy and it fell under the trusteeship of the Earl of Lauderdale and others.

Such a reaction surprised the new head of the Kyllachy family. In an age when trade was looked down on the professions were the main avenue for a poor man to make his way in fashionable London. Many leading lawyers had humble backgrounds, and some were eminent in politics. Moreover, provided he kept quiet about it, a barrister could supplement his income by writing for the press.

The next business letter from the north came not from Uncle John but his brother, Charles. Writing from Edinburgh on 3 March 1791 to explain the Earl of Moray, who held a mortgage on part of the estate, had decided to foreclose, he said:

> I am sorry to inform you that Lord Moray's men of business have some time ago intimated to me their intention of redeeming the Wadset of Daltonich at Whitsunday next, and they have already begun to take the legal steps for that purpose . . . They have applied to me to know whether you will dispense with legal formalities and grant a voluntary renunciation . . . I think it best to agree with a good grace to what you cannot prevent.

James went to plead with the earl at his London quarters, but found him 'politely evasive'.

Charles's letter also discussed arrangements for disposing of the estate in the event of Mackintosh's death, particularly the jointure or amount to be settled on Catharine. 'Do you mean your daughter to have your estate in preference to your Brother?' Charles asked. 'I think it right your wife's jointure should be heritably secured, but I do not see equal reason for granting heritable security to your sister. I even think her provision should be revokable by you at pleasure in case of her making an improper marriage.'

Meanwhile economy was required. The couple left their house in Buckingham Street, between the Strand and the Thames, and moved to the rural retreat of Little Ealing, Middlesex. While Catharine exercised her talents as a frugal housekeeper the future barrister could study and write without social distractions. For a time the plan succeeded, and Mackintosh turned again to pamphleteering.

Domestic politics were overshadowed by events in France, particularly the consitutional struggle between King Louix XVI, aristocrats, clergy, and reformers in Paris. Late in 1790 Edmund Burke published *Reflections on the Revolution in France*. With all the rhetoric at his command, he damned the revolution and forecast the strife it would entail. What is not always remembered is that the book carried the subtitle *And on the*

Proceedings in Certain Societies in London Relative to that Event. Burke's aim was to discredit not only French revolutionaries but their English sympathisers as well. This broadside was the more effective coming from a Whig who had championed the American rebellion against British rule. Its result was to split the party and alienate the author from his Commons colleague, Fox, who saw the situation of France in 1789 as similar to that of England in 1688 when parliamentary rule was firmly established.

Radicals and liberals sprang to their own defence. Some forty authors published answers to Burke in a few months. Nearly all of these, and the counter publications supporting his views, were uninspired and quickly forgotten. Mackintosh let it be known he was working on something substantial. When Tom Paine, who had sharpened his revolutionary pen during the American war, heard this he said to an acquaintance of the Ealing exile: 'Tell your friend that he will come too late unless he hastens for after the appearance of my reply nothing more will remain to be said.' Although James did hasten, Paine's *Rights of Man* did appear first. It proved to be an enduring work but it went so far towards what was then sneeringly called democracy that it caused many moderate advocates of change to accept Burke's forebodings of where this would lead.

Mackintosh's *Vindiciae Gallicae: A Defence of the French Revolution and its English Admirers,* published in April 1791, redressed the balance. It restored respectability to those who believed England as well as France needed reforms.

Poet Thomas Campbell caught the mood when he said:

> In the better educated classes of society, there was a general proneness to go with Burke, and it is my sincere opinion, that the proneness would have become universal, if such a mind as Mackintosh's had not presented itself, like a breakwater, to the general springtide of Burkeism . . . without disparagement to Paine, in a great and essential view, it must be admitted that, though radically sound in sense, he was deficient in the strategies of philosophy; whilst Mackintosh met Burke perfectly his equal in the tactics of moral science, and in beauty of style and illustration. Hence Mackintosh went, as the apostle of liberalism, among a class—perhaps too influential in society—to whom the manner of Paine was repulsive.

What had set out as a pamphlet turned into a book of some 50,000 words. Nobody can doubt the genuineness of the prefatory remark: 'Had I foreseen the size to which the following volume was to grow, or the obstacles that were to retard its completion, I should probably have shrunk from the undertaking.' The first part was already in the press while he struggled to complete the work at his home in Little Ealing. Lawbooks were neglected, for as a fellow-student said: 'The author was obliged at times to accommodate his studies to the departure of the penny-post, the clamours of impatient compositors, and eagerness of expectant printers' devils.' Catharine was enveloped in the turmoil. He liked her to be with him when he wrote but not to disturb him, so she had to sit still with a book. In the evening they would walk over the fields while he read the manuscript to her.

To compare it with the mighty *Reflections* is scarcely profitable today. Campbell exaggerated, but not wildly, when he spoke of the books as equal. Certainly Mackintosh wrote in much the same lofty strain and poured out his arguments with similar profusion as the man he once described as the most admirable person of the age. The verdict as to who won is probably best left to those intrepid characters who judge the merits of competing brass bands. But Burke had the unanswerable advantage that in a short time the Terror and guillotine proved him an accurate prophet. When James visited Paris eleven years later and received the compliments of Frenchmen on his defence of their revolution he replied: 'Messieurs, vous m'avez si bien refuté.'

That said, there are passages in the volume which can be read with pleasure and even profit two centuries later. Pointing out the state of France at the beginning of 1789 made change inevitable, Mackintosh wrote:

> The advance of Paris to light and freedom was greater in three months than it had been in almost as many centuries. Doctrines were universally received in May, which in January would have been deemed treasonable, and which in March had been derided as the visions of a few deluded fanatics.

Unfortunately he did not foresee where this brisk pace would lead.

But there were more down-to-earth passages which must have made reactionary ministers stir uneasily:

> There are two kinds of inequality; the one personal, that of talent and virtue, the source of whatever is excellent and admirable in society; the other, that of fortune, which must exist, because property alone can stimulate to labour, and labour, if it were not necessary to the existence, would be indispensable to the happiness of man. But though it be necessary, yet in its excess it is the great malady of civil society. The accumulation of that power which is conferred by wealth in the hands of the few, is the perpetual source of oppression and neglect to the mass of mankind.
>
> The philosophers of antiquity . . . wanted an engine wherewith to move the moral world. The press is that engine, and has subjected the powerful to the wise.
>
> The wealth of society is its stock of productive labour. There must, it is true, be unproductive consumers, but the fewer their number, the greater (all things else being the same) must be the opulence of the state.

Mackintosh made bold claims for his own class

> that middle rank among whom almost all the sense and virtues of society
> reside. Their pretended incapacity for political affairs is an arrogant fiction
> of statesmen which the history of revolution has ever belied . . . The
> oppression of England summoned into existence a race of statesmen in her
> colonies. The lawyers of Boston, and the planters of Virginia, were
> transformed into ministers and negotiators, who proved themselves inferior
> neither in wisdom as legislators, nor in dexterity as politicians.

By referring to the American Revolution, James was striking at its
champion, Burke. He did not shirk the issue of the blood already shed in
France, but remarked it should be compared with that spilt by Britain in
attempting to subdue America. He reminded readers also of the price
paid for their own country's Glorious Revolution of 1688:

> The disputed succession which arose from that event, produced a destructive
> civil war in Ireland, two rebellions in Scotland, and the consequent
> slaughter and banishment of thousands of citizens, with the widest
> confiscation of their properties;—not to mention the continental
> connections and foreign wars into which it plunged us.

These were evils on which the author could dwell with feeling; great-
grandfather Angus Mackintosh had been 'out' in the 1715 Rising, and
was imprisoned in London before escaping back to Inverness-shire. Then
there were the loss of Captain Angus in the American war, and the death
of Marjory Mackintosh in Gibraltar.
But he added:

> I do not say (God forbid!) that a crime may be committed for the
> attainment even of a good end; such a doctrine would shake morals to their
> centre. The man who would erect freedom on the ruins of morals neither
> understands nor loves either. But the case of the French revolutionists is
> totally different. Has any moralist ever pretended, that we are to decline the
> pursuit of a good which our duty prescribes to us, because we foresee that
> some partial and incidental evil would arise from it?

Interspersed with such arguments were deft descriptions of individuals,
such as 'the warm and wayward heart of Rousseau', while of Jacques
Necker, the finance minister who tried to avert revolution with tax
reforms, he wrote that he 'would have been adjudged by history equal to
his elevation had he never been elevated'.
Mackintosh declared of English reformers: 'Nothing can be more
absurd than to assert that all who admire wish to imitate the French
Revolution, the conduct of nations is apt to vary with the circumstances

in which they are placed.' He stressed what he and like-minded Whigs sought was not revolution but the redress of grievances: 'We desire to avert revolution by reform; subversion by correction.'

Yet he sounded a call that was to make him an object of suspicion to Tory gentlemen for the rest of the decade:

> A man who should pretend that the reason why we had the right to property is because our ancestors enjoyed that right four hundred years ago, would be justly condemned. Yet so little is plain sense heard in the mysterious nonsense which is the cloak of political frauds that the Cokes, the Blackstones, and the Burkes, speak as if our right to freedom depended on its possession by our ancestors . . . It is not because *we have been* free, but because we *have a right to be* free that we ought to demand freedom.

The *Vindiciae* ran through three editions. If Mackintosh did not quite wake up and find himself famous, he was certainly courted, probably more calculated to promote his career. He became known to Charles Grey, Fox, Samuel Whitbread and other leaders of the party he supported. Dr Samuel Parr, a strange mixture of practical piety and undigested learning who tried to model himself on Dr Johnson while deploring his politics, wrote to Richard Brinsley Sheridan: 'I hope you will read the mighty work of Mackintosh.'

Burke conceded his opponent had written in his own style. The fame of the Highlander, still only twenty-five, spread abroad. His sentiments were naturally popular in France, where part of the book was translated by a future king, and in America. Even Mme de Staël, who revered her father, forgave Mackintosh for his comment on M. Necker. But there were doubts in some quarters. Fox, too busy to read the book, told his nephew, Lord Holland, he heard that good though it was it went too far in some respects.

Apart from publicity the work produced money the author needed badly. Originally publisher George Robinson offered £30 for the copyright, but in view of its success paid more liberally, as Mackintosh wrote to Bailie John. This letter, as usual, struck an uneasy compromise between indignation at what he considered his relative's undue severity over his failings, and the realisation nobody else was capable of preserving his own inheritance.

Dated from Little Ealing 11 November 1791, the letter began:

> The length of my late silence to you demands an explanation, which, though it may not be satisfactory, will, I assure you, be sincere. I have really been considerably occupied, and I had real expectations of visiting the Highlands this season but I will not be so uncandid as not to add that the tone of your last letter was another reason for my long silence. I never,

indeed, questioned the right to admonish and to reprove, which, by so long
a series of benefits, you had so amply acquired . . . But I confess my surprise
that the proposition should have so suddenly estranged you. I was placed in
a situation where prudence exacted the preservation of my property, and
rational ambition my hopes. I have committed myself and my family in the
pursuit of a profession, and I have to conciliate, as well as I am able, that
pursuit, with the important object of preserving my property. The
proposition which I made appeared to me and others, an excellent mode of
conciliating these objects . . .

It having been my own good fortune to raise the money I wanted by the
unexpected success of my book, I have no further cause to keep alive
feelings which never could have been more than temporary . . . The general
popularity and the particular notice of distinguished persons which I have
been so lucky to acquire, have so smoothed the way to success at the bar
that the least sanguine of my friends are no longer doubtful of me. I may,
without vanity, say that the first literary and political characters of the
kingdom have courted my commission, and were I disposed to shipwreck
my future hopes by the prostitution of my character and pen, the
temptation of considerable income is not wanting.

After this display of bright hopes James was forced to conclude his
letter in a more familiar vein:

I am at present induced by various reasons to change my residence to
London . . . I move in two or three weeks to a small house I am about
taking in London. After so long a suspension of correspondence, I know not
how my affairs stand with you, but if they could bear a remittance of thirty
pounds it would be a great accommodation, as expenses crowd on me at a
moment of removal.

Whatever his feelings about this renewed restlessness and improvidence, the bailie sent the £30 and told the young man he
had read his book with interest and it had created quite a sensation in the
north.

Among proposals to Mackintosh was an unlikely reqest to turn his fire
on Dr Johnson. Sir George Staunton wrote to suggest Boswell's just-
published biography as a target: 'Samuel Johnson was a particular friend
of mine, and I admired his virtues and abilities; But I abominate his
political notions, and I am persuaded you do. He is an enemy worthy of
your pen.' This correspondent, a baronet who had been a diplomat in the
West and East Indies, concluded: 'I shall be proud to hear from you.'

Johnson and his biographer were spared. Instead James went in the
autumn to visit another formidable doctor, Samuel Parr, at Hatton,
Warwickshire. Dr Parr shared with his guest a passion for reading, and
displaying his capacious memory by quotation. He too loved an

argument; he once said of his wife, Jane, regarded by many of his friends as a vixen, 'She is wiser than myself, for she can confute Mackintosh and I cannot.' The doctor had been given the care of the parish at Hatton, where he settled with a library of 10,000 books, after a rather quarrelsome career as a pipe-smoking schoolmaster known for his love of cricket, boxing, and flogging.

Fox was Parr's hero. He called him 'the greatest statesman under the canopy of heaven' and poured out his wrath on anyone who hinted a reservation. Like Sydney Smith and other talented clergymen, Dr Parr felt only his liberal politics stood in the way of his promotion to the bench of bishops. None seemed to realise there might not be enough bishoprics to go round.

From Hatton the two friends went to Birmingham, where the doctor had many admirers among the dissenters. In the eighteenth century religious nonconformity was often associated with radical political views and humanitarian campaigns, such as the anti-slavery movement. On 14 July 1791 more than eighty leading Birmingham dissenters met at a hotel for a dinner celebrating the storming of the Bastille two years before. Shortly afterwards rioting broke out. Mobs chanting 'Church and King', the Tory battlecry, began to attack the homes of those they regarded as treasonable heretics.

There was more than a suspicion the rioters were encouraged by local magistrates and ministers of the established church. Eventually a detachment of dragoons restored order and two of the ringleaders were condemned to death. Mackintosh was taken on a tour of the buildings destroyed. They included the home and laboratory of Dr Joseph Priestley, chemist, author and Unitarian preacher who supported the French Revolution, two religious meeting houses, and the mansion of one of his wealthy patrons, William Russell. Both men later emigrated to America.

James had written of his abhorrence of the riots, in an additional section to the third edition of *Vindiciae Gallicae*; he was himself master of ceremonies at a 14 July dinner in London similar to the one which provoked the Birmingham troubles. Mr Russell and his friends invited him to produce a pamphlet on the subject for a fee of £200. Material was collected slowly for the publication, including shorthand accounts of the trial of rioters, and Mackintosh said he paid £50 for the insertion of a series of paragraphs in *The Morning Post*, of which Daniel Stuart had become publisher.

Although consultations continued the pamphlet hung fire until the atrocities marking the progress of revolution in France, and the alarm these excited in Britain, made it unwise and even unsafe to revive memories of Birmingham's unhappy experience. Mackintosh remained on cordial terms with the dissenters and they did not ask for the return of the £200. They must have realised it had already been spent.

Now that James and Catharine were back in London, living at 31 Charlotte Street, social and political activities increased their expense as he continued his studies. Direct evidence is lacking but it seems likely he undertook a regular engagement as a contributor to *The Morning Post*.

Journalism was a risky occupation; for some years judges held they alone were competent to assess whether published material was criminally libellous, leaving the jury to decide only whether the man in the dock had been responsible for publication. This was remedied when Fox piloted through Parliament his Libel Bill of 1792, reasserting the rights of juries to say what was a libel and what was not. This campaign was celebrated with a dinner at the Freemasons' Tavern, Covent Garden, Mackintosh, Sheridan and Whitbread being among the stewards. Guests included the American Radical Joel Barlow. Further dinners were held and the Bill's supporters formed themselves into The Friends to the Liberty of the Press.

Such associations were part of the political ferment of the time. They ranged from innocuous debating societies to bodies a suspicious government regarded as hotbeds of revolt. It seems to have been at one of the former, which met at the Clifford Street coffee house on the corner of Bond Street, that Mackintosh got to know George Canning, then a handsome man about town and rising Member of Parliament. While they differed in politics, they developed a respect for each other's abilities that lasted through life. Richard Sharp, a successful City merchant known as 'Conversation Sharp', also belonged to the Clifford, but already knew James through the more controversial Society for Constitutional Information which offered honorary membership to the author of *Vindiciae Gallicae*. Horne Tooke proposed this distinction, and other members included Dr Priestley and Barlow.

This had been active for many years, but some members felt it was becoming too involved with extremists. So in 1792 a new pressure group arose, the Association of the Friends of the People. Their declared purpose was to obtain parliamentary reform, with a wider franchise and more frequent elections than with the existing seven-year parliaments.

It was inaugurated at a dinner at the London house of Lord Lauderdale, the Scottish peer who was a trustee for Mackintosh's Kyllachy estate. James himself, Charles Grey (who became known to history as Grey of the Reform Bill), Brand Hollis, Sheridan, Whitbread and other moderate joined the Friends. Fox held aloof, and Grey later felt he made a mistake in associating with even mild agitators. When he raised the question of electoral change in the Commons, he was opposed by Pitt, and by Burke, who said there could be no such thing as temperate reform. Mackintosh watched this dismissal of his hopes in the Commons. In a pamphlet entitled *A Letter to the Right Honourable William Pitt* and signed 'An Honest Man' he launched a fierce attack on the Prime Minister, who seven years before had himself proposed a measure of reform, but abandoned it when outvoted.

'The debate on the motion of Mr Grey illustrated the fears of corrupt men and the malignity of apostates,' the pamphlet declared, 'the disgraceful triumph of that night will indeed long be remembered by those who were indignant spectators of it.' Telling Pitt 'I believe you to be the enemy of my country', Mackintosh turned on the premier's great ally, Henry Dundas, the home secretary notorious for manipulation of patronage in Scotland in support of the government: 'The frank and good-natured prostitution of Dundas, which assumes no disguise, and affects no principle, almost disarms censure;—one whom we can neither hate nor respect.'

'An Honest Man' stressed the recurring theme of his political philosophy—that if violent change was to be avoided, it was necessary to grant modest concessions. Suppression of all attempts to right manifest wrongs would, he warned, be 'as effectual in irritating some men into Republicanism, as Mr Paine's pamphlets have been in frightening others into Toryism'.

While political activity occupied her husband, Catharine produced their second daughter on 1 June 1792. She was christened Maitland, the family name of Lord Lauderdale. His brother Thomas Maitland was a fellow member with Mackintosh of the committee which drew up the manifesto of the Friends of the People.

Later the same year Mackintosh decided to visit the Continent. Writing to him on 8 July Dr Parr said: 'I entreat you, my dear friend, to get into no scrapes abroad.' He had in mind the spy mania spreading as Britain moved towards war with the revolutionary government in France. Typical was the suspicion aroused by the activities of Dr Thomas Beddoes, Mackintosh's acquaintance in Edinburgh student days.

On 1 December 1792 Evan Nepean, the principal official at the Home Department, wrote from Whitehall to one of his contacts in Shropshire: "It was yesterday intimated to me, that Dr Beddoes has lately been very active in sowing sedition in your neighbourhood, particularly by the distribution of pamphlets of a very mischievous and inflammatory tendency.' Most officials shared the view expressed by the spy who told Nepean: 'My opinion is, that the Reformers are full as dangerous as the Republicans.'

At a time when Mackintosh was trying to refute that judgement it is strange he should go abroad. The likeliest explanation is that he was collecting material for articles, since on 16 August *The Oracle* reported:

'Mackintosh (the *Vindiciae Gallicae*) is at *Boulogne*, not however vindicating the present Mobocracy of France.' Six weeks later it stated: 'Mackintosh rejected the proposal of being elected as a Member of the French National Convention,' and added he had returned to Margate.

At a dinner in Paris given by British supporters of the revolution his name was included in a toast to so-called British patriots. But by then he was safely home. One of his legal friends, Robert Cutlar Fergusson, a member of the Friends of the People, was in France. He contributed articles to *The Morning Chronicle* on which Mackintosh later commented.

It was the events of 1792 and early 1793 that led him to become deeply disillusioned with the French Revolution, whose beginnings, in common with many young liberals, he welcomed so heartily. At Boulogne he heard of the death of Theobald Dillon, a Dublin-born general in the French army, murdered by his own troops. Later came the storming of the Tuilleries palace, the massacre of political prisoners, and the death of Louis XVI and Marie Antoinette. In 1811, when he was thousands of miles from France, his journal still reflected the horror of those events: '2nd Sept; nineteen years from the massacre in the prisons of Paris.'

Yet on his return to London, he accepted from the revolutionary government's minister there, Bernard-François Chauvelin, a certificate of honorary citizenship of the Republic. It was a distinction he shared with George Washington and other foreigners. Since he preserved the certificate among his papers, 'Jacques Mackintosh' cannot have been displeased by the gift.

In November 1792 he and Catharine paid another visit to Dr Parr and Birmingham. They were kindly received, although all thought of the pamphlet on the city's riots had now been dropped. The doctor, in spite of his outspoken Foxite principles, and the freedom of his intercourse with unorthodox Christians, had an instinct for just how far it was prudent to go in politics. A month after this Birmingham visit he again wrote a warning note to Mackintosh: 'Pray my good friend take care what you say and what you do, and keep as close as you can to the friends of moderate reform. The cry here is against Presbyterians and Jacobins.'

Parr knew not all his friend's contacts were with aristocratic Whigs and moderate liberals. Through his work for *The Oracle* James had met Felix Macarthy, an Irish writer and rake who was an acquaintance of Sheridan. Felix was well-connected. An early biographer of the Prince of Wales said Macarthy was 'a man of infinite wit—at the same time destitute of all principle and honour. Still he was received at the table of his Royal Highness, to whom he was introduced by Lord Moira, who, though certainly the steadiest of his friends, was, on account of his improvidence, and his total ignorance of the value of money, a very unfit person to be the adviser of the Prince. His Lordship was continually in debt.'

Macarthy introduced Mackintosh to Joseph Gerrald, another flamboyant character, who had been a pupil of Dr Parr until he was expelled for what was described as extreme indiscretion. In spite of this the doctor admired his intelligence and loved him like a son. Parr seemed to have a real affection for scamps—he was devoted to Sheridan's son, Tom, another who came under his wing and his rod.

Gerrald had been disappoined in expectations of inheriting wealth from his family in the West Indies, and spent some time in Pennsylvania, where he met Tom Paine, before returning to England. There he plunged into revolutionary circles, and adopted the uniform of Jacobinism, long hair and open-necked shirts. It is easy to see why Mackintosh fell under his spell from this description by a contemporary: 'He was all fire—a real child of the sun—without deliberation or reflection.' But the observer, the Reverend William Beloe, did add: 'Like most of the lovers of reform, and advocates of liberty and equality, he was tyrannical, insolent, im-perious, and overbearing. He ultimately threw off all regard to decorum; lived in licentiousness, and indulged in every sensual irrregularity.'

Ignoring warnings of the danger, Gerrald became one of the delegates to a national gathering in Edinburgh late in 1793 which styled itself the British Convention of the Delegates of the Friends of the People. This was ominously reminiscent of moves which led to the revolution in France. He played a leading part in the proceedings, which called for a vote for every man and annual elections.

Mackintosh would have been startled if he had seen a letter sent by his brother-in-law, Charles Stuart, to the Home Office on 27 October 1793. In this, after offering to set up a system for managing the press to the Government's satisfaction, he added: 'You cannot be too vigilant about the Scottish meeting—Gerrald, one of the banditti delegates, is a man, I believe, that is very, very violent, he is an American and Creolian too— well-educated at Dr Parr's.' Just over a week later, the authorities pounced on the Edinburgh convention, arresting Gerrald and some of his colleagues.

They were charged with seditious practices. Released on bail Gerrald returned to London, where Mackintosh took him into his home. It was not a happy arrangement, especially as Catharine was pregnant again. James wrote later:

> Debauchery, political fanaticism and vulgar associates had by that time defaced his original self. He desired to remain in my small poor house by no means too large for my own family at a time when he had ceased to be an

agreeable inmate. He remained in it for several months. I was then very poor but he was still poorer. I respected the memory of his better days . . . notwithstanding the sanguinary violence of his conversation, the almost daily intoxication which he carried to the grossest extremity and the disgusting slovenliness which he ever affected.

It was not an exaggerated picture. Samuel Taylor Coleridge, who had at first admired Gerrald, wrote to a friend: 'I have been informed by a West Indian that to his knowledge Gerrald left a wife there to starve—and I well know that he was prone to intoxication, and a whoremonger.'

Justice in Scotland was in the hands of ultra-conservative judges. Anyone accused of being a Jacobin was treated as harshly as the Jacobites were fifty years before. Gerrald's friends urged him to flee abroad. Dr Parr, visiting the house in Charlotte Street, pleaded with his old pupil to escape, and Mackintosh himself advised against returning to Scotland. Gerrald replied he could not desert the men charged with him whom he had led into danger: 'Did I stand alone in the matter I would fly. Honour forbids my doing so.'

In Edinburgh he and four others were sentenced to fourteen years transportation. This was even worse than the punishment suffered by Jacobites, who were sent to southern American colonies. These were now part of the United States, so Australia had become the destination of prisoners.

Not long after the trial Catharine Mackintosh presented her husband with his first son, on 26 March 1794. Still a determined Whig, father named him Charles James Fox Mackintosh. It would have been a hard name to live up to; the baby died on 14 July.

Gerrald returned to London, but this time went to prison, where he remained more than a year awaiting transportation. Mackintosh wrote to Parr, who undertook to look after the prisoner's son: 'Poor Gerrald I have seen in Newgate. He is in pretty good spirits.' He also lobbied his Scottish friend William Adam, an MP and legal adviser to the Prince of Wales, about legal proceedings in Scotland. There could be no judicial appeal against the verdicts, so the only way of overturning them was through parliamentary action. But this move failed.

It was May 1795 before orders were given for Gerrald to be taken to Gosport, Hampshire, to embark for Australia. His friends received very little notice of his departure. James warned Parr what was happening and, together with Perry and his Morning Chronicle partner, James Gray, and other sympathisers, raised a subscription of between three and four hundred pounds. What was not needed for the prisoner's equipment for the voyage was held in trust for an illegitimate girl he fathered.

Parr wrote an affectionate letter of farewell which failed to reach Gerrald, a mishap the angry doctor blamed on Mackintosh. It seems strange Parr's biographer, the Reverend William Field, was able to quote this 'missing' letter in full. Either the doctor, in all the bustle of such a crisis, took the trouble to keep a copy with an eye to posterity rather than to his favoured pupil, or it was never despatched and remained among his papers. At the end of the five-month voyage to Sydney the unhappy man was suffering from tuberculosis and died in March the following year.

Success in breaking up the Edinburgh convention encouraged Pitt and his cabinet to move against other reformers with whom Gerrald had associated. They singled out the Society for Constitutional Information, claiming it preached republicanism. Horne Tooke and other leaders were charged with treason, and faced the death penalty. When Horne Tooke, who had been held at the Tower of London, appeared at the Old Bailey in November 1794 the Solicitor General, Sir John Mitford, stressed the moderate Association of the Friends of the People refused to cooperate with the Constitutional Information Society. Evidence was produced of Mackintosh being elected an honorary member of the latter. If Horne Tooke had been convicted few of his friends would have been safe. Charles Grey attended the trial and wrote to his mother 'I do not know how soon it may come to my turn'. Pitt had already told the Commons the evidence collected implicated many people.

But Horne Tooke won. He was defended by a brilliant Whig barrister, Thomas Erskine. Two years earlier Erskine was courageous enough to defend Tom Paine over *Rights of Man*. On that occasion his client was condemned to death in his abscence, and Erskine lost his appointment as attorney-general to the Prince of Wales. So heated did the Horne Tooke trial become that after the proceedings Erskine was overheard accusing the Lord Chief Justice, Sir James Eyre, of repeatedly insulting him, and offering to fight a duel. But it was partly the prisoner's own interventions in the proceedings, in which he poured scorn on attempts to portray his actions as treasonable, which led to his acquittal.

Ministers did not relent entirely. Nearly a year after the Old Bailey fiasco Pitt introduced what became known as the Gagging Acts, prohibiting meetings considered seditious, and making it an offence to ridicule the monarch. Mackintosh and some of his friends watched these motions go through the Commons. He wrote articles criticising the Government for *The Morning Post,* which now belonged to Daniel Stuart, but with the country at war against France even moderate reform was unpopular, and the Friends of the People soon broke up.

It was a time of confusion among the opposition. Mackintosh was not elected to the Whig Club, to which most leading members of the party belonged, until January 1795, for fear members might find his views too extreme. A friend wrote to Dr Parr complaining 'the club consists at present of Tories under the name of Whigs. They black-balled Mackintosh twice; there appeared amost as many black balls as white ones. I heard Mr Sheridan complain of this outrageous expression of Toryism . . . Mr Fox was much enraged when they black-balled Mackintosh.' Daniel Stuart was elected on the same day as his brother-in-law.

James visited the Highlands but without transacting much business. On 8 April 1795 an uncle, Duncan Campbell, who married the youngest daughter of grandfather James Mackintosh of Kyllachy, wrote: 'I am indeed much hurt to see your matters in this country in a state of ruin. It is true the subject is small, but were you worth £10,000 a year I beg leave to say the small property you have in Inverness-shire deserves some little attention. I have . . . never heard a sentence from you about the management of your estate since you left the country.' His letter closed with compliments to Mackintosh's sister, Anne, now in London, and a request for £60 he had paid to the British Linen Company Bank on behalf of his nephew

Three months after this unwelcome news Mackintosh took on more literary work, this time for *The Monthly Review*, an old-established publication owned and edited by Ralph Griffiths. At this time he was studying furiously, if belatedly, to qualify as a barrister, so it was appropriate his first contribution should be an account of a work by William Bradford, attorney-general of the United States, entitled *An Enquiry how far the Punishment of Death is Necessary in Pennsylvania*. This said capital sentences in that state had been commuted to hard labour for cases of unnatural crime, robbery and burglary, and the number of convictions had dropped. Mackintosh commented it 'might furnish useful hints for the reformation of the criminal law in England, which, in the form of proceeding and trial, is a most wise and merciful system, but, in the infliction of penalties, cannot be acquitted of severity and harshness'. It was an indulgent way to describe laws by which women and sometimes children were hanged for trivial offences. Many years later the student lawyer played a significant role in mitigating such barbarities.

James was not prepared to praise something just because it originated on the other side of the Atlantic. He said loftily:

> It deserves to be remarked . . . of this tract, that it is written with a purity and elegance of English style not very often observed in American productions; we find in it scarcely any of those licentious innovations, and unidiomatical combinations of words, by which the Anglo-American style has of late been too often disfigured; and which threaten, if it be not checked, to convert the English which is written and spoken on the different sides of the Atlantic into two different languages.

Political pamphleteering and being named in a treason trial were not recommendations for someone about to enter a traditional profession. When the Attorney General, now Sir John Scott, spoke in the Commons to support continued suspension of the Habeas Corpus Act, enabling ministers to hold suspects in prison without trial, he classed the writings of Mackintosh with Paine, Barlow 'and other champions of the revolution'. As the day approached when Mackintosh would present himself to the Society of Lincoln's Inn he wrote anxiously to Adam to ask him to stand security on his being called to the bar. He also asked him to solicit the attendance of friends who were Benchers of the Inn 'to insure against the possible bad effects of political prejudice and animosity'. All went well, and soon the new barrister was enjoying the company of men like the handsome and brilliant James Scarlett, and Spencer Perceval, who became prime minister.

To be close to Lincoln's Inn he moved into No 14 Serle Street. The street has been rebuilt, but Mackintosh would be pleased to know that St Thomas More, one of his heroes and a student of the Inn, is commemorated by a statue where it meets Carey Street.

He wrote from there to grandmother MacGillivray at Clune cottage on 16 November 1796. As letters from grandsons usually do, it opened with expressions of affection, gratitude, and profuse apologies for not having written before. He had to offer the similar regrets of his 27-year-old brother:

> John has a better excuse for his silence. He is not gone to India as you suppose. He found it impossible to raise money to carry him over in time for the voyage. His present situation poor fellow is very uncertain and he naturally wishes to put off writing you till he can communicate something more positive and more agreeable.

John's career made his brother's seem sedate. From 1790 to 1792 he served as what James called the youngest mate in the East Indiaman, the *Alfred*, on a voyage to Madras and China at midshipman's wage of 26 shillings a month. Judging from the regularity with which the ship's log recorded the death and burial at sea of members of the crew, and the need to confine others in irons, it was not a happy ship. Back in London he made an unsuccessful attempt to go into business as a wine merchant. Evidently he was now attempting to return to India.

The barrister's own prospects were brighter, he was engaged in actions which invariably followed parliamentary elections because of the corrupt and antiquated system of voting.

> For the short time that I have been at the bar I have been doing pretty well. The general election which took place very opportunely for me has thrown

about £300 in my way which has been a great lift. But the expenses of a family in London are so great and the appearance required by my professional character is so burdensome that I must expect for some time nothing better than a hard struggle. I have had no increase to my family since I saw you except one girl who was born about seven months after we left Scotland.

Thus casually did he announce the birth the previous year of Catharine, known in the family as Kitty. Probably the shock of losing his boy overshadowed the blessing of having yet another girl.

The letter did not mention a piece of legal business of a less profitable kind, an action in which Daniel Stuart had to pay £100 damages to a rival newspaper, *The Telegraph*, for deceiving it into printing a piece of foreign news designed to boost the stock market for his own purposes. William Adam appeared for Stuart, assisted by his newly-qualified friend.

One of Mackintosh's articles in *The Monthly Review* had happier results. Reviewing a pamphlet by Burke which came to be known as *Letters on a Regicide Peace,* opposing negotiations with revolutionary France, James praised his style while doing his best to refute the arguments—'no idea appears hackneyed in his hands; no topic seems common place when he treats it'.

The article, was anonymous, but in literary London it was not difficult to discover the author. Burke did so, and let it be known he had read the article and respected its talent. Hearing this, as he was probably meant to do, James wrote to the man whose works, he said, had been his chief study and delight in his youth. Explaining that events in France had to some extent modified his own views, he added: 'I cannot say (and you would despise me if I dissembled) that I can even now assent to all your opinions on the present politics of Europe. But I can with truth affirm that I subscribe to your general principles, and I am prepared to shed my blood in defence of the laws and constitution of my country.' He asked if he might visit Burke, now a sick and dispirited man living in retirement near Beaconsfield.

The sage replied in flattering terms, refering to Mackintosh as one 'from whom the world is yet to expect a great deal of instruction and a great deal of service'. But he wrote cynically to his confidant, Dr French Laurence: 'I forgot to speak to you about Mackintosh's supposed conversion. I suspect, by his letter, that it does not extend beyond the interior politics of this island; but that with regard to France and many other countries he remains as frank a Jacobin as ever . . . bad as he may be, he has not yet declared war, along with his poor friend Wilde, against the Pope.' John Wilde had written to Burke suggesting the Catholic Church could be equated with anti-Christ.

Burke was wrong: James was already discarding his belief in revolution abroad. But he never reacted into Toryism at home, and he doubted the wisdom of Pitt's policy of subsidising European monarchs to overthrow the French government.

Yet the meeting, over Christmas 1796 at Beaconsfield, was a success. It did not overturn the young man's Whig principles, but it confirmed his growing uneasiness about revolutionary excesses. As a contemporary put it: 'He renounced his early errors, and *received absolution.*' James was impressed by Burke's abuse of 'certain philosophers of the new school' whose object was to 'corrupt all that is good in man—to eradicate his immortal soul—to dethrone God from the universe'.

Three years later, Mackintosh, deeply attached to his own family, described what he called the astonishing effusions of Burke's mind in conversation, free from any affectation, and how he had entered 'with cordial glee, into the sports of children, rolling about with them on the carpet, and pouring out, in his gambols, the sublimest images, mingled with the most wretched puns'. In this account, recorded in the diary of a friend Thomas Green, he declared Burke was without any parallel, in any age or country, except, perhaps, Lord Bacon and Cicero. A bond between the two men was that, like Mackintosh, the Irishman had lost a son. He himself died eight months after their meeting. By that time James was overwhelmed by personal grief.

In its obituaries for 8 April 1797 *The Gentleman's Magazine* recorded:

> In her 33rd year, at her house in Serle Street, Lincoln's Inn, in child-bed, the Lady of James Mackintosh, esq, barrister at law; leaving to her husband no consolation for the irreparable and untimely loss of the partner of his youth, but the discharge of his duty towards her children, and the remembrance of the virtues of the most faithful and tender of wives and mothers.

He went to Brighton to recover, and there he opened his heart in a letter to Dr Parr:

> It is only now that I feel the value of what I have lost . . . an intelligent companion, a tender friend, a prudent monitress . . . Had I married a woman who was easy or giddy enough to have been infected by my imprudence, or who had rudely and harshly attempted to correct it, I should, in either case have been irretrievably ruined: a fortune, in either case, would, with my habits, have been only a shorter cut to destruction. But I met a woman, who by the tender management of my weaknesses, gradually corrected the most pernicious of them, and rescued me from the dominion of a degrading and ruinous vice . . . During the most critical period of my life, she preserved order in my affairs, from the care of which she relieved me; she gently reclaimed me from dissipation; she propped my

weak and irresolute nature; she urged my indolence to all the exertions that have been useful and creditable to me; and she was perpetually at hand to admonish my heedlessness and imprudence.

To her I owe that I am not a ruined outcast; to her whatever I am; to her whatever I shall be. In her solicitude for my interest, she never, for a moment, forgot my feelings or my character. Even in her occasional resentment,—for which I but too often gave just cause (would to God that I could recall those moments), she had no sullenness or acrimony; her feelings were warm and impetuous, but she was placable, tender, and constant: she united the most attentive prudence with the most generous and guileless nature, with a spirit that disdained the shadow of meanness, and with the kindest and most honest heart. Such was she whom I have lost.

Parr, not easily awed by anyone's eloquence but his own, replied: 'I never received from mortal man a letter which, in point of composition, can be compared with that which you wrote me.'

It was surely wrong to commemorate such a model of domesticity with a Latin inscription from his pen on a marble monument, in St Clement Danes, in the Strand. There had been unkind suggestions Catharine was considerably older than her husband; the memorial stated she was 32 years, 11 months and 21 days when she died.

Chapter Three

'A Time for Kissing and Quarrelling'

Late in the summer of 1797 two widowers left their law books in London and made separate ways to the west. One went in search of a wife, and was rebuffed; the other, bound merely for a visit to friends, found love.

The failed suitor was Basil Montagu, illegitimate son of the fourth Earl of Sandwich, and friend of William Wordsworth and Coleridge. They were living in Somerset, with William's sister Dorothy, and planning joint publication of *Lyrical Ballads*. After some time there Montagu hurried to Cote House, near Bristol, home of John and Jenny Wedgwood. The couple invited friends and relatives to celebrate the birth of their son Tom, destined to be a soldier and fight at Waterloo. Among them was John's sister Sarah, an eligible heiress since she shared with her brothers and sisters the fortune left by their father, Josiah Wedgwood, founder of the Potteries firm.

She rejected Montagu, who had no money and was not called to the bar until the following year. He had another motive for visiting Cote, he was anxious to see more of Mackintosh, whom he had previously met only in court. James followed a different route, first calling on James Greene, MP, at Llansantffraed, near Abergavenny in Monmouthshire. There in a farmhouse-mansion near an ancient church, both much rebuilt over the years, the Highlander met Catherine Allen, whose barrister brother he knew in London. What happened was described by Catherine in a letter to her youngest sister, Fanny:

> I have been a week in ye company of ye celebrated Mr Mackintosh at Llansantffraed, ye chief part confined by intolerably bad weather, wind and rain, to the house; but . . . I could not fancy myself in durance vile, particularly in the pleasure such a guest afforded us. John is acquainted with him and will not perhaps think I say too much in declaring him to be, as far as I can be supposed a judge, the cleverest and best-informed man I have ever known and withal of character and manners particularly interesting . . . He honoured me with very flattering notice, and if my memory was not a very treacherous one, I might have carried off from Llansantffraed information on almost every topic of conversation, for there was scarcely any that was not discussed; upon each of which he seemed enlightened in

39

his own mind, and clever and pointed in his statements, to the apprehension of others and certainly whenever I may feel it necessary for present satisfaction to look back to past scenes, ye pleasant week at L- - - - will not be forgotten. Mr Mackintosh gratified me very highly by discovering that he was very much pleased with John.

The attraction was not one-sided. Mackintosh moved on to the York House hotel at Bath, where he received a note from Catherine in which she said 'though I had flattered myself that you would retain me in your remembrance as an acquaintance, I was not vain enough to imagine I had made a conquest of your heart'. She agreed it was not desirable to enter into a formal engagement, assuring him a narrow fortune would not be an insurmountable obstacle, and adding: 'On Friday I mean to be at Bath, by the lower road, about one; and if it will be of any gratification to you to see me for a few minutes, I shall certainly be very happy to have your company from the entrance of ye passage to the North Parade to Mrs Nares' lodgings in ye South Parade.'

It was more than a few minutes they spent together. Three days later Mackintosh was back in London, and wrote to 'My Dearest Love' to say:

> You gave me the most delicious half hour of my life in our walk along the banks of the Avon. Let me indulge in the rapture of recollection that you owned you felt a stronger sentiment than friendship or esteem. There is no such sentiment but love. In the most severe calamities that may befall me I shall call to mind that I have even in the slightest degree been loved by Catherine Allen and be comforted.

It was not a complete case of off with the old and on with the new:

> I feel myself checked in the joy which that prospect inspires by a review of the difficult and distressed situation of which I am asking My Dearest Kitty to partake. I had a partner in that situation of such spirit and firmness and actuated by such zealous affection that she warded off almost every blow from me and preserved the tranquillity of my mind undisturbed by the difficulty of my circumstances. But she was prepared for hard fortune by her own humble origin and situation. What have I to offer to you to compensate for a situation the reverse of that in which you were born and have lived. Nothing Dearest Dearest Kitty (excuse my presumptuous fondness) but a heart as entirely devoted to you as ever human heart was to excellence.

He praised her

> happy mixture of gaiety and tenderness, of sincerity and gentleness—and above all the subordination of the whole soul to the rules of morals which

are the eternal laws of God and to the authority of the conscience which is the viceregent of God in the human heart. Never did religion appear to me so interesting nor Catherine Allen so amiable as when I knelt by her side.

Courtship at this pace was scarcely proper in the 1790s. But time was not on their side. With three young girls and an uncertain future, Mackintosh needed the secure home he had just lost. Catherine, like her suitor, was thirty-two and past the age when upper-class girls usually married, including several of her sisters. The Scotsman must have felt at home in entering an alliance with the Allen family, as deeply-rooted and many-branched as his own. There were nine daughters and two sons of widower John Bartlett Allen, who lived at Cresselly, Pembrokeshire. Like Captain John Mackintosh, he was a veteran of the Seven Years War. Two of his daughters were married to Wedgwoods.

Most of the Allen girls were good-looking and sparkling company; Jenny Wedgwood was outstanding on both counts. Husband John was more retiring, dividing his time between minimum duties as a gentleman partner in the London bank of Alexander Davison & Co, and tending his garden at Cote, where he grew grapes, pineapples, peaches and ornamental plants under glass. The Royal Horticultural Society was founded at his instigation a few years later, and he became its first treasurer although his career showed finance was not his strongest point.

Cote, a fine mansion in pleasant country between Bristol and Westbury-on-Trym, gave Mackintosh another opportunity to meet Catherine. He also renewed acquaintance with Dr Beddoes, who had established himself at Bristol, where he mixed common sense hygiene ahead of its time with alarming experiments with drugs and laughing gas.

Catherine had intellectual and religious tastes. She was an admirer of Coleridge, even at that early date, and anxious to assist him. In his letter about their Bath tryst, Mackintosh wrote: 'Send me Coleridge's address I think I have hit upon the means of procuring him a guinea a week with little literary exertion.'

At the time Coleridge subsisted mainly on small loans and gifts in kind from friends, and it seems he applied to Mackintosh for money, unaware the barrister was even more in debt than himself. James wrote back in embarrassment:

I have long been an admirer of your genius but it was not till my late visit to Mr Wedgwood's that I felt an interest in your character almost equal to my admiration of your extraordinary powers. From the reports of Dr Beddoes and of my amiable friend Miss Allen I found that you were not less interesting as a man than as a poet and I heard with the most sincere regret that like many other good men and great poets you had not been so kindly treated by fortune as by nature. Had I been possessed of opulence I should certainly have thought your permission to assist you one of the greatest honours of my life and the power of aiding such a man to be the chief enjoyment and blessing of wealth. But I am poor.

James then transmitted an offer from Daniel Stuart to pay Coleridge a guinea a week for contributions in prose and verse to *The Morning Post,* with the prospect of an increased salary if the arrangement satisfied both sides. Although Coleridge became only a fitful contributor to the *Post,* his introduction to Stuart provided one of the few sources of remunerative employment he enjoyed in life. Mackintosh continued to offer practical aid to the poet from time to time over thirty years, undeterred by his hostility. Coleridge resented the Scotsman's failure to see the latent genius of Wordsworth, whom Samuel worshipped at that time. He also found Mackintosh was not prepared to play the part of the captive audience Coleridge preferred when expounding philosophy.

Conversation was not the poet's strong point. As Wordsworth once remarked 'we had some good haranguing, talk I cannot call it, from Coleridge'. Mackintosh preferred the cut-and-thrust of an argument, in which the knowledge from his vast reading could be deployed. Coleridge may also have envied the charm with which the barrister, throughout his life, found it possible to surround himself with intelligent, lively women. The poet, in his Somerset days, was extremely vain, reported one young woman.

James had been invited back to spend Christmas 1797 at Cote—John Wedgwood was his banker, which cannot have been an easy task. But first there was other business to complete. He called at Donington Park in Leicestershire, home of the Prince of Wales' friend, Lord Moira, whose improvidence placed Mackintosh in an embarrassing position. Moira, a man of stately presence who fought in the American war with a mixture of bravery and ruthlessness, was concerned in negotiations earlier in the year aimed at ousting Pitt as prime minister and installing the earl in his place.

When the manoeuvres failed, Mackintosh 'ghosted' a pamphlet for Moira, putting his role in the loftiest light, and denying he agreed to lead a government which expressly excluded Fox. The pamphlet took the form of a letter to Colonel John McMahon, secretary to the Prince. Subsequently the earl wrote to James saying he felt he should have something to 'make up the loss to which I subjected you' by diverting him from more profitable activities. Regretting he himself had 'not a sixpence at his command' Lord Moira explained Colone McMahon would pass money to Mackintosh and added:

I have made him understand thoroughly that this is not a price paid for your performance, which would lower the rate of the service rendered by you; but that it is a compensation dictated by honesty for the expenditure of your time, in the discharge of which I have an interested view of future advantage. The day may come when it may be important for me to employ your ability.

Whatever James felt about this gauche exposure of his activities in the twilight world between hired hacks and dedicated pamphleteers, he was not averse to possible favours from a powerful friend. Mackintosh told Catherine he hoped to obtain a commissionership of bankrupts, a sinecure which was the first step on the road to fortune for many a young barrister. At Donington they discussed the crisis in Ireland, whose grievances Lord Moira espoused, but he apparently said nothing about a post for his friend. From there James went on to Hatton, where Dr Parr was polishing his Latin inscription for the monument to the first Mrs Mackintosh; and so to Cote House and the second.

Coleridge showed no immediate resentment over his failure to borrow money from Mackintosh. On November 20 he replied:

> I do not complain of my lot. It is true I have long been grappling with poverty; but she has never been permitted to overthrow me; and although since I left college, I have known more than the name of misfortune I have been always preserved from the two heaviest calamities, Debt and Desertion. My religious and political creeds had in some measure alienated me from my own family; but I have found more than a compensation in the friends, who attached themselves to me from principle, and from the firmness of principle have retained their attachment; and from time to time I have discovered many among those, whom I had honoured at a distance without dreaming that they had even heard of my name.

He requested Mackintosh's help in finding out what had happened to a play he submitted to Sheridan, hoping for performance at Drury Lane:

> The name of my tragedy is *Osorio*. I have completely reconciled my mind to the idea of its rejection by the Manager—and that I have heard nothing concerning its fate I attribute to a cowardice in giving pain, common in minds framed as I conjecture Mr Sheridan's to be . . . I suppose that as a composition it is not on the whole inferior to many that have succeeded. But its defects may unfortunately be the very ones which render it unfit for the stage and of its fitness for representation I cannot say that I am an imperfect judge, for I am no Judge at all . . .
> It has one great defect—the virtuous characters (whose tale and feelings I intended to be only secondary to the development of Osorio's character and passions) are never during the piece in a state of actual distress—and the pathos arises, if any, from the fainter feeling of recollected anguish. The plot

too, the outline of which was suggested to me by the tale of Lorenzo in the
Ghost-seer, is not an interesting one; and in the three first acts effect and
situations, altho' I imagine sufficiently dramatic, are not always tragic.

Coleridge sent a copy of the play to Mackintosh, and ended his letter:

> If you would point out to me any faults in it, which I myself have not
> detected, I should consider myself as essentially benefited. I am happy that I
> have to add the sense of private obligation to the high respect with which I
> have always been, very sincerely yours, S T Coleridge.

He added a postcript:

> You have probably heard that I commenced Dramatist in consequence of a
> message from Mr Sheridan thro' the Revd W L Bowles. Possibly a delicacy
> arising from this circumstance had made him keep the business in suspense
> longer than he otherwise would have done.

Sheridan's delicacy proved insurmountable. Nearly three months later
Coleridge wrote to Mackintosh from Stowey, in Somerset:

> Six weeks ago I wrote to Mr Sheridan, entreating from him a definite
> answer respecting my Tragedy—as I wished to publish it. I have received
> no answer. Will you call on him, and procure for me an answer—whether
> the play be so radically vicious, that no alteration in parts will fit it for the
> stage—? If Mr Sheridan reply in the affirmative, as I doubt not, he will—
> will you desire him to send me back the manuscript?—You see, my Dear
> Sir! the freedom with which I treat you. If you find it troublesome, you
> must attribute it to your own kindness. The Lime, that has honey on its
> leaves, and honey in its blossom, will always have an importunate multitude
> of Bees and Flies, humming and buzzing about its branches.

Meanwhile letters passed between James and his dearest Kitty. They
followed the pattern common to those contemplating matrimony; his
notes pleaded for an early wedding, mingled with remorse at his tangled
finances. She, while assuring him of her love, dwelt more on upholsterers
and dressmakers, and the necessity of the house in Serle Street being
thoroughly aired before they moved in. Postage was expensive in
Georgian days, most letter-writers evaded this by getting peers or
members of parliament to frank their mail to go free. In one of her notes
she observed: 'By ye different franks I receive from you I conclude
indeed that our present connexion is known and our intended one
surmised by half ye House of Commons.'
She was adamant the wedding could not be brought forward from the
planned 10 April 1798: 'I have so many good reasons for not marrying

till ye 9th or 10th that any different arrangement on this head is quite out of the question. I dont choose to be married in Passion week or on Easter Monday because Monday is a very unlucky day to be married on. My mother was married on a Monday and used to tell us "Girls do not marry on a Monday". Tuesday the tenth is the soonest you can receive my vows.' Catherine, who had a horror of debt, went on: 'The next point of business is the diamond ring which I interdict, you will *mortally offend me* if you mention such a thing again. We must not throw away a guinea and I require no such proof of your affection.'

In between writing love letters, Mackintosh was pursuing his career. One note from her was endorsed on the outside, 'The sweetest of letters from the sweetest and best of women—received Feb 28th 1798 the day of ye conviction of my client Sinclair for perjury.' From Maidstone, where he was attending court, he made a last attempt to hurry his bride to the altar, dangling the unlikely bait of the chance to see a treason trial involving Arthur O'Connor, a case which was to have a dramatic ending. James told Catherine:

> While the judges are gone to church previous to the opening of the court I sit down to scribble . . . I last night was supping here with the brawling mob of vulgar and ungentlemanlike men who form the great majority of our circuit . . . O'Connor's trial comes on at this place before a Special Commission which is now intended to be in Easter week.
>
> What do you think of my proposal of marriage a few days sooner. The lodgings where I am now writing will accommodate you very comfortably and though the bed in which I slept last night was not very large yet on going into it I thought I could without much difficulty have made room for Kitty Allen, though she was represented as such a porpoise by the philosophical Miss Wordsworth.

His invitation was refused, but in consolation she told him her brother John, a man of considerable charm whose opinion she respected, had written to tell her

> I cannot help repeating what I have often said of M- - - - that he is almost the only man whose abilities seem to encrease upon acquaintance and his modesty with all his talents and reputation is marvellous, he certainly will not go out of ye world without making some noise in it.

More materially her father, whose relations with his daughters were far from placid, gave his blessing to the marriage with a present of £800. Mackintosh had a bill to meet of £200 in April, and was also in debt to his Llansantffraed host. Catherine wrote: 'Without there are more pressing debts to discharge I should like you to put it to liquidate part of ye debt to Mr Greene.'

Help came from an unexpected quarter. Daniel Stuart offered his sister's widower a share in *The Morning Post*, but he hesitated to accept because of his professional status. His sweetheart exhorted him:

> An offer of receiving an addition of 3 or 400£ per annum to your income is of very essential importance indeed in our circumstances, it is as they say, a Godsend, I think and ought to be immediately closed with, it comes at a very critical juncture when more of my friends are beginning to despair of our being able to unite ourselves and little fortune together so soon as April . . . I see not ye least objection to accepting the engagement. It may be kept I should think entirely secret and yet if by accident it should transpire it is not of a nature to throw surely ye least reflection on any part of your character.

Stuart's account, written some thirty-five years later, said Mackintosh bought some shares in the paper, which he soon sold, and agreed to write for it at a salary of £200 a year. James himself said 'in the ten or eleven years between 1790 and 1801 I wrote nearly as much in the periodical press, and in magazines and reviews, as any man of my time'. But in 1803 he denied he retained any influence over the paper's policy, and the growth in his law practice and other preoccupations indicate he was right in suggesting 1801 was the last year he had leisure for regular journalism.

Catherine was deeply attached to her sisters' brother-in-law, Thomas Wedgwood, a chronic invalid who inherited his father's interest in science, and dabbled in studies relating to the connection between physical sensations and mental attitudes. She was concerned that Thomas, whom she nicknamed Polydore, seemed indifferent to Christianity: 'I am deeply disappointed at finding I had only conjur'd up a phantom in my own imagination and called it Polydore, I think my scheme of converting him to acknowledge our faith and to revere just and unsophisticated morality ought not to be abandon'd.' She went on to ask James: 'Whenever you may happen to be in his company to dilate your sentiments on morals and religion in neither of which is his opinion or his faith orthodox.'

On 22 February 1798 'C.A.' wrote to him from Cote House: 'Coleridge is now with us for a day or two in very good spirits and very pleasant.' Urging her future husband to try to push the merits of *Osorio* with Sheridan, she added: 'I am quite interested for Coleridge, he appears amiable . . . I wish by the way you were fonder of music.' She was musical and Mackintosh was tone-deaf, a source of contention during their married life. There were other indications in the correspondence the second Mrs Mackintosh would not prove the self-effacing partner Catharine Stuart had been.

He was pressed to persevere with a piece of translation for which he had been offered £50. But James was still the convivial improvident man who preferred the dinner table to the study, and talking about literature to writing it. One evening in February 1798 at his house in Serle Street it was proposed he and some friends should form a club. This was christened The King of Clubs by Robert Smith, known by his schoolboy nickname of Bobus, brother of the Reverend Sydney Smith.

Founder members included Samuel Rogers, the banker-poet, Richard Sharp, and James Scarlett. Others were added in the next twenty years, but it was always select, and invitations to the monthly dinners at the Crown and Anchor Tavern in the Strand were prized. One of Mackintosh's guests, Thomas Campbell, described it as a gathering of 'the reigning wits of London . . . a lineal descendant of the Johnson, Burke and Goldsmith Society', devoted to 'literary conversational rivalship, maintained, to be sure, with perfect good nature . . . Every one of these brilliants goes there to shine; for conversational powers are so much the rage in London, that no reputation is higher than his who exhibits them to advantage'.

It was the age of eloquence, men were expected to sparkle over their claret, having perhaps already delivered speeches in the Commons or the courts. Mackintosh was not himself a wit, he was kindly by nature and his sharpest sallies were reserved for the privacy of his letters. But he had a strong sense of fun, and was respected for the readiness with which he could produce quotations to support his arguments.

It was at Westbury-on-Trym, in a church originally part of a monastery, that James and Catherine were married by licence on 10 April 1798. Two witnesses signed the register, John Wedgwood and John Mackintosh. The bride, who was stately and black-eyed, wore a habit 'of the darkest blue I could get with yellow buttons'. Campbell described Mackintosh at this time as regularly handsome, well-made and above middle height, but Catherine had criticised his tailor for making him a coat with 'flaps almost down to his ankles', no doubt an attempt to emulate the dandies. She wanted him to marry in one of the same hue as her habit, but could not spare a piece for a pattern, so assured him 'as long as our minds are in somewhat similar livery it is not at all necessary that our coats should be of the same shade'.

In spite of her efforts to bring order to their finances, he remained an inveterate borrower. A month after the marriage he wrote to a barrister friend and wealthy Irishman, George Moore, acnowledging receipt of a letter containing £100, and expressing the hope he would be able to repay the total of £400 outstanding when he sold his Kyllachy estate.

By August the newlyweds and the three daughters of Catharine Stuart were at Broadstairs. Catherine wrote to her younger brother, Lancelot

Baugh Allen, that they were 'very comfortably situated having an entire house to ourselves small and neat without the town or more properly village looking over a field to ye sea' at only 30s. a week. George Moore, and another friend of Mackintosh's, Patrick Byrne, were in lodgings nearby, and Fergusson also visited Broadstairs. Her letter remarked:

> The more I see of Byrne the more I see to like in him though I dont give myself heedlessly to admiration as *heretofore* for I wont put it into the power of *man* again to put my good opinion to shame; my *brothers even cant deceive me* now I have eaten of the fruit of good and evil I see men and women now more *in needibus* than I used to do. I form no longer romantic ideas of, or romantic expectations from either sex but I must here hint that there is at least one human being with whom I ought to be satisfied. *It is flat* to mention his name for besides being a lover which singly would sound very well, truth obliges him to own the more vulgar title of husband.
>
> This same gentleman is studying away very diligently as I hope to his future honour and emolument. Ye sea air and bathing agrees amazingly with him, his appetite is enormous, his spirits exhilarated . . . I feel myself more in my own element here than in Serle Street.

They remained there into October, having been joined by three of Catherine's sisters. The eldest, Bessy, was married to Josiah Wedgwood, known in the family as Jos. to distinguish him from his father. Jos. was the most practical of the three Wedgwood sons—the competition was not keen—and Bessy played a big part in bringing up her sisters after their mother's death. She reported to yet another sister by letter that 'Mr M. still continues the fondest and the best-humoured husband I ever saw. The children are very manageable and the least troublesome of any I ever saw, and what will give you pleasure, I think she makes a very kind and attentive stepmother.'

Mackintosh's studies at Broadstairs included the works of Bacon, as he noted in his copy of them at the time. He was about to make one of his spectacular displays of intellectual power and bring himself again into public notice, this time as a lecturer.

On 26 November 1798 he wrote to 'the Benchers of the Honourable Society of Lincoln's Inn' proposing he should use their hall to deliver a series of lectures on the 'Law of Nature and Nations' for the benefit of students and practising lawyers. In a letter to William Adam, James explained he intended to discuss the general principles of morality, of politics and of law as well as the rights and duties of nations in relation to each other. In this way he could occupy the leisure his slow progress at the bar entailed, and enhance his reputation.

He encountered unexpected opposition. The benchers hesitated to consent, not on the grounds a barrister with three years experience could not have much wisdom to impart, but for fear the author of *Vindiciae Gallicae* might preach some form of Jacobinism. Adam reported to James some objected to lecturing in any form, and promised a 'canvass of three old fogies whom we have not yet sounded'. Another influential friend, the Reverend Robert Nares, joint editor of the *British Critic* and keeper of manuscripts at the British Museum, wrote: 'I will not say that I have found it easy in some cases, when I have expressed a desire of promoting your design, to remove the impression caused by your former book, and some other circumstances.'

It would have damaged his career prospects as a young barrister had it become known the benchers of his own inn considered him unsound politically. Mackintosh rushed into print *A Discourse on the Law of Nature and Nations* containing the substance of his opening lecture, setting the guidelines for all thirty-nine talks. He sent copies to ministers and to sympathetic legal men. One of the shrewdest, Scarlett, wrote praising the publication but pointing out the test would be how well the lectures measured up to this prospectus, 'They will never pardon you if any relaxation of your zeal should disappoint their impatience to see fully completed the noble work of which you have so admirably sketched the outline.' He knew the lecturer's failings.

Partly through the good offices of George Canning, the Speaker of the House of Commons, Henry Addington, lent his support, and prime minister Pitt wrote to Mackintosh: 'I have no motive for wishing to please you; but I must be permitted to say, that I have never met with any thing so able or so elegant on the subject in any language.' Nonetheless it was not until the lord chancellor, Lord Loughborough, himself a member of Lincoln's Inn, told the benchers the lectures would be 'of great utility and of much ornament to our profession', that use of the hall was granted.

James and Catherine spent Christmas at Stoke D'Abernon, in Surrey, where Jos. Wedgwood lived the life of a country squire in a manor house with Bessy and their two children, one of whom was the third generation Josiah, known as Joe. Mackintosh reported to his grandmother he had enrolled 150 pupils at five guineas each.

From February to June he delivered his lectures, breaking off when court duties called him away. He told his audience he would outline the state of laws governing men and states, embracing 'the events of history, the opinions of philosophers, the sentiments of orators, and poets, as well as the observations of common life'. These, he declared, were 'the materials out of which the science of morality is formed; and those who neglect them are justly charged with a vain attempt to philosophise without regard to fact and experience,—the solid foundation of all true philosophy'. Prominent in his illustrations were quotations from Cicero and Burke, 'who have, in a few words, stated the substance, the object, and the result of all morality, and law'.

Mackintosh later confessed that only when he took part in actual court cases on international law did he realise how little he knew about it. Writing to George Moore he said: 'I trusted more than I ought to have done to my general habits of reflection on the subject. When I came to the execution of my plan I found it more toilsome than I imagined. I have however upon the whole been more successful than I had any right to expect.' He added six peers and a dozen MPs attended, although all but two were Tories. He reflected he received more kindness over the lectures from ministers than 'eight years of faithful attachment have ever procured me from my friends in opposition'.

His success was striking. This was apparent even from William Hazlitt's tongue-in-cheek account written many years later, describing the effect as 'electrical and instantaneous', but adding: 'Dazzling others by the brilliancy of his acquirements, dazzled himself by the admiration he excited, he lost fear as well as prudence; dared every thing, and carried everything before him. The Modern Philosophy, counterscarp, outworks, citadel, and all, fell without a blow, by "the whiff and wind of his fell doctrine", as if it had been a pack of cards.'

Hazlitt complained the lecturer dealt mainly in quotations, expressing contempt for visionary sceptics and believers in utopias:

> Poor Godwin, who had come in the *bonhommie* and candour of his nature, to hear what new light had broken in upon his old friend, was obliged to quit the field, and slunk away after an exulting taunt thrown out at 'such fanciful chimeras as a golden mountain or a perfect man' . . . Those of us who attended day after day, and were accustomed to have all our previous notions confounded and struck out of our hands by some metaphysical legerdemain, were at last at some loss to know two and two made four, till we heard the lecturer's opinion on that head.

Philosopher William Godwin's book *Enquiry Concerning Political Justice* exercised much influence on young men already fired by the French Revolution. It preached a gentle form of anarchy, a world in which the need for laws, and for matrimonial and family ties, would be superseded by universal brotherhood, and presumably universal motherhood. Jos. Wedgwood, whose brother Tom was a keen disciple of Godwin, declared such 'writings tend to make a foundling hospital of the world'. The philosopher himself made no attempt to practise his precepts—apart from the belief that men of genius, like himself, should be subsidised by richer men, such as Tom, and Percy Bysshe Shelley, who became his son-in-law. But earlier in the decade he had discussed his book before publication with a number of friends, including Mackintosh, then fresh from his attack on Burke's *Reflections*.

Godwin considered the ridicule of his views on the perfectibility of man was a betrayal. With a touch of vanity he suggested both that, because he had not been named in the lectures he had no opportunity to refute them, yet because he was clearly the target there was a risk the government would prosecute him for sedition, or the mob might attack him. In fact ministers had long since decided his book was too intellectual to be dangerous, and the lawyers who had paid five guineas to listen to the lecturer were not likely to turn into a lynching party. However, James admitted later he had been unjust to his former friend and did his best to make amends. His denunciation probably owed much to Catherine's anxiety over 'Polydore', and Burke's condemnation of irreligious philosophers.

This one took his revenge by portraying Mackintosh as a modern counter-part to a Spanish Inquisition prosecutor in a novel, *St Leon*. It was typical of Godwin that the book dwelt at length on family virtues he previously held to be unnecessary.

Both Hazlitt and Godwin missed the point of the lectures. An inn of court was hardly the setting for philosophical revolution; it was in any case as difficult, and as unnecessary, to invent a new morality as a new sin. Near the end of his life, Coleridge was reported by a young enthusiast for German philosophy, John Stuart Blackie, to have said 'he had thrown all such speculation overboard, and found perfect satisfaction in the first chapter of the Gospel of St John'. The key to the lecturer's approach was in his declaration, 'Morality admits no discoveries.'

Godwin appealed to Samuel Parr in his dispute with Mackintosh, but the doctor responded with a blistering attack on the philosopher. His motive, he declared, was that Godwin had undermined the faith of three young men. One was undoubtedly Joseph Gerrald; the others may have been Basil Montagu and Tom Wedgwood.

One case in which Mackintosh was engaged during his lectures was the sensational trial of his old legal and journalistic friend, Robert Fergusson, and the Earl of Thanet at Westminster in the King's Bench Court on 25 April 1799. It says something for the Scotsman's reputation that other counsel for prosecution and defence included two future lord chancellors, three who later served as lord chief justice, and others who became judges. James had been a guest at the home of Lord Thanet, Hothfield House in Kent, where he was presented to the Prince of Wales.

Charges revolved around an affray a year before at the Maidstone Assizes from which James had written to Catherine before their marriage. There Arthur O'Connor was acquitted of high treason after leading Whigs, including Lord Thanet, gave evidence for the defence.

When O'Connor was immediately approached by Bow Street officers seeking to rearrest him on further charges he leapt from the dock and tried to escape. The case against Lord Thanet was that he said 'it is but fair that he should have a run for it' and then with Fergusson, a defence counsel, impeded officers trying to detain the Irishman. Both were sentenced to a year's imprisonment, the peer serving his sentence in the Tower of London.

On 26 May 1799 Elizabeth Vassall Lady Holland noted in her journal:

> Mackintosh is the man who wrote a vindication of the French Revolution in the beginning of it. He was then exclaimed against as a furious Jacobin. Nay, two years ago he wished to come here, and I refused seeing him on account of his principles, as I have always dreaded this house becoming a *foyer* of Jacobinism, and have invariably set my face against receiving all who are suspected of being revolutionists etc etc. However, since M. has regained his character, and is become a friend of Canning's etc, I admit him; and he yesterday dined here with a numerous party.

She did not mention that a month earlier, in his lectures, this carefully-vetted guest to Holland House attacked divorce. Marriage, he declared, could only be a life-long contract, anything else meant 'cohabiting during pleasure', and he swept aside conventional arguments for divorce, saying 'extremely unhappy marriages are as rare as extremely happy'. As Lady Webster, she had been divorced by her much older husband after spending some flirtatious years abroad; she then found happiness in a second marriage with Lord Holland, whose unfailing good spirits provided the stability she formerly lacked. Since she made it her business to know all the gossip of the day Lady Holland was certainly aware of Mackintosh's onslaught on divorce, especially as her husband attended the lectures. She must have been curious to see the moralist, and anxious to deflect his fire.

So he entered Holland House, a mansion already historic in its associations with great men before the Hollands turned it into a place where the most brilliant and famous gathered to enjoy the best food and talk in London. Because of her suspect past Lady Holland was not welcome at fashionable houses, apart from those of Lord Holland's numerous relations and some other Whigs so aristocratic they could ignore convention. In retaliation she ruled like a queen over her own table, and there was no shortage of men eager to be invited to dinner. James became one of her willing subjects, and in later years regarded Holland House as a second home, sometimes his first.

Catherine was expecting a baby in mid 1799, and went to her sister's house at Stoke D'Abernon, where two others, Jessie and Fanny, joined her. What happened next is not clear. According to a law student, writing his recollections more than thirty years later, Mackintosh was handed a note one day while lecturing and broke off in agitation, saying his wife had given birth to triplets. 'The children died shortly afterwards,' the student said. *The Gentleman's Magazine* for May carried the announcement: 'The wife of Counsellor Mackintosh, three children, one of whom is since dead, but the others, with the mother, likely to do well.' No Mackintosh births or deaths were recorded in the Stoke D'Abernon parish register although there is an entry for the christening on 12 May 1799 of Henry Allen Wedgwood, son of Jos. and Bessy.

Children were not mentioned when James wrote anxiously to Catherine 'I was very severely disappointed by Jessie's note to find your recovery has been so slow,' adding, 'I was mortified to hear from Fanny that even the opium had not made you sleep comfortably.' His unspoken thoughts perhaps dwelt on the fate of his first wife. In August they began a lengthy visit to Cambridge to speed her recovery, and enable him to collect material from university libraries for his next course of lectures.

Writing to his grandmother in November, Mackintosh said: 'Though still poor I have thank God of late escaped embarrassment and distress and what is most important of all I have less cause to be dissatisfied with my own conduct than at many former periods of my life.' He praised Catherine as mother and governess of his three children, saying: 'Little Kitty who was originally very weakly is under her love becoming a fine girl. She is naturally the sweetest tempered child in the world.'

James used his influence to obtain the post of captain paymaster in the Sixth West India Regiment for his brother, and he told Mrs Mac-Gillivray: 'I have had one letter from John since his arrival at the Honduras coast where his regiment is quartered. It is dated June. He had an attack of the fever on his arrival in the W. Indies but had recovered . . . Notwithstanding the fairest promises I was disappointed in every effort to get a place for my sister's husband.'

Sister Anne was in disgrace in the Highlands, for the letter went on to seek forgiveness for 'your granddaughter . . . orphan daughter of my most worthy mother, she whom I had seen you nurse with most tender care as an infant', adding Anne 'had claims on me which no misconduct of hers could cancel'. This reference to Anne and her husband in 1799 is mysterious, for it was not until 22 February 1802 that Anne Mackintosh married James Cochrane at the same St Mary le Bone church where her brother was united with Catharine Stuart. Perhaps the ceremony was necessary because of some irregularity in an earlier wedding. This could account for the accusation of misconduct, and for Charles Mackintosh's advice to James to guard against Anne making an improper marriage.

Jos. Wedgwood moved from Surrey to Dorset, and on 27 October 1799 he wrote to Mackintosh that he and Thomas had bought an estate at

Tarrant Gunville, five miles from Blandford, 'which we must pay for at Christmas'. He reminded his correspondent: 'When I had the pleasure of advancing you a small sum in November last you mentioned that you would certainly be able to repay it in a twelvemonth. I do not write to urge it if it should be inconvenient to you, but if it should not, it would be very desirable to me to receive it by Christmas Day.' According to notes preserved by the Potteries firm, the sum was £150.

James swiftly disillusioned him. He explained his ability to repay depended on selling the Kyllachy estate and there had been much haggling over price: 'In the Highlands the sale of an estate is more like a transfer of sovereignty than a transaction about an article of commerce.' His description is borne out by the deeds, four pages of cramped legal jargon, with much reference to the granting of land to his ancestors early in the seventeenth century, and feudal rights enjoyed by the Earl of Moray. These included the duty to serve the earl and his successors 'against all mortals (our sovereign Lord the King and the heirs of the deceast Sir John Campbell of Calder, knight, only excepted)'.

This decision to part with his inheritance drew a protest from John Wilde, who wrote from Edinburgh:

> James Mackintosh, what is it I have seen in the newspapers! . . . the sale of —— I will not write the word. If you love yourself, if you love me, if you have any regard whatever for my peace of mind, in all my life to come, do not, do not do it. What can be the reason. You cannot be in debt nearly so much as you have been, when you had no such intention . . . Think, James, of all your ancestors. Think of the hills themselves . . . Think of the water of Findhorn, think of the possibility of your passing that road, and saying these are now the lands of a stranger!

His plea was made more poignant by the fact Wilde's mind was shattered later. Mackintosh did not heed him but two years passed before the sale was completed, and it did little to reestablish his finances; of the £9,000 purchase price, only £300 was transmitted to him, the rest swallowed up by his own drawings in advance of the sale, and by payments to Lord Lauderdale, Uncle Duncan Campbell, and others with claims on the estate.

The Mackintoshes spent Christmas with their relatives at Cote House, and on 6 January 1800 he wrote from there to George Moore, about his next round of lectures, and expressed final disillusionment with France, where a coup made Napoleon virtual dictator with the title of first consul:

> The last extraordinary Revolution in France which has rooted up every Principle of Democracy in that country and banished the people from all

concern in the government . . . The whole power is now vested for ever in Bonaparte and a body of his creatures . . . I greatly admire your honesty and magnanimity in openly professing your conversion. I think I shall have the courage to imitate you. I have too long submitted to mean and evasive compromises. It is my intention in this winter's lectures to profess publicly and unequivocally that I abhor, abjure and for ever renounce the French Revolution with all its sanguinary history, its abominable principles and for ever execrable leaders.

In a letter from Serle Street two weeks later Mackintosh confided to Jos. Wedgwood the number of paying pupils for his lectures had dropped to sixty, and he did not think it worth while attempting a third round. Politics still fascinated him: 'I passed six and a half hours in the gallery of the House of Commons on Monday in expectation of a debate which went off from Pitt's illness which some say arose from his port and others think was imported by the Hamburg mails from Berlin'—a reference to unpalatable war news. William Bayley Wallace, who wrote a biographical sketch of Mackintosh after his death, said as a result of his lectures he was offered an undersecretaryship by Pitt, but declined because of loyalty to Fox and other Whigs.

In spite of his Cambridge research, the lecturer still depended largely on memory in his second course. The same student who retailed the triplets anecdote said he took notes during the earlier series, and James borrowed them saying he had lost his own memoranda.

In the audience was Coleridge, then working for Daniel Stuart on *The Morning Post*. He wrote to Jos. Wedgwood: 'I have attended Mackintosh regularly. He was so kind as to send me a ticket, and I have not failed to profit by it.' Three months later he wrote from Somerset to William Godwin in a different tone. Saying he had met Humphry Davy, then an assistant to Dr Beddoes at Bristol and later a distinguished scientist: 'He always talks of you with great affection and defends you with a friend's zeal against the animalcula, who live on the dung of the great Dung-fly Mackintosh.'

Coleridge sided with those who felt Godwin was unfairly attacked in the lectures. He and others were shocked when James announced publicly his repudiation of the French Revolution in the words of the recantation of heresy he employed in his letter to Moore. It was a decade in which many men regretted their earlier enthusiasm for an experiment which dissolved into bloodshed and tyranny, especially those like Mackintosh with first hand experience of the situation in France. William Wordsworth and Robert Southey, outspoken Radicals in youth, quickly became reactionary Tories; Lord Castlereagh, conservative at home and abroad, started his political career as an Irish Whig. Coleridge himself wrote two years earlier to a brother complaining his reputation as a democrat and seditionist had clung to him:

> A man's character follows him long after he has ceased to deserve it, but I have snapped my squeaking baby-trumpet of sedition, and the fragments lie scattered in the lumber-room of penitence. I wish to be a good man and a Christian, but I am no Whig, no Reformist, no Republican.

He wrote a poem called *Recantation*, later discreetly retitled *France: an ode*. Those who retained youthful illusions, like Hazlitt, were forced to pretend Napoleon, the child of revolution, was its upholder. In a Napoleonic world Hazlitt's own writings would have been ruthlessly suppressed with other symptoms of dissent.

It was not so much Mackintosh's change of heart as his open proclamation of it, with the unspoken implication others should do the same, that made his hearers uncomfortable. Some of his associates, jealous of his success, suspected him of wishing to placate the ministry engaged in war with France.

There seems to be no evidence he was offered a junior post in government but he was certainly courted by people in touch with the prime minister. Among these were the Duchess of Gordon, a formidable hostess whose Pall Mall house was a rallying point for Tories, and William Windham, one of a group of Whigs who joined Pitt's administration. Mackintosh wrote to Moore in March 1800:

> On Thursday evening Mrs M and I were at a numerous and brilliant party at the Duchess of Gordon's where for the first time for several years I saw and conversed with Windham. His conversation is full of sense, knowledge and vivacity and his manners very gentle. We talked with equal enthusiasm of Burke and with equal abhorrence of Democrats and Philosophers.

Major Pryse Lockhart Gordon stated: 'Jane, Duchess of Gordon, who, at that time had considerable influence in Scottish affairs, and was intimate with Pitt and Dundas, told me that she had in vain tried all her persuasive powers, and they were not small, to detach him from his party.'

But he kept in touch with Canning. Dr Parr had fallen foul of this senstive politician, and Mackintosh tried to arrange a dinner of reconciliation at his home. Canning replied immediately that, while willing to dine with James himself, and to welcome him as a guest at his own table, he must decline to meet Parr: 'The language, in which, as I have reason to believe, Dr Parr has been for some years past in the habit of indulging himself respecting me, is such as, according to my way of thinking, no political differences of opinion could justify.'

With his lecture fees shrinking, and his family growing—Catherine was pregnant—Mackintosh approached Canning about obtaining an appointment as a judge in India. In two letters in June 1800 he made it clear he was not promising political support for the government, in which Canning was at the board of control responsible for the subcontinent and patronage there: 'I have no possible claim to favour—I have rendered no services and I have no influence . . . you have never shewn friendship to one less capable of returning it by any services.'

Mackintosh learned that year his brother had died in the West Indies, where losses in the forces because of fever were high. In July he lamented 'the death of my most excellent grandmother', recalling 'her tender care of my infancy and youth'. *The Morning Post* obituary described her as 'Mrs MacGillivray, widow of the late Alexander MacGillivray Esq Merchant of Charlestown, and daughter of Alex Fraser, Esq, late of Balnain. Her sense, honesty and kindness, her blameless and useful life, will be long affectionately remembered by her numerous friends.' In a letter to his Aunt Mary he promised to arrange for monuments to be placed at Dunlichity for his grandmother, and at Petty for his father. She replied: 'I well know you tenderly loved our valuable parent and was by her most tenderly beloved, often in her last illness did she pray God to bless you and yours.'

Late in the summer Catherine stayed with her father at Cresselly to await the birth of her child. The atmosphere was tense. John Bartlett Allen was a foxhunting squire who, after dinner, would sometimes crash his fist down on the table and order those daughters still at home, Jessie, Fanny, and Emma, to entertain him with conversation. However, it made them articulate when they moved in society. Nor was the strong will all on one side. After the death of his first wife, Captain Allen married the daughter of a collier on his estate, and had three children by her. His daughters forbade him to bring this second family into the house, an eighteenth century building which has since been enlarged.

Catherine was close to her father—some of her sisters thought their temperaments were too much alike. In spite of her sufferings the previous year, she was in high spirits when she wrote to her husband on 16 August:

> Your expressment to hear from me on Saturday I feel very flattering . . . ours is not at least a dull state of matrimony thanks to the frequent boilings of my Welsh blood, an insipid state of general regard and gentle dullness I humbly deprecate as a very intolerable one. I would rather know that I had a heart by its achings than feel as if I had no heart at all. One might as well not exist at all as not feel that we do exist, therefore long life to kissing and quarrelling with our lovers and our husbands.

By the bye in reading just now an extract from Burns life in the papers I
fancied a resemblance of character between you and him as you must have
been in your early days, both a similar propensity to science, love and
poetry . . . Burns continued to cultivate his love for the fair, where they are
fairest amidst the innocent occupations of a remote country life while you
repair to the smoking Dunghills of an Edinburgh University where low
debauchery, vulgar dissipation and vain and pernicious sciences are learnt in
pretty equal proportions . . . had it been our fortunes to have met when we
should have been both strangers to the vices or sufferings of life perhaps you
might with more justice than since have thought me as Burns did his first
Goddess at the pretty age of fifteen 'A bonnie, sweet sonsie lass' and what
do you think I should not have found you?—why every thing I could have
wished all my own from the beginning.

Her husband arrived at the end of August, and set about charming the
poor prisoners as he described his sisters-in-law. Fanny Allen related: 'I
shall never forget that time; he delighted every one who saw him, by the
readiness and pleasantness of his conversation. His good spirits prevented
the constraint and awe that superior understandings so often excite.' Even
Captain Allen thawed. Bessy Wedgwood, who had also made the
journey to be with her sister, told Jos.: 'I think my father begins to relish
society more than he did. I fancy he was a little afraid of Mackintosh at
first, but he has now found out that he is by no means overbearing, and
he finds himself comfortable in his company.'

The baby kept them waiting, but Mackintosh wrote cheerfully to
George Moore, warning him to avoid boredom: 'One great remedy is
marriage, which, if it were only good for stirring the mind, would by
that alone make up for all the noise of the nursery.' This time there were
no complications, and the child was christened Frances Emma Elizabeth,
a compliment to her attendant aunts. She was to be her father's favourite
daughter.

Christmas 1800 was spent with the Wedgwoods in their new home,
the manor house at Tarrant Gunville; two or three months later the
Mackintoshes left their Serle Street home for a larger house, 60 Upper
Guilford Street, Bloomsbury. The lectures had attracted notice; he
appeared in cases of constitutional and international law brought before
committees of the House of Commons, and the privy council. He
reported to Moore he was enjoying a steady flow of business at the
Cockpit, the nickname for Westminster Hall where judges presided
before the Strand lawcourts were built.

He was equally bullish about the country assizes, to which judges,
barristers and officials went in a kind of travelling circus for weeks at a
time. 'I was busy on circuit where I have had uncommon success.' he told
Moore. Writing to Catherine from Thetford, Norfolk, on 18 March

1801, Mackintosh said he made a speech of an hour and three-quarters in a defence of a clergyman accused of challenging an officer to a duel. But he expressed doubts about the assurance he received from his client that half the court were drowned in tears.

An example of the Scotsman's talent was given by Scarlett:

> A cause between two Frenchmen had been referred to arbitration; he was counsel for the plaintiff. The defendant, a noble emigrant, pleaded his own cause in person. When the parties were assembled before the arbitrator, the defendant complained of the hardship to which he was exposed from his imperfect knowledge of English, having to combat a gentleman of such extraordinary talents as he who appeared for his opponent was known to possess. Mr Mackintosh, to accommodate him, without further preparation, made his speech, and conducted the whole controversy in French, with a facility and elegance that were applauded by all who heard him.

Presumably the arbitrator was equally gifted.

Life was not unclouded. In the Thetford letter he expressed pleasure his wife had made up a quarrel with sister Jessie: 'That two such women as you should not love each other would be too bad.' In Buckingham four months later he was suffering from toothache, and found lodging with a surgeon a doubtful advantage: 'The laudanum which my landlord applied to the tooth stupefies me and pain irritates me.'

He remained a voracious reader and anxious to put his knowledge to account. He confided to George Moore:

> I am in treaty with the body of London Booksellers about a new edition of Johnson's Poets which is intended to be *Corpus Poetarum* from Chaucer to Cowper and for which I am to write lives and criticisms for all the poets before Cowley with whom Johnson begins and since Gray with whom he ends. The ancient poets will be very troublesome especially Chaucer and Spenser, but I console myself for my ignorance of our ancient literature by the reflection that criticism in such a work as this ought not be very learned and recondite but such as every man of good taste can feel and that if I were learned in the literature of the middle ages I ought to keep back my learning in a popular book. Johnson's own criticism is popular. Is this a sufficient excuse for my undertaking to criticise writers whom it requires a vast portion of all such reading as was never read thoroughly to understand?

The treaty remained unsigned. It was Thomas Campbell who produced the *Specimens of the British Poets* nearly 20 years later. Another scheme which failed was a proposal to launch a twice-weekly literary journal, in which his collaborators would have been Bobus Smith, Scarlett, Rogers and Sharp. The suggested title, *The Batchelor,* does not sound inspired, and the project foundered when Smith accepted an

appointment as advocate-general for Bengal, a post Mackintosh would
have liked. Perhaps discussions about *The Batchelor* had some influence
when Smith's brother Sydney helped to launch *The Edinburgh Review*
shortly afterwards.

James could congratulate Bobus with good grace on his appointment,
since the prospect had opened up of a career even more to his taste.
Marquis Wellesley, governor-general in Bengal, and acting as if he knew
one day the title would be viceroy, realised the need for an efficient civil
service to administer the territories. These were expanding, partly
thorugh his own policies, in which he had the military support of his
young brother, the future Duke of Wellington. He wished to establish a
college at Fort William, Calcutta, where the motley collection of young
civilians sent to India in search of fortune could learn the elements of
their role as combined magistrates, rulers and commercial ambassadors
among millions of people whose beliefs and customs differed totally from
their own.

Mackintosh wrote to James Greene to say he had received a letter
inviting him to become professor of ethics, politics and public law in the
college: 'The salary is £3,000 a year with a house and a pension of which
the minimum is £1,000 after seven years service . . . It seems to be
generally thought that I may return in 10 years with £50,000 and my
pension. This temptation is so great that most of my friends think I can
hardly hesitate.'

Negotiations dragged on, made more complicated by the dual nature
of the British presence in India. Theoretically it was commercial, guided
by the East India Company and its court of directors. But for some years
over-riding political decisions had rested with a government minister at
the head of the board of control. In between was the governor-general;
since it took at least six months to send a letter from Calcutta to London
and receive a reply a forceful man like Lord Wellesley could act as a rajah
in many respects. But the college meant long-term expense, and he was
finally defeated by the directors, who pleaded that however great the
fortunes made by their servants, the East India Company was losing
money. When a college opened at Fort William, it was on a much
smaller scale than Lord Wellesley hoped; Mackintosh played no part in it.
During these manoeuvres Catherine Mackintosh started a diary,
beginning on 5 June 1801 and ceasing, as far as surviving pages go, on
July 28. Most entries were unremarkable, covering singing lessons, acting
godmother to a child of James Scarlett, and taking 'a mess of pottage and
pudding' to a poor boy and his mother. Other entries illustrated the way
in which, while Georgian husbands dined out unaccompanied by their
wives, these felt free to attend mixed parties without their husbands,
which might be frowned on even now. It was worth remarking when

'Mackintosh had invitations to dinner for today from Lord Rosslyn and Lady Melbourne but he declined them and dined alone with me'.

Stately Catherine had a dark, troubled side to her nature which even her sisters could not penetrate. On the first page of this fragment of diary she spoke of 'my present unmerited happiness which I hope to deserve in future better than I have hitherto deserved it'. Three days later she felt her 'mind and feelings in a comfortable state, my repining of the past subsiding gratefully'. While her husband was away on circuit, she wrote: 'In the house all day till night when I walked alone in the New Square and pondered on my past life till I shed tears plentifully of regret and vexation. Weather charming.'

On another occasion she 'felt quite sick and faint before my supper came because, as I suppose I had *not taken* my . . .' What Catherine had not taken is unrecorded, because a corner of the sheet is obliterated by a stain. One of Mrs Mackintosh's problems was lacking the talent to be hostess to a man who liked to entertain beyond his income: 'For once in my life I was satisfied with my own dinner which Escudier dressed very well indeed. In ye evening Parr very gay.'

In June 1801 Sydney Smith visited London and wrote to his friend in Edinburgh, advocate Francis Jeffrey, that he had been impressed by Mackintosh: 'He does not wish for the best in politics or morals but for the best which can be attained; and what that is he seems to know well.'

During the summer Mackintosh learned he had lost another army relative, 21-year-old Angus Campbell, son of the Duncan who did his best to look after Kyllachy. James wrote to William Adam asking whether it was possible to approach the Duke of York about 'the means of bringing to justice a commissary who appears to have murdered a young cousin of mine, Captain Campbell of the 37th in the West Indies. The matter would I conceive be best put into a train of inquiry by application to the Commander in Chief.' How the commissary, in charge of supplying food, caused this tragedy was not explained. When Margaret Campbell, the young man's mother died four years later, the inscription on her monument at Peterhead said she never recovered from the shock.

With memories also of his brother's fate, Mackintosh naturally hesitated about accepting an offer late in July from ministerial sources to become judge of one of the vice-admiralty courts being established in Jamaica and Guadeloupe. He still hoped for the Calcutta professorship. He asked for these manoeuvres to be kept secret, but inevitably they were not.

A bitter lampoon on him as a place-seeker in a radical newspaper, The Albion, ran:

> Thou'rt like Judas an apostate black,
> In the resemblance one thing thou dost lack;
> When he had gotten his ill-purchas'd pelf
> He went away and wisely hang'd himself:
> This thou may do at last; yet much I doubt,
> If thou hast any Bowels to gush out!

Felix Macarthy was a contributor to the paper, but the lines were written by Charles Lamb. Lamb's view of the Scottish barrister could have been coloured by Coleridge and Godwin, a much milder philosopher by that time than the muddled anarchist of the early 1790s. Lamb had contributed the prologue and epilogue to Godwin's play *Antonio* which was damned by *The Morning Post* when presented at Drury Lane at the end of 1800. The *Post* was not alone in this, the play was virtually unactable, and the first night audience had been hostile.

There seems to be no evidence that Mackintosh was the dramatic critic concerned, but he certainly endorsed the attack, and suggested the philosopher based his hero on someone in his novel, *Caleb Williams*. Writing to Jos. Wedgwood he expressed himself with a sharpness he rarely used even in private letters:

> You have probably heard of the damnation of Godwin's tragedy. *He has shamed the rogues by printing it.* His principal character is a very bad copy of Falkland. The madman of honour again commits assassination and to make the matter more complete it is on a woman! The man has it must be owned excellent notions of a Castilian Cavalier of the fifteenth century. This gives me still higher esteem for polite literature as a test of a man's real merit. As long as Godwin lurked in the gloom of metaphysics his nonsense could not easily be exposed to the vulgar. But when he ventures into the broad daylight of human life the meanness of his puny talents is conspicuous to the whole world.

In September 1801 the Mackintoshes visited Edinburgh, renewing acquaintance with Sydney Smith, and the Highlands. There James reflected on the fate of two of his fellow students in the 1780s. Charles Hope was lord advocate, and among prisoners under his control was Thomas Addis Emmet, held in Fort George for his activities as an Irish nationalist. Emmet survived to become a New York barrister. Mackintosh also spent two days with Henry Dundas, who apparently bore no grudge for the contemptuous terms in which he had been described in the *Letter* to Pitt some years before. The former secretary of state resigned with the prime minister when the King opposed any relaxation of restrictions on Catholics.

The return south was enlivened by a visit to Liverpool. Among barristers James mixed with in London was Thomas Creevey, known to posterity for the mischievous indiscretions of the 'Papers' he left when he died. Creevey's friend James Currie, a Liverpool doctor, liked to entertain legal men with business in Lancashire. Dr Currie wrote to Creevey on 11 February 1802:

> I never had an opportunity of thanking you for your skill in showing off Mackintosh. He is a wonderful Lion: not what you would call a Scotchman—but an indolent, thoughtless, innocent sort of man that will be continually in scrapes, and that will not get forward with all his extraordinary talents, unless somebody take him up and push him on.

On 13 January 1802 Sydney Smith wrote to James from Edinburgh about the proposal to launch *The Edinburgh Review*: 'What do you think of the form of publication, and the probability of sale? We wish to weigh the matter well, and if your literary experience can suggest anything for the improvement of the plan, we shall be extremely thankful to you for your counsel.' He invited James to become a contributor, a suggestion not taken up, perhaps because in the first year no payment was made to authors. The clergyman added a typical quip about the promotion of his friend's Edinburgh University relative: 'Tytler has been long in anticipation of the judge's gown, and is so totally disqualified in every respect for the office that I am rather surprised his appointment should be so long delayed.'

On 18 February Mackintosh once more had a son. The boy was probably delicate, since Robert was not baptised until 24 July at St George's church, Bloomsbury. On circuit, the father wrote from Thetford, Norfolk, on 21 March:

> It was really vexatious to see ten civil causes at Cambridge without one brief for me which I am convinced arose from the report of my going to India. Yesterday I was employed from 8 till 3 in the defence of two unfortunate wretches who were convicted of uttering forged banknotes on the evidence of the miscreants who had *tempted* them. I bullied and blasted the accomplices in examination . . . My clients were convicted and will I fear infallibly be hanged.

Later in the year Catherine wrote from Cresselly: 'My father observing as I read your letter the goodly size of the paper and the well filled pages said in a *lively manner for* him that among so many briefs as you mentioned missing it was evident you had not sent me *one*.'

Another crop of contested parliamentary elections gave James an opportunity to display his legal-historical knowledge. If he had any doubts about the need for reform these hearings before committees of MPs dispelled them. Following a poll at Taunton he appeared with

Adam for a candidate who claimed his opponent was the returning officer and refused to acknowledge votes cast against himself. At Boston, Lincolnshire, bribes of five guineas were offered. Some were taken by men ineligible to vote, leading to a wrangle over whether it was unlawful to bribe a non-voter. One of Mackintosh's clients, elected for Hereford, admitted paying five shillings each and providing modest refreshment at inns; his defence was all candidates had done the same 'with the commendable intention of preventing those enormous expenses and scenes of debauchery, which too frequently attend popular elections'.

In 1802 the peace concluded at Amiens gave Europe a pause in what became known as the Napoleonic Wars. Britons streamed across the Channel to Paris and beyond. Among them were James and Catherine, but first he was presented to the king in London. This paved the way for him to be introduced formally to the French head of state, Napoleon. Through some mishap the man ahead of Mackintosh in the queue, William Frankland, was complimented as the author of *Vindiciae Gallicae*, while he himself was asked whether he had ever been lord mayor of London.

Catherine was presented at what amounted to the court of Josephine. She wrote home describing Bonaparte reviewing his troops before the Tuilleries: 'The little great or rather the great little man sat on a beautiful white horse with a scarlet saddle cloth laced richly with gold, he rode near enough to the windows where we sat to see his extreme pallidness.'

During this month's stay in the autumn of 1802 Mackintosh met many ministers and other leading citizens. He prophesied the country's fate in a letter to Dugald Stewart:

> It appeared to me, that all the elements of a free, or even of a civil government, have been broken and dispersed in the course of the Revolution. Nothing, I own, would surprise me more than to see any authority in France not resting chiefly on military force; the Revolution unanimously condemned; a dread of change greater than the passion for change was in 1789; a broken-spirited people, and a few virtuous and well-informed men, without adherents, without concert, without extraordinary talents, breathing vain wishes for liberty:—these were the features which most struck me in the political state of France. Frenchmen seem destined to be the slaves of a military chief, and the terror of their neighbours for a time.

These views were unpalatable to many Whigs, particularly Fox, who thought the fragile peace could be preserved by accommodation with Napoleon. When he encountered Mackintosh in the Louvre, he passed him with a brief nod, and later told his companion, Samuel Rogers, he was angry with the Scotsman for seeking a place in India from a Tory government. But Fox's uncle, General Richard Fitzpatrick, told Rogers the real reason was Mrs Mackintosh had not paid a formal call on his wife. Formerly Mrs Armistead, she had been Fox's mistress, and even when they married it was kept secret for some years. People who flout the conventions often expect others to be punctilious in observing them.

The Whig leader's charm and oratory brought him whole-hearted admirers. Creevey declared his own creed was 'devotion to Fox . . . the imcomparable Charley!' But it has been well said he would make any sacrifice to his friends short of taking their advice.

Mackintosh's admiration for Burke did not endear him to the Foxites. When, as a gesture of posthumous reconciliation, he asked Fox to take the lead in suggesting a memorial to his former friend, Fox replied:

> There may be a good deal in what you say concerning the propriety of my moving some public honours to Burke, but whether it be owing (which I think very likely) to want of magnanimity or to whatever other cause I cannot bring myself to do it, tho' I should not oppose but rather support a proposition of this kind if made by another. At the same time I am satisfied that your motives in suggestting such a measure can not be otherwise than kind to me.

Unfortunately Coleridge then launched an attack on the Whig leader in *The Morning Post*. He was urged to do so by Daniel Stuart, who was upset by so many Britons rushing to Paris. The editor told Coleridge: 'Pray write the letter to Fox—and pray abuse those coxcombs who pay adoration going to Bonaparte—Erskine, Mackintosh etc.'

The poet obliged. He had already sent to the newspaper verses on Mackintosh even more virulent than the rhymes by Lamb. They referred to him as a 'counsellor keen . . . with a waxy face and a blubber lip, and a black tooth in front to show in part what was the colour of his whole heart', and indicating the Devil would one day claim 'This Scotchman compleat'. Stuart deleted the most obvious references to his brother-in-law and his broken tooth. But they were widely circulated; when Coleridge issued his collected poems after the victim's death he passed them off as 'mere sport'.

Why Coleridge hated his benefactor is not clear; seeking motives in a mind as mercurial as his, then beginning to sink under the influence of opium, is hazardous. There were obvious points of friction, the difference of opinion over Godwin, and their involvement with *The Morning Post*. Stuart declared Coleridge was a more valuable contributor than Mackintosh, but the poet may have been uneasily aware his rival was more dependable. James himself said the enmity dated from their first meeting in 1797, and it was presumably from him Stuart heard the story, which he repeated when both Coleridge and Mackintosh were dead, that the Scotsman had flustered the poet in conversational combat on philosophical subjects. Coleridge's early letters to Mackintosh do not reflect this hostility, it became apparent only in London, where he came under the influence of Godwin.

On 30 January 1802 James sent a cordial invitation to Coleridge to dinner with 'my friends Sharp and Bobus'. But mixing with brilliant talkers gave him an inferiority complex, a disagreeable experience for a man accustomed to a captive audience. An entry he made in his notebook after Mackintosh had been knighted ran: 'When I am in company with Mr Sharp, Sir J Mackintosh, R & Sydney Smith, Mr Scarlett etc, I feel like a child, nay rather like an inhabitant of another planet. Their very faces all act upon me, sometimes, as if they were ghosts, but more often as if I were a ghost among them—at all times as if we were not consubstantial.'

The *Letter to Fox* suggested by Stuart was followed by another attacking him for going to Paris and consorting with Napoleon, who was also bitterly abused. Coleridge signed the articles with thinly-disguised initials, and on 9 November 1802 this second letter declared: 'Your name and your authority have drawn over to Paris, and to the consular levees, a cluster of your Parliamentary friends.' He described as 'Bonaparte's courtiers' the 'group of degenerate Englishmen (though indeed to the honour of that name the greater number have been Scotchmen and Irishmen)', and added: 'Some of your fellow-courtiers had procured themselves to be presented at St James's purposely and solely to enable them to appear at the levees of . . . this low-born Corsican.'

Apart from resenting criticism of himself, Fox suggested the attack on Napoleon was a cause of the renewal of the war six months later. Inevitably, Mackintosh was suspected of having a hand in the *Post* letters, but he later stated he had no communication with Coleridge on the subject, pointing out it was well-known he was 'a man not well disposed to receive suggestions or materials from any one'. He declared: 'I had no control over the editor of the paper which could have prevented the publication of the letters in which I was myself by very clear implication abused.'

Mackintosh's feelings about Napoleon were revealed when he accepted a five-guinea brief to defend Jean Peltier, a French royalist refugee to England. The charge brought by the government was criminal libel over articles in his newspaper *L'Ambigou* alleged to be an incitement to assassinate the first consul who, during the peace, was regarded as the head of a friendly power. Since there was no doubt this was Peltier's intention, James turned the defence in the Court of King's Bench on 21

February 1803 into an indictment of Napoleon for trying to suppress freedom of speech in Britain: 'I consider it as the first of a long series of conflicts between the greatest power in the world, and the only free press remaining in Europe.'

Running to more than 20,000 words drawing on precedents from the days of Queen Elizabeth and William III, and decorated with Latin quotations, the speech probably did little for his client. But it was praised highly by other barristers. Peltier was convicted, but renewal of the war meant he was never sentenced. This saved ministers some embarrassment, since it transpired he was a paid agent of the government; the prosecution was, as Mackintosh alleged, instigated by Napoleon.

A month after his great speech, while on circuit, he received a letter form Catherine, headed 'Mr Swann's near Terrace Walk, Hampstead' telling him:

> You little know how ill your little boy is he was taken with convulsion fits on Sunday night which have increased ever since in frequency and violence. Since Monday morn I have not had my clothes off or been in bed and I have this instant left my little angel's crib to write you that you may be sure I leave nothing undone in this case so near to me that can be done. I left town on Tuesday forenoon and have been here since in a state of equal hope and fear.

On 25 April Robert was buried in Hampstead churchyard. Mackintosh was again without an heir, his anxiety increased by the knowledge his wife was pregnant. In Wales Grandfather Allen was similarly agitated. Fanny Allen wrote to her brother Baugh: 'I think I have never seen my father so animated as he is at present about all his children and particularly Kitty, it would be a good weight off his mind to hear of her confinement and he is very impatiently looking for it every day.' But the Cresselly captain died before Elizabeth was born in the house in Guilford Street on 13 June.

James finally received an appointment as a judge, filling the vacancy caused by the death of Sir William Syer, recorder of Bombay. His friends, George Canning and William Adam, used their influence, and it was providential that the prime minister was now Henry Addington, who as Speaker supported him over the Lincoln's Inn lectures, and knew of his disappointment at missing the Calcutta professorship.

He must have realised accepting even a non-political office from a Tory government would further alienate his friends, especially as the appointment carried a knighthood with it. Nor would those who opposed the war be likely to approve of his joining the Loyal North Britons, one of many volunteer battalions which sprang up to defend the country against invasion by the French. He took the chair at a meeting of

400 men eager to support the unit on 1 August 1803 at the Crown and Anchor, meeting place of the King of Clubs, and delivered a stirring speech. He said: 'Though no man living loves the country in which we now reside more than I do, yet the place of my birth will ever be peculiarly dear to me, and I shall always consider it as one of the distinctions of my life, to fight the battles of the British Empire in the ranks of a regiment of Scotchmen.' He had the candour to admit he would himself soon leave the country for a distant part of that empire.

James was elected a captain. John Mackintosh would have been proud of his son, though puzzled by the speed of his promotion.

Dr Parr made no secret of his disapproval of the recorder of Bombay, his pugnacity perhaps increased by a serious illness in 1803. A story circulated that Mackintosh was discussing a treason trial in which an Irish priest named James Quigley was condemned to death, and called him a rascal. Parr rejoined: 'Yes, Jamie, he was a bad man, but might have been worse; he was an Irishman, but he might have been a Scotchman; he was a priest, but he might have been a lawyer; he was a republican, but he might have been an apostate.'

This anecdote smells more of the study lamp than after dinner candles. Those who recorded it agree it happened in a large company, but seem always to have heard it from somebody else. Samuel Rogers learned of it from Fox; evidently the great Whig leader enjoyed repeating it. However, there was certainly an occasion when James lost his temper, a rare occurrence, with Parr, as he admitted in later correspondence.

Mackintosh had a brush with another fervent Foxite, James Perry. The newspaper editor continued to administer funds for Joseph Gerrald, using the money for the maintenance and education of his natural daughter. Some cash was left in the hands of those who collected it until needed, including about £20 held by Mackintosh. On 13 July 1803 Perry wrote asking for this money, but it was not forwarded for six months.

Although aware of the undercurrent of hostility against him, Mackintosh was too proud and busy to meet it as it arose. During his years in London the young Highlander was more than a little of a social and intellectual climber, seeking the best and most stimulating company. In accepting the post he could plead support for the Whigs had brought him no advancement, no offer of a seat in the Commons at the disposal of his aristocratic friends.

Yet he was not a political turncoat. If he had accepted the Duchess of Gordon's blandishments to turn Tory he would have received something better than a distant judicial post. Writing to Adam, James said: 'I have no claims on Addington—I have rendered him no services—I never conceived myself to contract any political obligations to him. You know better than I can tell you that the favours he has conferred on me were strictly personal arising from accidental intercourse about the college and with no other motive but a desire to make up for my disappointment in the failure of that plan.'

Nor did his strictures on the French Revolution arise through political opportunism. As early as 1792 he wrote to Parr that since publishing *Vindiciae Gallicae* 'many of my principles are not a little mitigated and qualified', and remarking that in it 'I may have stated principles too widely, and expressed sentiments too warmly (it was easier to imitate my illustrious antagonist in these defects than in his inimitable excellencies)'. Perhaps Addington and his cabinet felt, after the Peltier trial, it was desirable to remove such a powerful Whig orator far from Westminster; but the opposition had shown no inclination to put him there.

Meanwhile Mackintosh made a circuit of the country sessions—he earned £1,200 from his profession in this final year—and hurried to Wales. There John Hensleigh Allen had succeeded his father as squire of Cresselly, making it a happy place for his unmarried sisters and visiting relations.

On this occasion the focus of attention was a few miles away, at the seaside resort of Tenby, where James and Catherine, and the five children, passed the late summer and autumn. Fanny Allen, who was twenty-two, wrote:

> We were a large family party, collected to pass as much of our time together, before the departure of Mackintosh and his family for India, as circumstances would allow of. It was a delightful autumn. A little memorandum of M.'s that I saw many years afterwards, mentions this time as one of the happiest of his life. He made the delight and joy of our circle; his spirits were gay, no care oppressed him, and his anticipations of the future had all the brightness of early hope.

This was succeeded by farewell parties in London, among the attenders being the Sydney Smiths, now living near the Mackintoshes, Rogers, Scarlett, Sharp, and Amelia Sloper and her father. As a last extravagance James had his portrait painted by Sir Thomas Lawrence, and his wife's by John Hoppner, two artists who joined the celebrations. For Fanny Allen the festivities were enlivened by a beau, Sharp's city partner Samuel Boddington, who received £10,000 damages when his wife eloped with his cousin Benjamin in 1797.

On 21 December 1803 Mackintosh was dubbed knight at St James's Palace. Lady Mackintosh was presented at court, causing a flurry of quills between those of her sisters who saw the event and others in the country. In spite of the attack in *The Morning Post*, James still admired Coleridge—

3 Lady Mackintosh, believed to be by John Hoppner.

2 Sir James Mackintosh. An engraving after a portrait by Sir Thomas Lawrence.

Marriage *James Mackintosh of the Parish of St Church Dured in the County of Middlesex*
of Parish
and *Katharine Allen* of the
were
Parish
Married in this *Church* by *Licence*
this *tenth* Day of *April* in the Year One Thousand Seven
Hundred and *ninety eight* by me *Tho. Broughton Minister*
This Marriage was solemnized between Us { *James Mackintosh*
{ *Catherine Allen*
In the Presence of *John Wedgwood I. Mackintosh*

4 Extract from Westbury-on-Trym wedding register. Reproduced by permission of the Diocese of Bristol.

5 Aldourie in 1851.

Sydney Smith declared the Scotsman had no gall bladder—and offered to get him an appointment as part of his staff in Bombay. The offer was rejected contemptuously.

Instead Mackintosh engaged William Erskine, a young Scotsman, as secretary, with the promise of later advancement. Erskine was a friend of Francis Horner, a rather solemn Edinburgh advocate who settled in London and was destined to shine as a Whig politician. Horner told William in a letter:

> As to books you will hardly find it necessary to carry out any. Mackintosh carries out an immense and well selected library. It contains all the classical writers, ancient and modern, including the German; every scrap, I believe, that has ever been printed about Asiatic history, antiquities and topography; a more extensive collection than I ever saw elsewhere, of metaphysical writers—good, indifferent or execrable. . . he carries out to Bombay the folio vols of Aquinas and Duns Scotus.

Permission to transport his library free was granted by the East India Company, which under the complicated system of administering the country paid the recorder's salary. Out of his £5,000 a year Mackintosh received an advance of £3,000 before sailing, so he entered his new life as he lived the old—in debt.

With a governess, Miss Amelia D'Aubigne, the family left London at the end of January for Ryde, Isle of Wight. There, while waiting for favourable winds they were joined by friends. Among the last letters James received in England was one from Sharp telling him: 'I owe much to your society . . . I have received more advantage from it, than from that of all my other companions.'

A few last embraces and handshakes and the *Winchelsea*, commanded by Captain Walter Campbell, set out for what was then a 15,000-mile voyage on 14 February 1804.

Chapter Four

Lawgiver of Bombay

Their passage was swift and uneventful. Lady Mackintosh wrote from sea to her sister Harriet Surtees, married to a Gloucestershire clergyman:

> Nothing could have been more prosperous than our voyage. The Bay of Biscay even put on a countenance more flattering than usual . . . We expect to be at Bombay by the "King's Birthday'. Since I have been *introduced at court* you see this is my courtly method of computation. I meant by the way to have written you an account of her Majesty's gracious reception of me and what a little insignificant hideous ill-draped dwarf she appeared to me by way of a Queen.

She reported Captain Campbell was handsome, spirited and unaffected. For fellow-passengers they had half-a-dozen army and navy officers 'all very obliging and good-humoured', though 'as to understanding, acquirements and conversation they are certainly below par and poor Mack misses in consequence the society he has left behind him'. For her there were compensations: 'During the fine moonlight nights we had a very pleasant and picturesque dance on the deck which I began to enjoy very much.'

When the naval escort left half-way to their destination, the *Winchelsea* was exposed to possible interception by French privateers. Sir James, on the strength of his title and captaincy in the Loyal North Britons, took command of a party of pikemen, ready to repel boarders. Several alarms occurred at the approach of vessels, but none proved hostile.

He took Sunday services on the quarter deck. But most of his time was occupied by study, reading to daughters, or improving his German with the help of their governess. His aim was to tackle that country's philosophers, though he never seemed to relish the task. It was not long before he turned to Italian literature. However much he missed the King of Clubs wits, he enjoyed the company of young people anxious to add to their knowledge, and made himself popular by chatting with officers and cadets in the poop in the cool of the evening.

In less than three and a half months they reached Bombay but misfortune struck shortly before they did so. He recorded:

We suffered nothing from ill-health till the last week when Lady M by a little run along the quarter deck with her youngest child brought on a miscarriage which unfitted her for encountering the fierce sun which we found burning over our heads on our arrival and which has since produced disagreeable consequences.

Two days later on Monday 26 May 1804 the recorder took his seat, to a salute of 17 guns from the battery at the city's fort, and prepared to hear his first case. Probably to his relief this case, an allegation of rape, was dropped. Bombay had only one judge, assisted by magistrates; there were no juries in civil cases, throwing an extra burden on him. But the following day Mackintosh made it plain to his compatriots in the corner of the Empire he meant to put his own stamp on proceedings. Before the court was a young European accused of assaulting a native.

The *Bombay Courier* reported:

> The facts were clearly proved, and the Recorder informed the Jury that it was their duty by their verdict to make known to the world, that men of every colour and race and nation and religion in India were, under the British laws, equally protected; that they equally enjoyed the rational rights of men and the civil privileges of British subjects; that the law was no respecter of persons, but would protect with as strong an arm the poorest wretch in the most despised caste of India, as the proudest peer in the British Empire.

Fining the defendant 600 rupees, the judge recommended the money be paid to the victim. A rupee was then worth half a crown, one eighth of one pound sterling.

Since there was no official residence for the recorder, the Mackintoshes accepted an invitation from Governor Jonathan Duncan to occupy his country house at Parel, some five miles north of the city. In the days of Portuguese occupation this was a Jesuit monastery. The chapel had been turned into a banqueting hall, with a ballroom above, and there were fine gardens and a lake. Unfortunately malarial mosquitoes bred in its swampy surroundings, and the building's modern fate has been to serve as a plague laboratory.

At first Sir James regarded this as a temporary home, and sought permission from the East India Company, whose directors met in the City of London, to have part of the courthouse premises in Bombay converted for his family. But Governor Duncan, who lived in his town house, wrote to him:

> You are, I assure you, as welcome as can be to retain the use of Parel House, for your accommodation and that of your family. In your doing so, I shall have more satisfaction than in occupying it myself—for I have, for the most

part, only done so in a desultory way . . . Allow me then, my dear Sir, to consider you as the fixed tenants of Parel, as long as I have the disposal of it . . .

With respect to the other proposition, it is very reasonable; and there ought not to be much difficulty in acquiescing in it, but you have no idea with what a jealous and inquisitorial eye the court of directors take up even the smallest addition to our present establishments, in reference to which it would almost make you smile to observe, the detailed and cautious steps and contrivances, by which, it became at all possible, to fix the courthouse, where it now is . . . if you can assist me, in the means of obviating the ready objections from Leadenhall Street, I will be extremely happy to see you accommodated in that respect to your liking.'

Eventually an apartment was provided for occasional use.

Back at Parel Lady Mackintosh organised a ball. She also headed the subscription list with a donation of a thousand rupees for the relief of famine in the neighbouring territory, and her husband drew attention to the high deathrate among refugees pouring into Bombay. The couple found it as difficult to economise in India as in London.

Sir James urged his friends to supply him with letters and among the first to arrive was a typical one from Sydney Smith:

I strongly recommend you to take bribes, not small ones . . . you will be punished in another world for it but you will be highly respected in this if you employ your wealth in expensive equipage and savoury repasts . . . My dear Mackintosh, prosper and return to many years of laughing and controversy with your friends.

To a more serious correspondent, Richard Sharp, Mackintosh wrote

The governor, who has been very civil to us, is an ingenious, intelligent man, not without capacity and disposition to speculate. Four and thirty years' residence in this country have *Brahminised* his mind and body. He is good-natured, inclined towards good, and indisposed to violence, but rather submissive to those who are otherwise.

They discovered the climate worse than anything they imagined:

Even in the evening, when we were tempted abroad by a sunless sky, we found the atmosphere like the air of a heated room. In about a fortnight the rains began, and tumbled from the heavens in such floods, that it seemed absurd to call them by the same name with the little sprinkling showers of Europe. Then the air was delightfully cooled, and we all exulted in our deliverance; but we were too quick in our triumph; we soon found that we were to pay in health for what we got in pleasure. The whole frame is here

rendered so exquisitely susceptible of the operation of cold and moisture, by
so long a continuance of dry heat, that the monsoon is the usual season for
the attack of those disorders of the bowels which, when they are neglected
or ill-treated, degenerate into an inflammation of the liver, the peculiar and
most fatal disease of this country . . .

Having been obliged to take one dose of Madeira, and another of
laudanum, I have this day put on an English coat and waistcoat, though the
thermometer be (I dare say) at 84°. After the use of medicines, so violent,
both of which continue to be with me equally unusual, you must not
wonder that I am somewhat dull this morning.'

While admitting the beauty of Bombay and neighbouring islands, and
the agreeable grounds in which their home was set, he grumbled the heat
kept them indoors most of the day, and their short evening walk
involved keeping watch for cobras. Mackintosh found society narrow
and dull, and he seized on the visit of an artist brother of the royal
academician, Richard Westall, as an opportunity to promote a young
man's career and secure stimulating company in a tour of Hindu monuments in the local caves, of which the best-known was at Elephanta:

As soon as I heard of his being here, I unearthed him. I offered him a room
in my house. I offered to go with him, in two or three months, when the
weather is cooler, to all the caves in this neighbourhood (some of them
more remarkable than Elephanta), to write a description for his prints, a
text for his Voyages Pittoresque des Cavernes, which, with my name,
might, I thought, more rapidly introduce him to the public after his return.
He was proof against all these offers, and returns with the same ship which
carries this letter. Love, I understand, prevails over his curiosity and
ambition, and he will not go to our cave, because his Dido is not here to
enter it with him.

His mind was full of projects, including a book on the principles of
morals. More immediately, in Bombay he planned to achieve 'the
reformation of the police, of the administration of penal law, and
particularly of the prison; which, as I intend, if possible, to return to
Europe with a bloodless ermine, will be my principal instrument of
punishment'. He regretted that, as the jail had been rebuilt recently, he
could not introduce Jeremy Bentham's scheme for a prison called a
panopticon. This was fortunate since, while dealing with existing abuses,
it involved constant surveillance which would surely have driven both
jailed and jailers mad.

In a letter to William Adam, James complained of the 'dulness and
lethargy of the English here, especially the civil servants', and added 'my
mind is in a desert and my body too often in a crowd'. He wrote to Basil
Montagu, suggesting he should take a vacant post at the Bombay bar.
Montagu made enquiries about the climate, and declined.

The chief centres of British rule in India were Calcutta, seat of the governor-general, and Madras. Bombay, an island port on the west coast, was the least important of the three presidencies, as they were called, and the most expensive because it was far from the larger concentrations of population and trade. But for the same reason Governor Duncan, assisted by a council, exercised considerable power. In this small world Mackintosh, the fount of justice, ranked number two and as the governor lacked a wife, Catherine was first lady. They found this eminence alternately flattering and irksome, involving large parties, small talk, and the risk of violating protocol.

Court sittings occupied only one day in four. On others, he confessed to Sharp he lounged, wrote, and 'alas! oftener loiter away the forenoon in the really beautiful apartments that contain my library'. Evenings without social engagements were spent reading to his family—their education was always an anxious concern of their father. He told his correspondent, in a letter dated 24 February 1805:

> Another variety of our life is a monthly meeting of the Literary Society, which I founded and opened by a discourse *de ma façon*, in November. I thought it a sort of *duty* to try something. All that I mean to do is, to tell others what they are to pursue, why they ought to seek, and how they will best attain it. The comparative value of different parts of knowledge, the intrinsic value of each, and the rules for its successful cultivation are discovered, estimated and taught by philosophy. To contemplate oriental matters in this point of view, is not to be an orientalist, but a philosopher. Now, philosophy is my trade, though I have hitherto been but a poor workman.'

His society inspired some officials and military men to undertake research into Indian affairs—William Erskine, who became secretary, developed into a considerable Persian scholar, and worked for many years to produce a book of Indian history. The institution was based on one founded in Calcutta by Sir William Jones, and both survived as branches of the Asiatic Society. Having set others to work Mackintosh was characteristically slow to do so himself, in his opening discourse he commented: 'Those philosophers who have denied the influence of climate on the human character were not inhabitants of a tropical country.'

He told Sharp: 'I observe that you touch me with the spur once or twice about my book on morals: I felt it gall me, for I have not yet begun ... what has either really or apparently to myself retarded me; it was the restless desire of thoroughly mastering the *accursed* German philosophy.' He never did master it. Writing to another friend, George Philips, the would-be-philosopher declared:

On the whole, your literature has not, during the last eighteen months, been brilliant. But what nation produces much in eighteen months? Except, indeed, my friends the Germans, who, in less than that time, generally produce two or three entirely new systems of the principles of human knowledge.'

His literary society caused fresh perturbation at the East India House in Leadenhall Street, from which the directors sent a despatch to the governor:

We have taken into our consideration the petition of Sir James Mackintosh on behalf of the Literary Society of Bombay praying for permission to raise by Lottery a Sum of Money to enable the Society to establish a Library and purchase a philosophical Apparatus, and also to erect an Observatory for the purpose of facilitating the objects of this Institution.

Although it is probable that a Lottery at Bombay is not equally liable to the objections which exist against lotteries in this Country, yet it would certainly have been desirable if the Funds for the purposes of this New Society could have been raised by some other means, but as this does not appear to have been practicable, and as we very highly approve of the objects of the Society which have in view the more general improvement and diffusion of Knowledge and Science, we are disposed on the present occasion to acquiesce in the permission granted by you to the Society to resort to Lottery for raising the Funds in question.'

Undaunted by his failure to cope with German philosophers, Sir James contemplated another large work. In a letter to Lord Wellesley on 16 July 1805 he said he had been considering compiling *The History and Present State of the British Dominions in India* for the use of young men entering the civil and military service. He commented: 'The curiosity of learned Englishmen has hitherto been directed rather to the antiquities, than either to the certain history or present condition of India.' Mackintosh sought the governor-general's help in inducing officials throughout India to provide statistical information for a survey. But his lordship had troubles of his own with Leadenhall Street, and was about to go home.

Anyone who reminded Mackintosh of his youth was welcome at Parel, and he was delighted to find a captain in the Bombay artillery was the youngest son of his Fortrose schoolmaster, William Smith. This led him to set down the reminiscences quoted in the first chapter of this book.

'Whether England will ever feel any curiosity to know the events of my life and the feelings which they excited in my mind I cannot presume even to conjecture,' he wrote. 'The utmost extent of my presumption is to have *hoped* that at some future time I may *hope* to be better known to the public than I now am.' He mused on the problem facing autobiographers—that readers were more interested in the writers' failings than virtues: 'If what they say appears to entertain their hearers they have reason to dread that it is not very creditable to themselves and if it be honourable to themselves they may in most cases be sure that it is tiresome to all their indifferent hearers.'

Perhaps this was the reason he abandoned his sketch when he came to his departure from Scotland. Later he wrote volume after volume of journals, but these were chiefly diary letters to his wife rather than memories recollected in tranquility. Catherine suffered from the climate, and was indisposed each autumn. Housekeeping posed problems, for she complained the servants 'never told the truth if a lie did as well'. Then there were five daughters to educate and protect from sickness and other hazards—a small colony with a preponderance of young men was a forcing house for teenage girls. Some difference arose with the governess.

On 10 November 1805 Fanny Allen wrote from Cresselly to her brother Baugh expressing pleasure the latest letter from India showed sister Catherine was in good spirits 'undisturbed by that mortal plague Miss D'Aubigne', adding: 'The best thing Mackintosh could do, would be to give her away with the next vacant place in his disposal, and the man that takes the one must have the other also.' By that time the troublesome girl had left Bombay.

James wrote to Sydney Smith and other friends asking them to send a replacement. For a salary of not more than £120 a year he hoped for someone well qualified as to 'morality, temper, age, ugliness, love of reading and acquaintance with good English writers, modern languages, music and drawing'. Smith informed Jos. Wedgwood: 'We have not heard of any governess yet for Lady M. but I hope we shall soon. One we have rejected on account of her beauty.' Presumably the Mackintoshes were reluctant to pay the passage of someone likely to be snapped up as a bride soon after landing.

The recorder's interpretation of his duties, which savoured more of the law-giver than judge, caused consternation in the community, particularly his reluctance to impose the death penalty. In a letter to an old friend and fellow-member of the King of Clubs, Swiss writer Pierre Etienne Louis Dumont, Sir James said:

> I hope I shall be able to give this system a fair trial notwithstanding the sneers of those who surround me who, supposing that I can act only from constitutional good nature, seem to think such a quality very much akin to folly when its objects have a black complexion.'

Such was certainly the view of Stuart Moncrieff Threipland, prosecuting counsel for the East India Company against a sepoy who admitted murdering with a hatchet another Indian whose wife he coveted. Threipland observed that if any persons were disposed to be sceptical with respect to brutal insensibility forming a predominant feature in the characters of the natives, this was one of many examples calculated to remove all doubts. Sir James told the prisoner he deserved death, but instead sentenced him to be transported for life to Prince of Wales Island, in the Far East. About the same time he drafted an advertisement for a jailer stipulating 'he must have the most unexceptionable recommendations for sobriety, firmness and humanity'.

His attitude to debtors and corruption disturbed some of the men he met at dinner parties. In India as at home it was common to send men to prison for debt, depriving them of any prospect of earning the money that could free them. His own financial carelessness probably gave James special sympathy with offenders. He explained his policy when writing to Lord Moira, another spendthrift:

> Our courts in India have a power of fixing a sum for their respective jurisdiction below which relief may be afforded to prisoners for debt . . . I thought it fair to convert this discretion into an instrument for relieving debtors from the capricious tyranny of their creditors and for subjecting their cases to the impartial determination of a court. I therefore raised the sum from 3,000 rupees at which I found it fixed by my predecessor to 12,000 rupees which includes all the prisoners now in jail . . . If it should appear necessary I shall not shrink from a still farther stretch of my power . . . It amounts substantially to a reform in the Debtor Laws.

He also tried to ensure a fairer distribution of assets in cases of bankruptcy. Too often wealthy merchants on the spot benefited from knowing when a firm began to get into difficulties and could withdraw their money swiftly; not so retired India hands and widows living in England whose capital was still invested in the city. They might be ruined, without hope of redress.

Eighteen months after his arrival he had to preside over a case of corruption involving the local custom master, Robert Henshaw, whom he later described as an old rogue whose official income was £10,000 a year. The prisoner enjoyed much sympathy, as the recorder explained in a letter to Sir William Scott, judge of the court of admiralty in London:

> A trial has taken place before me of a considerable civil servant for peculation in which by the mere discharge of my duty I have incurred a degree of animosity which cannot very easily be conceived by those who know only the calm and unobstructed course of criminal law in England. The hostility is not indeed avowed—but it is very discoverable and in a small society very vexatious.

Politics increased his unpopularity, for Bombay citizens were predominantly ultra-Tories. They reacted strongly to parliamentary attempts to impeach Viscount Melville, as Henry Dundas had become, for careless handling of public money while first lord of the admiralty. Mackintosh told Sharp: 'I have been more than once almost insulted in company for taking the part of the House of Commons against Lord Melville for whom the people here feel the strongest attachment on account of the very striking resemblance of his delinquency to that of the Custom Master.'

Prominent among those who made life unpleasant was Charles Forbes, acknowledged leader of the commercial community, who sometimes served as foreman of the grand jury which considered cases before they were brought to trial. Nor did Mackintosh enjoy the backing of Governor Duncan, whose inclination was to avoid controversies that might agitate the governor-general in Calcutta, or the directors in London. However Sir James did put forward proposals for judicial reform, notably the need to have two judges for mutual support and to switch trials of prominent residents to another city; these were adopted, although too late to benefit him.

One of his greatest pleasures during what he regarded as exile—his letters often reflected Cicero's sentiments when banished from Rome— was to open the cases of books and reviews sent from England. Then there were visits from Inverness-shire kinsmen, especially those of Lachlan Mackintosh, who had met John Mackintosh during his one voyage to China, and settled down in Calcutta as a merchant.

At the beginning of 1806 news arrived of the death of Tom Wedgwood, the ailing Polydore whose scepticism had once distressed Catherine. His death at thirty-four was an embarrassment to Mackintosh. Tom dabbled in metaphysics and philosophy, and made a deep impression on all who met him at Cote House or in London. A wealthy, generous young man, of self-effacing manners, was bound to be popular, but he was genuinely admired by men as different as Wordsworth, Godwin, Sharp, and Thomas Campbell.

Among his preoccupations was the relationship between time, space, and physical sensation. Persistent headaches and abdominal pain, relieved only by opium or tramping with a gun through the country, prevented him doing more than jot down his ideas. Mackintosh offered to put these into coherent form and accepted a gift of £100 to do so. In 1801 he wrote to Tom:

> I have not forgotten our metaphysical discussions and I continue anxious (in spite of my laziness) to be your midwife. I have talked of them to some of the Scotch metaphysicians with various results. Coleridge promised me a

long account of the notions of Kant on time and space to enable us to judge how far they coincide with yours which he thinks they do very remarkably. For my part the more I think of your speculations the more I am satisfied both of their justness and importance. Indeed I think I see every symptom of a revolution in metaphysics.

Coleridge predicted, accurately, that in spite of good intentions, the Scotsman would never fulfill his promise. Robert Southey scoffed at the whole project in a letter to a friend in 1802:

> A great metaphysical book is conceived and about to be born. Thomas Wedgwood the Jupiter whose brain is parturient—Mackintosh the man-midwife—a preface on the history of metaphysical opinions promised by Coleridge . . . Time and Space are the main subjects of speculation. I am afraid the book will add nothing to what I have already learnt from the clocks and the milestones.

James took the notes with him to India, and on Tom's death he was urged by Jos. Wedgwood to complete the work. It was never written and the notes vanished, although he did once sit down to sketch out the theories, judging from some sheets of paper preserved among his manuscripts at the University of Keele. Failure to keep faith with the dead man was a bad lapse in what Mackintosh himself described as a life of mixed projects and inactivity.

The most charitable explanation is that he came to doubt the value of the speculations, and the wisdom of publishing them, a possibility borne out by a letter to Sharp written four years later:

> I am now in the midst of poor Tom Wedgwood's philosophy. It will soon be finished and I think it will be impossible for me not to subjoin a good many notes or short dissertations. At the end I am unfeignedly afraid that I shall not do him justice. My notes are so imperfect, my memory of conversations so faded away, his notions so singular and belonging to that part of the metaphysical philosophy the least cultivated by me that I shall not wonder if doctrines should appear absurd from me to which he might have ensured general acceptance.

Certainly the brief notes on other topics published in *The Value of a Maimed Life* more than a century afterwards do not suggest the powerful intellect his contemporaries detected in Tom. They show the influence of Godwin's belief in the perfectibility of man, and the ideas on education foreshadow Aldous Huxley's *Brave New World*. He tried, in all seriousness, to balance the pleasure a man derives from shooting an animal against the loss it suffers by early death, coming down in favour of the blood sports he enjoyed.

In February 1806 Mackintosh reported 'two or three twitches of a bilious disorder which though trifling in themselves were sufficient to admonish me that in three or four years I might feel an imperious necessity of flying from this climate'. The subcontinent was notorious as the place from which men carried home fortunes and diseases of the liver.

He paid a visit to Poonah, the first of several journeys he undertook during his years in India; there he encountered oriental splendour at the court of Bajee Rao, known as the Peshwa, and enjoyed the company of Colonel Barry Close, British resident or adviser, whom he described as 'by far the most considerable man whom I have seen in the East'. Describing the trip in a journal letter to Lady Mackintosh, he said he felt some alarm that being met by ceremonial elephants would 'discompose the tranquillity of my Lord Chancellor of a horse', but 'Signor Cavallo beheld them undisturbed', even when joined by a thousand Mahratta horsemen. He found the rounds of civilities tiresome, especially when it involved squatting on a carpet: 'As I had on leather breeches, and had not been bred a tailor, I found the operation troublesome, and the posture not very agreeable.'

But he approved of the ritual washing of hands in rose-water by which the host signalled an interview was over: 'It would be a good expedient in Europe to get rid of bores.' Although he considered the Peshwa's manners and appearance superior to the other heads of state he had met, George the Third and Napoleon, he dismissed him as 'a superstitious voluptuary'.

Lady Mackintosh meanwhile was not so happy. Apart from having to nurse a sick Elizabeth, her younger daughter, she was brooding on what action to take over the slighting behaviour of a Bombay acquaintance. She must have fallen foul of local etiquette, for in referring to a planned ball she wrote from Parel: 'Today I issued forth cards for 160 including every body I believe rag, tag and bobtail from alpha to omega so I think it is impossible that I can offend this time.' But she closed her letter:

Believe me more in inclination than in duty bound to subscribe myself

> My dear Mackintosh's
> tender and *proud* wife, Mistress
> Friend and chere Compagnon
> mais non pas du Voyage
> C.M.

Evidently part of her displeasure was sorrow at not being able to join him on his journey.

On 4 February 1806 Catherine sent her sisters an account of the ball at Parel, given to Admiral Sir Edward Pellew and the officers of his squadron:

I heard that it was thought to have gone off vastly well . . . a very fine ball and supper room elegantly lighted, a plentiful supper, and the front of the house or strictly speaking the gate, which is a very handsome one, and the shrubbery before the door very brilliantly illuminated which had a very gay and striking effect. The company were nearly 200 . . . I danced with Sir E. Pellew, a Lieutenant Gordon, a brother of Lord Aberdeen, and another gentleman from Calcutta

The *Bombay Courier* spoke of a 'brilliant assemblage of ladies and gentlemen comprising all the taste, fashion, and beauty of our little settlement . . . the whole happily arranged in that peculiar style and taste, that so eminently characterises her Ladyship's entertainments'. William Erskine, secretary to Sir James, had become editor of the paper. It is not known whether the recorder retained his youthful love of dancing.

Two months after the ball he presided over the trial of two British officers, Lieutenants Bryan Maguire and George Cauty, found guilty of plotting to ambush two Dutchmen involved in a civil action against them. Before passing sentence, he told the court:

I conceive it to be the first duty of a criminal judge to exert and to strain every faculty of his mind to discover in every case, the smallest possible quantity of punishment that may be effectual for the ends of amendment and example. I consider every pang of the criminal not necessary for those objects, as a crime in the judge.

Sentencing them to 12 months imprisonment, he observed he had not been influenced by learning Maguire tried to carry into court loaded pistols in a portable writing desk, intending to assassinate his judge before committing suicide.

Politics at home were transformed by the death of Pitt, whose career as a war minister was eloquent but unsuccessful. 'At the close of every brilliant display,' Sydney Smith said, 'an expedition failed or a kingdom fell. God send us a stammerer.' His wish was granted when Viscount Castlereagh began to dominate foreign policy.

News of Pitt's death reached Bombay in mid-1806, and brought fresh unpopularity to Mackintosh. He told his correspondents at home: 'The people here had the folly to ask me to preside at a public meeting for a statue to Mr P. and to be angry that I did not go . . . I have been almost persecuted for non-conformity to the idolatrous worship of Pitt which has been founded in this island.' Leading his attackers was James Morley, a barrister whose conduct to clients had been censured by the recorder. At the statue meeting Morley made an impassioned speech praising Burke and hitting at British Jacobins.

It was tactless to refuse to honour the prime minister's memory, but Sir James had good reason to proclaim his lifelong Whiggishness at that time. He had learned Dr Parr was blackening his name, accusing him of disloyalty to Fox. In addition he spread the story Mackintosh never intended to write the account of the Birmingham riots for which the dissenters paid him £200, and worst of all, had appropriated for his own use £20 Parr sent for Gerrald before he was transported to Australia. James Perry added to the scandal by recounting Mackintosh's tardiness in paying over the £20 in 1803.

Sir James wrote to Parr asking him to deny these stories; the doctor did not at first reply, and grumbled some officious friend had caused trouble by telling the absent Scotsman what was being said. Dr Parr, it seemed, saw nothing wrong in character assassination provided the victim did not know he was dead.

This was a shattering blow to Mackintosh, who thought of the doctor as his friend. He poured out his woe in a letter to Lord Holland, proclaiming that although he did not always agree with Fox, notably in relation to France, he never ceased to consider himself a loyal follower of the great Whig. It was apparent James, whose early life lacked the presence of his own father, was transferring the filial feeling he had for Parr to Lord Holland—not a happy choice.

His sufferings were increased by the months it took to receive a reply from England. By the time Lord Holland's answer arrived Fox was dead after a brief spell of office in the Ministry of All the Talents. The peer sent a soothing letter stating he never heard Fox indicate any belief in Parr's suggestions; but he did admit members of the party resented Mackintosh accepting a post making it impossible for him to lend active support.

Of the other accusations, Mackintosh pointed out the Birmingham dissenters had never asked for the refund of their money, and welcomed him cordially on his return to the city; moreover Dr Parr remained friendly with him long after this episode. He expressed astonishment at the suggestion he had defrauded Gerrald, whom he sheltered in his own home. Parr later wrote a placatory letter, but the breach was never truly healed, for the story of Gerrald and the £20 reappeared in various garbled forms for many years. Fanny Allen confided to Baugh nothing but a horse-whipping would do for Parr 'and if I was M. I would cross the ocean for the pleasure of making that old treacherous rogue wince'.

Basil Montagu managed to extract a joke from the situation, reporting an encounter with Parr and deriding his hopes of becoming a bishop:

> When calling to see Opie's picture of you, just after the death of Bishop Horsley, I observed the Doctor, who was in imaginary lawn sleeves in the episcopal palace, put his hand upon your portrait. I am afraid it is the only episcopal blessing he will give you, for I understand that his preferment is to be the deanery of Lincoln.

7   Fanny Mackintosh by George Richmond.

6   An engraving after John Opie's portrait of Mackintosh.

Writing to Mackintosh on the same subject, Jeremy Bentham delivered from his London home a sharp attack on Fox which probably embarrassed the recipient:

> My expectations were never sanguine. He was a consummate party leader; greedy of power, like my old friend, Lord Lansdowne,—but, unlike him, destitute of any fixed intellectual principles . . . When I saw you enlisted in the defence of a castle of straw, which I had turned my back upon as fit for nothing but the fire, I beheld with regret what appeared to me a waste of talents so unprofitably employed.'

With disarming candour the designer of the panopticon said he refused to attend Mackintosh's lectures because 'smoke I abhor, and not the less for its being illuminated with flashes'. Later, Bentham continued, he heard 'Cicero had got a provision which, for the first time in his life, would enable him to do real service to mankind, and that he had always manifested dispositions to apply his talents to that use. Then, for the first time, began the hermit of Queen Square Place to think of the man of eloquence with pleasure.'

In Europe the war was going badly. Sir James wrote to a friend, Friedrich von Gentz, who had taken refuge in Saxony after Napoleon's victories over the Austrians: 'I believe, like you, in a resurrection because I belive in the immortality of civilization.'

Fortunately 1806 ended with two events which brought the family pleasure. On 9 December Mackintosh wrote to John Allen at Cresselly to say he was on the verge of being out of debt, and requesting a present of '10 dozen of your finest Welsh Ale'. On 22 December Robert James was born; for the first time Sir James had an heir who would outlive him.

Answering requests for friends to keep him in touch with events at home, Amelia Sloper interpreted this as an invitation to pass on scandal: 'It is a considerable pleasure to me that Mr Sharp has again come amongst us and that though I have not been able to contribute to the happiness of his life I have at least ceased to be any source of uneasiness to him.'

Referring to an Oxford clergyman she declared:

> I think you did not believe me when I assured you the Seraphic Coxcomb had never thought me worthy of being his companion through life and that my friend Miss Tate was the object of his peference. Yet such was the case and not having been able to succeed with her he is now about to marry Miss Bailie—a handsome girl with £10,000 . . . Lady Caroline Ponsonby's marriage with Mr Lamb pleases the family exceedingly. They are extremely attached to each other and both so clever and singular in their notions that they seem particularly adapted to each other.

Amelia seemed determined to involve every available man with Miss Tate—even John Hensleigh Allen, the young squire of Cresselly, who cherished a hopeless love for a married woman. She told Sir James:

> Mr Allen proposed leaving Town today . . . I believe I mentioned in a former letter that he seemed much taken with one of my cousins—but this year I think his attention more chiefly directed to my friend Miss Tate. I suspect him of being a great flirt, tho' à ce qu'on dit—he is very constant to the real object of his idolatry, Mrs Waddington. She is a beautiful creature and has considerable talents . . .
>
> God bless you. I will not put my name to my letter lest it should fall into the hands of the French and be published.

In another letter, dated 2 February 1807, she declared Boddington, who that year became an MP, was foolish not to pursue Fanny Allen.

Many letters to Parel expressed appreciation of the hospitality relatives and friends received there. A favourite guest was Joshua Allen, a cousin of Catherine's. Nicknamed Caliban by the Mackintosh girls, he was a lieutenant in command of an East India Company vessel. In September 1807 two newcomers joined the household. One was Claudius James Rich, a handsome talented young man in the company service, the other Miss Johnson, governess.

It is not recorded whether she met the standards of intellect and ugliness Mackintosh stipulated, but a letter from Basil Montagu was not reassuring: 'She staid some time with Lady Bush and about a year with my brother Admiral Montagu . . . I hope that Miss Johnson may be of service to you, had I been consulted it is probable that she would not have been sent.' Two years later James reported to Sharp the governess was 'worse than useless. She only stays here because she cannot afford to go home. I cannot afford to send her.'

In addition to his duties as recorder Sir James was appointed judge of a court of vice-admiralty set up in Bombay, dealing with maritime cases, especially disposal of captured vessels. He received no extra pay for this work, but it concerned international law, in which he was interested, and enabled him to find a post for Erskine as registrar of the court.

Naval officers were keenly interested in the prize money dependent on some of his adjudications. When he freed an American ship, the *Minerva*, detained on the ground it had been trading between enemy ports, the reverberations reached London. His cautious kinsman, Aldourie-born Charles Grant, chairman of the directors of the company, wrote to him: 'It has given me some concern to understand that the opinion of the legal authorities here does not accord with yours . . . I cannot but feel this event may have rather an unfavourable effect on your interests.' His decision on the *Minerva* was influenced by fear British highhandness on the high seas might lead to war with America, as finally happened.

More cheerful was a letter from Daniel Stuart, although again Mackintosh may have winced at contemptuous references to Fox's role during the Whig ministry which George III dismissed in 1807:

> He seemed to think France only desired to see him Minister to grant us good terms of peace, and he set about it so hastily and carelessly that in the end he made a most pitiful figure . . . The Prince of Wales called himself the head of the party and assumed to himself the actual power of patronage. Places and pensions he gave away to worthless persons; some of his friends were selling seats in parliament, places and titles and many disgraceful stories are in circulation.

Stuart's views were coloured by some change in his own politics. He had sold *The Morning Post* and bought *The Courier*, an evening paper whose editor, Thomas George Street, believed in supporting ministers without too much regard for their policies. He went on: 'I saw Sheridan lately. He did not conceal how inconvenient it was for him to be turned out and how much Mrs Sheridan disliked relinquishing his splendid palace at Somerset House.'

Late in 1807 Lady Mackintosh suffered a severe illness, and the couple took a cruise to Goa, the Portuguese colony south of Bombay. There they attended a cathedral service, of which Sir James recorded:

> I was called into the choir, and had the honour of sitting next the first Inquisitor, a tall monk, of a coarse and savage countenance, who looked as if he would not object to the effective revival of the functions of his office, which even here have almost dwindled down to formality.

Perhaps the recorder remembered Godwin comparing him to an inquisitor. Also in the cathedral were three judges in black robes. He thought they looked dispprovingly at his own white waistcoat and breeches, and green silk frockcoat.

It was Christmas Eve when the couple returned home. Awaiting them were two heartening letters. One from Spencer Perceval, now chancellor of the exchequer and soon to be prime minister, was primarily a letter of introduction for a young doctor about to start a career in Bombay, but expressed 'the pleasure which I shall have in renewing our acquaintance on your return', a sentiment faithfully honoured.

In the other James Scarlett reassured his friend nobody who knew him well credited the slanders of Dr Parr. He wrote of Fox:

> I had long known that a certain number of inferior persons who had too much influence over his good nature and who envied your reputation made

it their business to sneer at your supposed change of principles . . . I did not
hear Mr Fox say a word to your prejudice, nor did I ever hear from others
that he had.

Sir James also found his eldest daughter, 18-year-old Mary, and
Claudius Rich were in love. They married on 22 January 1808. Two
weeks later they left Bombay in the *Princess Augusta*, commanded by
Joshua Allen, for Bagdad where Rich was to represent the East India
Company as resident to the Pasha.

The illegitimate son of an Army colonel, Rich was handsome, proud,
a dashing horseman, gifted linguist and fond of expensive clothes.
Mackintosh, although devoted to his children, viewed them with
detachment. He wrote to John Allen that Mary 'though so destitute of all
pretensions to beauty has got a husband who might satisfy at the same
time the proudest beauty and the coolest parent'. To his daughter he said:
'My affection for Rich and my choice of him as a son-in-law depended
so entirely on his personal qualities that would not have been in the least
affected by the circumstances of birth and descent. These are indeed
matters to which I ascribe a very secondary value.' His judgment was
vindicated by a supremely happy marriage.

Bagdad was an important post politically; there was much intrigue in
that part of the Turkish Empire, and fear Napoleon might send an army
overland to invade India. Letters and news travelled faster through the
Middle East than by sea route around Africa. But the area was of minor
commercial value, so friction arose between the authorities in Bombay,
anxious to restrict expenditure, and Rich who was extravagant and knew
the importance of display to impress the despots with whom he had to
deal.

In between was the recorder, urging restraint on his son-in-law and
forbearance on Governor Duncan. Writing to Rich on 8 March he said:

> Allow me with the liberty of warm affection earnestly to exhort you to
> exert every power of your mind in the duties of your station. There is
> something in the seriousness both of business and of science of which your
> vivacity is impatient. The brilliant variety of your attainments and
> accomplishments do I fear flatter you into the conceit that you may indulge
> your genius and pass your life in amusement . . . What is amiable gaiety at
> twentyfour might run the risk if it were unaccompanied by other things of
> being thought frivolous and puerile at fortyfour. I am so near fortyfour that
> I can give you pretty exact news of that dull country.

Among other recommendations to useful activities, he suggested Rich
should investigate the ruins of Babylon. This resulted in two books on
archaeological exploration, and probably influenced Claudius to become

a collector of eastern manuscripts and coins. Mackintosh reported the collapse and death of the local commander with brutal brevity:

> General Bellasis died one morning at the military board, the only military death to which a Bombay general is likely to be exposed. There followed the usual panegyrics on his exploits which as usual had during his life been perfectly unknown—at least to the enemy.

The cynical dismissal of Major-general John Bellasis, who was decorated for bravery, reflected the disgust Sir James felt at corruption in India. Writing to John Whishaw a few days earlier he said:

> The extent of the peculation practised at least in this presidency especially by military officers would appear incredible if it was accurately stated. The eagerness to gain fortune is so undisguised, the means of concealment through native agents so great, the sums which pass through their hands so enormous, and their distance from such means of check and control as we have at the presidencies often so immense, that you must at once see it is impossible it should be otherwise . . . a few months of a distant expedition always makes the fortune of the commander and his whole staff, just beforehand loaded with debt.
>
> I caught one of these plunderers once in my court, but the general policy of the company and its governors is to bury such enquiries in obscure committees, and in the few cases where enquiry is made to do no more than send the flagrant official home to enjoy his fortune with credit—indeed one of these persons suspended here for peculation after one of those private enquiries has been sent back by the court of directors and recommended for promotion!

He added:

> If I were to attempt to state the tenth part of the abomination and abuse of this system, I should write a volume which indeed if I ever escape, I may perhaps do.

He escaped but never wrote the volume, since both Rich and Erskine were in the company's employ and at the mercy of the regime he wished to attack.

James continued to read widely if not always well. The volumes of Madame de Staël's *Corinne* were quickly finished, and he revised his views on Wordsworth. Writing in his journal, he dismissed Jeffrey's famous attack in *The Edinburgh Review* as 'very unjust and anti-poetical'. He confided to a correspondent: 'I have just got, by a most lucky chance, Wordsworth's new Poems . . . Perhaps it might please him to know, that his poetry has given these feelings to one at so vast a distance: it is not

worth adding, to one who formerly had foolish prejudices against him.'
When the message reached Wordsworth he accepted what he called the
'recantation'. This was presumably a jocular reference to Mackintosh's
public repudiation of the French Revolution. But with Wordsworth you
cannot be sure.

The exiled Scotsman probably had his own chequered career in mind
when he wrote to his relative, Lord Woodhouselee:

> I have just perused with equal instruction and pleasure your excellent Life of
> Lord Kames. His was indeed one the few cases where the Life of an author
> is really more important than his works. It is not so much by classical and
> permanent works as by the impulse which the national literature received
> from his active and powerful mind that he will attract the notice of
> posterity. The details of his life were necessary to show that he possessed
> more mental power than many who merely by a more discreet application
> of it have produced works which will continue longer to be read. He
> scattered in endless books, in professional labour and in voluntary public
> service much of that understanding which more prudent followers of fame
> have concentrated on one object.

In the privacy of his journal he was less complimentary about the
biographer, whom he described as 'a man of letters without philosophy,
and hostile to it', writing the life of 'a metaphysician without literature'.

Early in 1808 Lachlan Mackintosh, the Calcutta merchant, left for
home with a fortune. He was anxious to help his less provident kinsman;
they discussed a scheme for James to enter Parliament with an annual
retainer of £3,000 a year from the merchants of India, on the
understanding he would represent their interests against the monopoly
exercised by the company. They particularly disliked being excluded
from trade with China. As he genuinely believed they were right he saw
nothing wrong in such a course, pointing out that Burke had acted as the
agent of New York Province. But Bobus Smith, earning £10,000 a year
at the Calcutta bar, advised strongly against the plan, and it was frowned
on by friends at home.

James submitted reluctantly; he was desperate to return. While his
friend, Thomas Erskine, was lord chancellor briefly in the Whig
administration there was some chance of transferring to a more congenial
appointment. Now he could see no escape but resignation. Soon he
would be too old to start a new career, and halfway through 1808 his
health began to decline sharply.

Local irritations continued, including a clash with Sir Harford Jones,
an overbearing character appointed by the government to proceed on a
mission to Persia. He suggested the recorder could call on him in
Bombay. Mackintosh insisted that, since he was second only to the

governor in the presidency, Sir Harford should first visit him; to do otherwise might set a precedent with other men of rank passing through the territory. Sir Harford finally complied, but took his revenge by not inviting Catherine to parties held when he left the city.

This absurd incident may have contributed to a cooling of relations with Governor Duncan, for in spite of his open-ended offer of the loan of Parel he reclaimed it late in the summer of 1808. The Mackintoshes, who had grown fond of their residence, moved to Tarala, a house on the east of the island, about half way between Parel and the city of Bombay. They were still handsomely accommodated; Tarala—the name means Palm Green—had a spacious library on the top floor, surrounded with a verandah enclosed by venetian shutters.

Riding was the recorder's only exercise. He preferred tranquil mounts, and his horse was named Sir Charles Grey. When compiling his father's memoirs Robert James took care to say this was because of its colour. At home Aberdeen University made its graduate of twenty-four years before an honorary doctor of literature.

Soon he was called on to do doctoring of a different kind. Taking another journey through the interior, this time to Hyderabad, he reported:

> We have been pestered by a mob of diseased persons who suppose all Europeans especially those who do not wear red coats to have a sort of medical omniscience and omnipotence . . . I gave them some pills and drops which I thought proper but rather with a view to soothe them than with any hope in such circumstances of being very useful.

Arriving at Beejapore he recalled the Persian poet, Hafez, was invited to the court there in the fourteenth century

> but got so sick on board ship that he relanded and returned to drink his shiraz. He afterwards wrote an ode against the folly of crossing the seas in search of wealth which I ought to have read and considered in 1803.

At Golconda, the ancient capital, he was entertained to dinner by Captain Thomas Sydenham, resident to the Nizam of the Decan, in tents:

> Mrs Orr, the sister of Captain S. has an agreeable countenance is very cheerful and perfectly unaffected. She also plays as they say wonderfully on the piano. The only merit in that way of which I can judge is that she did not seem displeased at my entire neglect of her performance.

For much of the journey he travelled in a palankeen, a curtained litter carried by bearers. When taken ill one day he thought of 'the stories I had heard of unfortunate gentlemen dying in their palankeens, and being carried forty or fifty miles after they were dead by the bearers'. Having spent much time interviewing people in authority, Sir James again dismissed the local rulers as 'mere voluptuaries' who 'exercise no functions of government, except that of collecting the revenue. In every other respect, they throw the reins on the horse's neck. In their dominions there is no police—no administration of justice; sovereignty is to them a perfect sinecure.'

From Bombay Catherine sent news of the family. Little Robert had been ill, but 'your darlings Fanny and Bessy I never saw look so well. Bessy is become quite beautiful and will give our Fanny the go-by in this respect if she does not advance quicker. Bessy . . . is so innocently gay that it is delightful to see her.'

Some friends from Goa, Major William Campbell and his wife arrived unexpectedly at Tarala: 'I was amused at your politeness in expressing yourself pleased *on my account* that the Campbells with their squealing boy and four servants were here to *amuse* me in your absence. If my Muse awakes again it will certainly be to tune an Ode to Solitude, though so often sung never was it by a more impassioned votary than myself.'

Servants remained a problem: 'Antonio gives us both dinner and breakfast an hour and a half after the time I order it. Hitherto I am all patience and I hope that will last or Antonio will alter. He has however on the whole behaved better than I expected and bating obstinacy and entire ignorance of his business he is a pretty good servant.' Much was excused Giovanni Antonio, a Sardinian who had been a slave in an Arab ship until Sir James secured his release.

Lady Mackintosh was anxious to preserve the dignity of her station, not always easy with her love of dancing:

> You may probably hear of a Bengal officer of the name of Brown having danced with me for he made such a sudden and bold push for that honour that I was taken too much by surprise to refuse him which I ought to have done as he was not introduced to me. I took my revenge however by dancing in perfect silence without opening my lips to him.

More   gratifying was the attention shown at Sunday service by General John Malcolm, a soldier-diplomat who was a friend of the family:

> The general came with me in the coach and handed me up the aisle in grand etiquette. The governor was there to do him honour I fancy as I believe he has not been before but once this year, though that is oftener than somebody that I know. After the service was over they both came together to open my pew.

Husband and wife complained of the narrowness of Bombay life. But in May 1809 the ship *Cornelia* brought them company that sometimes proved too lively. Among the passengers was Maria Dundas, later well-known as Maria Graham, whose mother was born in Virginia. The daughter was intelligent and well read, having spent part of her youth in Edinburgh mixing with people Mackintosh knew. Perhaps Sydney Smith had her in mind when he claimed that as a couple flew by him in a reel at the assembly rooms he heard one girl say to her partner: 'Why, Sir, if you mean love in the abstract . . .'

As there was no hotel fit for ladies Maria, with her father, George Dundas, a naval captain, sister Agnes and young brother Ralph, took up temporary quarters at Tarala. Maria was charmed by the Mackintoshes, particularly with the conversation and library of Sir James, but appalled by the social etiquette: 'At dinner we sat down 36 persons, strangers, who stared as if we had been wild beasts; very formal and sitting still, *sans parler.*'

Her host was equally impressed with Miss Dundas. Writing to Rich he said she was 'clever, accomplished and agreeable, such a girl in short as is rarely exported to Bombay', adding: 'Her superiority of understanding is you know an unpardonable crime. It has already excited a cry against her. She lives at our house which does not facilitate her pardon.'

During the voyage from England she became engaged to a naval officer, Thomas Graham. She also enjoyed the company of Lieutenant Charles Tyler, son of an admiral of the same name related by marriage to Lady Mackintosh. Although only twenty-five he had travelled widely and fought in Europe as a freelance officer. He became a favoured guest at Tarala as he waited impatiently for promotion and command of a ship, the fate of many young men in the Napoleonic era. Sir James told Rich: 'He has been sent to India as the climate most likely to cure a man of heroism and unless his distemper be very far advanced his recovery may certainly be expected in this country where the pursuit of rupees occupies every mind.'

When William Erskine sought permission to marry Maitland, second daughter of her father's first marriage, he demurred, since she was sixteen and Erskine was twice her age: 'You have heard of Erskine's proposal to her and of our wish to delay the match a few months on account of extreme youth. He has not behaved quite so reasonably as I expected from his character.'

Maitland became ill, with a chest complaint, and was sent to Madras to stay with friends. Erskine visited a brother in Calcutta, and on his way back called at Madras, where the couple married on 27 September 1809. Sir James gave his consent, but neither he nor Catherine attended the wedding. Just as the Allen girls had escaped from Cresselly by marriage twenty years before, the daughters of Catharine Stuart wanted to get away from their stepmother.

Mary, writing, to Maitland, complained of 'the tyranny, ill-treatment, and neglect of one who, I fear has not done her duty towards her husband's children'. Such censure from a stepdaughter who was only twenty, and devoted to an indulgent father, must be viewed with suspicion. It certainly made little allowance for Lady Mackintosh's ill-health and the difficulty of protecting three girls in a hothouse society, at the same time nursing her own young children and fulfilling the duties of a judge's wife. A breach occurred between her and the Riches which led to an angry exchange of letters.

Against this tense background Lady Mackintosh left for home at the beginning of 1810, for the sake of her health and that of her son and daughters. She made a conciliatory gesture before leaving. Fanny Mackintosh wrote to her stepsister in Bagdad: 'I send you a locket with Bessy's and my hair in it which Mama bought for us to give to you as a little memorial of gratitude for the affection you have always shown us and of our affection towards you.'

James accompanied his family to Ceylon, from which they sailed in the *Cumbrian* on 23 February 1810 on a voyage which did not bring them to England until early July. His wife carried with her a medical certificate to reinforce his request to retire as recorder with a pension. Lonely and dispirited he returned to Bombay with his son's terrier, Tartar, and wrote to her: 'On coming here the library and nursery struck a deadly cold into my heart.' Their parting had not been amicable. He expressed the hope 'that absence has dispelled every cloud that hid any part of my heart from you. I acknowledge the faults of my conduct—but indeed they were external and superficial.'

Lady Mackintosh felt, with some justice, her husband was too easy-going with his elder daughters and their husbands. She would have been less than human if she did not also feel jealousy at his admiration of the talents of Maria, now married to Captain Graham. Left with fifteen-year-old Kitty, Mackintosh had proposed the Grahams should move into Tar-ala to provide suitable protection for his daughter and agreeable company for himself. This arrangement came to nothing, for Graham was posted to Madras and his wife went to live with her father and sister, who had earlier quarrelled with Lady Mackintosh. Kitty was looked after by Luke Ashburner and his wife who lived in Salsette, to the north of Bombay.

Mackintosh was an intellectual philanderer, who regarded his platonic relations with women as above suspicion, and those he admired as similarly protected, although he could be caustic in comments on any he disliked. He was shocked when he learned unfounded rumours had circulated in Madras that Maria Graham, not long married, had visited Ceylon to give birth to a baby. No doubt spice was added to the rumour from this visit taking place while he was there to see his wife off.

His long journal letters home became a mixture of hypochondria as his health sank, of records of his reading, of exhortations to speed the arrangements for his own return, and of titbits of what he called parish scandal. It seems his friend Captain Sydenham had a mistress, for Sir James wrote to his wife: 'Sydenham came here in July with an intention of going home overland. But as he must in this case have dismissed *La Reine de Golconde* her secret influence was sufficiently exerted to make him change his mind and go to Madras in the Lushington which agreed to carry both to Europe.'

Anxiety to resign his post was tempered by need to secure the pension of £1,200. Each time a ship arrived from England without news for him, he attributed it either to forgetfulness on the part of Catherine or a disinclination by the government to accept his retirement: 'I am now afraid of every word that I may write endangering my pension— insomuch that I could not now print even poor Tom Wedgwood's papers but some freedom of speculation might displease the unworthy dispensers of pensions.' His years in India failed to produce the fortune he expected when quitting England, at most he would carry home £10,000—'I am ashamed of my poverty . . . I can no more learn to play the game of life than that of whist.'

Having decided philosophy was too risky a subject, he considered spending the rest of his life writing 'The History of Great Britain from the Revolution in 1688 to the French Revolution in 1789, to which is prefixed a Preliminary Discourse on the Progress of Government, Laws, Opinions, Taste and Manners in England from the Earliest Time'. He visualised it as running to the length of Gibbon's masterpiece. But he still had thoughts of a parliamentary career.

Sometimes he was an optimist: 'The evening of life may prove the most cheerful as well as the calmest part of it. We may both repair in the fourth act the negligences and blunders of the three first.' He teased her about claims the Allen family had links with the Cecils, reminding her of the Countess of Salisbury's role in the founding of the Order of the Garter. Whatever the history of the Allens and Cecils, late in the nineteenth century the Mackintoshes' great-niece, Georgina Alderson married the Marquis of Salisbury, who became prime minister. His father disapproved of the match.

At other times he was obsessed by fears he would never see his family again, and burdened his wife with plans for the welfare of their daughters and son:

I have very extensive and encyclopaedical plans of education for poor Robin. One circumstance I mention because I feel my own defect. I anxiously wish him to be early inured to manly and daring exercises and sports. I cannot help thinking that they give vigour not only to the body but to the mind and contribute at least somewhat to that bold and military cast of character which is necessary to manhood and peculiarly indispensable in the approaching state of the world. Let him be a capital rider and much given to boxing . . .

If I should never see you do not suffer your visions of unattainable purity to blind your great understanding in the education of poor Robin. Consider that the common frailties of young men are not so pernicious or contemptible as timidity, constraint or hypocrisy.

He referred to his family as Fanny the Clever, Bessy the Gentle, Robin the Bold, and 'Imperial Juno the mother of the Celestials'. The rather tactless likening of Catherine to that stately beauty is borne out by the Hoppner portrait of her.

In her own letters Catherine made it plain she would rather hear of progress on his history than the expenditure of so much time on journal-letters to her. In London she and the children received a warm welcome from her own family, and from Daniel Stuart and his sister, known as Betsy. But she experienced difficulty in extracting a firm pledge from ministers to allow her husband to retire with a pension.

In July Mary Erskine was born, making Sir James a grandfather for the first time. He reported: 'Maitland's little girl is a stout healthy good-natured child but so very serious that I call her Grand Mama.'

While his own career languished, Mackintosh put much effort into pushing on the young men who visited Tarala. Charles Tyler spent nearly a year there, restless for his promotion, and planning to assume a Lawrence of Arabia role if the feared French invasion materialised, as Sir James explained: 'Tyler means to put himself at the head of a band of Arabs to rob the French in the desert as they pass to and from India. He has promised particularly to take care of all French and German Journals in the plunder for me—in whatever oasis I may have my old age.' Only when Admiral Edward O'Brien Drury died did Tyler become a captain and depart for Java. His host commented: 'Admiral Drury died on the 6th of the consequence of a mad fit of anger which appears to have lasted since he met Admiral Bertie at the Isle of France. He has behaved so ill to Tyler that I care very little about his death.' This naval engagement occurred when Vice-Admiral Drury, commander-in-chief in India, having planned to capture Mauritius from the French, arrived on the scene to find himself under the command of superior officer Sir Albemarle Bertie, from the Cape of Good Hope.

Joshua Allen also received promotion, having distinguished himself in action against pirates in the Gulf. He looked magnificent in his captain's uniform, Sir James said, but before 1810 was out he died of fever: 'He was interred at six, with less light than I have before seen at a funeral, which heightened a little the melancholy feelings with which I saw the remains of so worthy a man laid in the dust.'

Another young man presented himself at Tarala that year. The host wrote to William Frend, a London mathematician he met some twenty years before in Belgium:

> I received your letter of the 29th December and your nephew who is now passing some days with me in this house and who seems an amiable and promising young man. I have caused enquiries to be made respecting the best arithmetical books of the natives. I shall supply your nephew with such as I can find and shall have great pleasure in contributing to your collection of comparative arithmetic.

To the courteous recorder, other men's studies took priority over his own.

When Sir James received news William Windham had died, he commented: 'Had Windham possessed discretion in debate, or Sheridan in conduct, they might have ruled their age.'

His strained relations with official and unofficial Bombay came near to snapping during a sensational trial over which he presided. There was resentment among native officials when George Cumming Osborne, recently appointed to the treasury department, began a drive against corruption. Some attempted to assassinate him, but he fought them off. They then offered a bribe of 3,000 rupees to the police superintendent, Charles Joseph Briscoe, to secure their release. The trial of Briscoe, and the refusal of Governor Duncan to suspend him before he was convicted, as suggested by the advocate-general, Hugh George Macklin, caused controversy in the small city.

Stress made Mackintosh ill in the final stages, but he had the satisfaction of knowing most of the community, even Charles Forbes, had come to respect him by the time he sentenced Briscoe to twelve months imprisonment. The recorder had always been dissatisfied with the conduct of the local police, with Briscoe exercising the power of sentencing minor offenders to be flogged or deported.

By March 1811 bouts of ill-health were relieved only by convivial evenings which made James worse. Telling his wife he was going to a birthday party given by Robert Rickards, a member of the colony's governing council, he said: 'I have drunk nothing but water for nine days—and I quaff the sparkling champagne in fancy as it is uncorked—though I have had heartburn and headache even with my abstemiousness.'

Three weeks later came the laconic entry in his journal-letter: 'Court in the morning and headache in the evening.' He took perverse pleasure in writing to her:

> I forget whether I have reminded you of the fate of the performers at your musical parties here— Briscoe in jail for corruption—Mrs Daw committed (to use an incorrect expression) of crim. con.—Padre Jackson suspended for drunkenness and Mrs Conelly—not suspended for the same vice—not to mention Mr Lemesurier obliged to abscond because his taste in love rather differs from our national prejudices.

Her own letters were not always consoling. She had sharp words for his sister Anne, who returned to London after spending some time in Scotland, complaining of the way relatives there treated her. Catherine wrote:

> You may make yourself quite easy about your sister if indeed she is your sister which since my return I have often wished I could have doubted but she has here and there in her person a very untoward resemblance to you. I am afraid you must believe little or nothing of what she has told you about her reasons for leaving Scotland for I have ascertained beyond a doubt that your friends behaved very kindly to her . . . She got herself as it was reasonable to conclude into all sorts of scrapes by her boarding house in London from which I extricated her and paid her debts etc at the expense of 70 and 80 pounds and to ensure her from any future distress or misconduct I have put her to board with a good sort of woman who finds her in every thing for her 50 pounds. I purposely do not tell you where she is for there is no occasion for your writing to her before you return.

Anne was now a widow, and according to Daniel Stuart she died soon after her brother returned home.

James at last heard his resignation was accepted, and waited only for his successor as recorder. He solved the problem of disposing of 16-year-old Kitty by sending her under the guardianship of a diplomat, Sir Gore Ouseley, and his wife to join her sister Mary in Bagdad. Mackintosh wrote to Catherine: 'The only material event is the engagement of Kitty . . . On the voyage Sir William Wiseman, Bart, second lieutenant of the Lion, made love to her.' Sir Gore, he added 'gave his consent to their being immediately married by Captain Heathcote of the Lion. Captain Heathcote behaved like a gentleman and father. He positively refused and disapproved of any step taken without my consent.'

The girl continued her journey to Bagdad, while Sir William returned to Bombay to stay at Tarala. There, after a term of probation, he received permission to marry Kitty. His prospective father-in-law summed up: 'He is not in the least degree lettered. He is not handsome or brilliant—but perfectly exempt from the least approach to vulgarity or folly.'

Mackintosh reported Governor Duncan was dying:

> He is said to be haunted with the horrible idea that he has no friends and that all mankind have requited him with the blackest ingratitude . . . I have endeavoured by every attention in my power to soothe his dying moments and to convince him of the reality of that compassion and good will which I certainly feel though I can entertain neither esteem nor affection for him.

One more ordeal faced the recorder. He had dispensed the law for seven years without capital punishment, sometimes undoubtedly by bending the rules of clemency but, as he asserted, without any increase in murders in a crowded community. At last he found it necessary to sentence a man to death, a British artilleryman guilty of the wanton murder of an Indian at Goa.

Sir James watched from his courthouse quarters as the prisoner, handcuffed and with a rope round his neck, was taken to the place of execution, the esplanade of the port on 20 July 1811. About 50,000 Indians and most of the European population gathered 'to see a sight which after the last seven years they must think very extraordinary'. The prisoner confessed his guilt at the last.

Approaching repatriation did not lift Mackintosh's spirits unduly. Some reprimands in his wife's letters led him to quote Thomas Gray's lines in The Hymn to Adversity:

> Oh gently on thy Suppliant's head
> Dread Goddess lay thy chastening hand

For good measure he told her:

> It seems now to be your determination not to be on speaking or writing terms with my two eldest daughters as long as you and they live. I need not say how bitterly I am mortified by the reflexion that I who once aspired to teach and influence mankind have not importance enough in my own family to prevent so unseemly a spectacle.

His farewells were attended with tributes of more than ritual fervour, a great public dinner at the city's theatre, and addresses from the grand jury and the literary society, with requests that a portrait and bust be commissioned for them. Perhaps more to his taste was a last evening at Parel, which evoked his pleasantest recollections of Bombay. He would have smiled had he known he and the late Jonathan Duncan would share, with other local worthies, the distinction of having their relief portraits decorate the frontage of the former India Office looking into the Foreign Office quadrangle in Whitehall.

Before he went on board the *Caroline* he arranged for William Erskine to fill the newly-created position of second magistrate at an annual salary of 18,000 rupees. In addition he negotiated a settlement of the allowances to be paid to his other son-in-law, Rich, who ran into debt in maintaining his position in Bagdad. A small staff appointment was found for a cousin, Lieutenant Alexander Brodie Campbell, brother of Captain Angus who died in the West Indies. Nor were lesser dependants neglected. One of the recorder's last acts was to obtain a pension for a native official at his court.

His parting thoughts turned again to his favourite Roman, and he wrote home:

> Cicero said to Pompey 'You should never have coalesced with Caesar, or never quarrelled with him'. The first would have been honourable, the second prudent. Certainly a friend might say to me, you should either never have come to India, or have stayed there three years longer.

Sir James embarked on 6 November 1811. The principal event during his voyage occurred elsewhere, in Bagdad two months later, when Kitty was married; or, as the officiating clergyman William Canning, cousin of George, informed her father:

> On Wednesday the 8th instant between four and six in the afternoon the family in the residency having assembled in the harem, I joined the hands of your daughter and Sir William Wiseman . . . I really believe, if good sense and good temper contribute to connubial happiness, as much as they are reputed to do, Sir William and her Ladyship are likely to experience as much real enjoyment in their journey through life as falls to the lot of the most favoured of their fellow creatures.

Theirs proved an eventful journey. Perhaps the setting of the marriage was responsible; in the building used for the residency the harem was the only part suitable to accommodate Mary and her sister.

Chapter Five

Orator and Clubman

Ill-health and uncertainty about his future made the journey home melancholy for Sir James. He continued to write a journal for his wife and children, although it could not be delivered until he met them. Some desultory work on his history of England suffered from distraction by fellow passengers in the 450-ton vessel, including ten unruly children—'the severest test to which the power of attention of a student of philosophy was ever subjected'. He reflected it was good practice for a man who might have to contend with hostile voters on the hustings of Covent Garden. His principal consolation was the company of the terrier Tartar.

He was touched when, during a bout of violent sickness, he received kind attention from his former adversary, Charles Forbes, travelling home to round off his career by becoming an MP, baronet and public benefactor to his native Scotland. Only when the *Caroline* put in at Cape Town and passengers put ashore for nearly the whole of January 1812 did the retired recorder's nerves relax. There he was at ease in the company of charming and intelligent women.

They included Lady Hood, whose husband Sir Samuel was on his way to command the navy in India. She knew his cousins, the Grants, and Mrs Fraser who had shown her the burn where young Dr Mackintosh went bathing with the key of the wine cupboard in his pocket. He recorded in his journal: 'She showed me a great number of letters to her from Walter Scott . . . He passed some time with the Hoods at Tunbridge about three years ago.'

On a visit inland Sir James discovered Maria Graham in her passage home had stayed at the cottage of Lady Anne Dashwood, a married sister of his friend Lord Lauderdale: 'To every body else she seemed a monster but Lady A. like her without being blind to her foibles.' It was not long before Lady Anne was sharing scandalous gossip with her fellow-Scot: 'I had heard before that Fox's dumb son was by his Aunt Lady Sarah Lennox Bunbury Napier. Lady Anne affirms it to be so.'

He was even more taken with one of·the Dashwoods' guests:

Mrs Cockell the wife of General Cockell a neighbour came to dinner—a
vulgar-talking, good-looking, good-natured woman from Leeds whom
everybody likes and laughs at. She and I entered into many ludicrous
controversies and we had a laughing afternoon. She would not allow a
husband even to have a literary flirtation and seemed to have a shrewd
Yorkshire suspicion that it must always end in 'solid pudding and
substantial pye'.

Presumably Mackintosh did not fear Catherine would apply this to
himself.

He was not blind to the darker side of life at the Cape: 'The cruelty of
the Boers to their slaves seems to be shocking. One slave who had
conspired to kill her mistress at Stellenbosch ate a hearty breakfast on the
morning of execution and said it was the first comfortable half hour she
had passed for twentytwo years!' He became one of the leaders of the
anti-slavery movement in Britain.

Gloom returned when the *Caroline* resumed her voyage, made worse
by contrary winds. Early in April his journal-letter to Lady Mackintosh
declared: 'Oh how I long for a sight of you!' History studies were
abandoned while he composed a poem of seventy-four verses in
celebration of their wedding anniversary. His inspiration was
Shakespeare, for he assured her *Venus and Adonis* was as warm as anything
by Thomas Moore: 'Though I always thought Venus very little better
than she should be I cannot bring myself to think her quite so shameless a
strumpet as she appears in this poem.'

Hopes of a career in Parliament were fading: 'You need no assurance
that I never will accept any political situation from Ministers whom I
disapprove and that I expect such a situation very little from those whom
I might approve.' But there were posts he felt he could accept, without
political strings, first among them that of ambassador to America,
'although I have no more chance of it than of the Crown'. As envoy to
that country, whose cause he supported during the War of Independence
and more recently in the prize court at Bombay, there would be scope
for his powers of conciliation: 'I am familiar with American politics and
have a sort of liking for the nation though not for individuals.' As James
feared the two countries were on the edge of a war which brought little
profit or credit to either.

But a day's illness—he seems to have suffered from recurring malaria
and jaundice—shattered his dreams: 'I fear that all I can carry to you will
be a broken constitution little capable of discharging those large arrears of
the business of life which I have so sadly suffered to accumulate.' He
landed at Weymouth on 25 April 1812.

Nor did he return to a family in robust health; the youngest daughter,

Elizabeth, had always been delicate, and her mother suffered from what used to be called nerves, now recognised as stress, producing depression, headaches, and minor ailments. Mackintosh hurried to London, anxious to renew the social life he had known at the turn of the century. Among friends who called at the family's temporary home in New Norfolk Street were Daniel Stuart, Sydney Smith and Bobus, Samuel Rogers, Samuel Boddington, Amelia Sloper and Charles Grant; he also met Canning, and attended the King of Clubs. This had lost some of its sparkle and meetings became steadily less frequent before ceasing altogether in the 1820s.

Invitations included one to 10 Downing Street from Spencer Perceval, Tory prime minister since 1809. He would probably be almost forgotten today if he had not been assassinated by a madman in the lobby of the House of Commons. Perceval offered Mackintosh the early prospect of a seat with hints of advancement in the government. He did not press for an early answer, and treated the returned judge with great courtesy.

It was a tempting prospect; there had been no approach from his Whig friends.. 'I promised an answer in 4 or 5 days, not that I hesitated for it had long been my fixed determination not to go into public life on any terms inconsistent with the principles of liberty which are now higher in my mind than they were twenty years ago,' Mackintosh wrote in his journal, 'but I wished to have an opportunity of sending a written answer to prevent misconstructions.' Having drafted his refusal with the help of Bobus and another barrister friend, John Whishaw, he 'was preparing to send it on Tuesday when about seven o'clock in the evening Jos. Wedgwood came into the parlour of our house in New Norfolk Street with information that about five Perceval had been shot through the heart by one Bellingham, a bankrupt ship-broker'.

Loyalty received a quick reward. The day Perceval died, 12 May, James Scarlett called on Mackintosh to ask him to stand at the next election for the county of Nairn. This seat was controlled by Baron Cawdor, who owned the castle of that name, but preferred to live at his mansion in Pembrokeshire. The prospective MP soon found himself involved in political manoeuvres. In the crisis caused by the prime minister's death Lord Wellesley tried to form a broadly-based cabinet, and Canning was deputed to suggest to Mackintosh he might be appointed to the board of control responsible for India. But he again declined when the Whig leaders, Lords Grey and Grenville, found the terms offered to them to join the government unacceptable.

Although his finances were as precarious as ever, and MPs received no salary or allowances then, he bought 15 Great George Street, close to the parliamentary Palace of Westminster. It would be interesting to know if the security forces of the day were aware a Mr Fawkes occupied the house three doors away.

In the middle of this activity *The Gentleman's Magazine* announced: 'Sir James Mackintosh, during his residence in Hindoostan, has compiled a history of England, since the Revolution . . . It is said that the booksellers have engaged to give him £6,000 for the copyright.'

The work was, unfortunately, scarcely begun. The author retreated to Cheltenham, to drink the waters before setting out for his future constituency. On the way he and Catherine held a reunion with Allen and Wedgwood relations. Jos. and Bessy had moved to Maer Hall, Staffordshire, to be nearer the pottery at Etruria, which had suffered from the reluctance of the Wedgwood brothers to play an active role. John Allen had abandoned his devotion to Mrs Waddington and married Gertrude Seymour, so the three unmarried Allen sisters, Fanny, Emma and Jessie left Cresselly. They were on a protracted visit to Maer when the Mackintoshes arrived. The fine Jacobean house, which still stands, and its landscaped grounds ornamented with a lake became a favourite rendezvous with all the family's connections including the Shrewsbury household of Dr Robert Darwin, husband of Susannah Wedgwood and father of Charles Darwin.

It says much for Mackintosh's charm and for Jos. Wedgwood's forbearance that they renewed their friendship without apparent strain. James still owed money to his host, and had failed to produce the promised book on Thomas Wedgwood's time and space theories; he claimed the manuscripts were lost during his voyage home. Not a very likely story, although it seems he did lose some papers which were later recovered in France in mysterious circumstances.

From Maer he and his wife visited friends in Manchester and Harrogate before calling on the Wordsworths in Lakeland. Then came an extended tour of Scotland, passing rapidly through Edinburgh, Glasgow—'we had a singular navigation of two miles on the firth of Clyde in a steam boat, the first vessel navigated on that principle on the eastern side of the Atlantic'—and on to Iona and Staffa. There followed a visit to his home county, as he related in a letter to his daughters still in the East: 'About four miles from the western end of Loch Ness, on the southern side, at a lovely place called Glendo (where my grandmother was born), the carriage had a most tremendous overturn, in which Lady M. (then alone in it), narrowly escaped with her life: she was, however, only slightly hurt . . .

> We slept two nights at the place of my birth, Aldourie, now inhabited by my cousin, Mr Tytler, the sheriff of Inverness-shire . . . We soon reached Cawdor Castle, an old and striking castle in a romantic situation, which was our headquarters during our residence in the Highlands. We slept just under

the bedroom shown to travellers as that in which Duncan was murdered by Macbeth.

Their host at Aldourie, William Fraser-Tytler, was a son of Lord Woodhouselee. It was principally to meet the handful of county freeholders expected to vote for him that Sir James had travelled to Nairnshire. He was flattered to receive his burgess ticket as a freeman of Inverness, but it was discovered he could not be a parliamentary candidate. Differing reasons for this setback were published. One said his association with Nairnshire was too short.

An alternative reason given in the London press was that he was ineligible 'from his retention of a trifling place under government'. This was plausible, for on 10 December 1812 he wrote to Sir William Scott: 'On resigning the office of recorder of Bombay I accidentally omitted to send any formal resignation of that of judge of the court of vice-admiralty.'

In either case it seemed a strange mishap for a constitutional lawyer to suffer. The difficulty was overcome by an obliging relative, Hugh Rose of Kilravock, holding the seat temporarily and applying for the Chiltern Hundreds in the following June. His resignation left the seat vacant for James, who was elected unanimously.

This game of political chairs was enlivened by further attempts to detach him from the Whigs. The first was made by the Prince Regent, through his secretary, Colonel John McMahon, who reminded Mackintosh of his pamphleteering when the Prince first hoped to become regent in 1788. His royal highness was reconciled to the existing ministers, who proved understanding in settling his debts, but he knew the administration, now headed by Lord Liverpool, needed strengthening. James respectfully pointed out he was already committed to Lord Cawdor and the Whigs.

A more down-to-earth proposition came through Street, Daniel Stuart's partner and editor of *The Courier*. On 10 March 1813 he wrote to Mackintosh he had been told by Charles Arbuthnot, a treasury official concerned with patronage and the press: 'There is a place now vacant of £1,000 a year, not tenable with a seat in Parliament but of which government would feel honoured by your acceptance until, upon ascertaining your wish to be in Parliament and take an active part with the government, a seat will be vacated for you and a more efficient office proffered for your acceptance which might be held with a seat.' He added this offer was 'expressive of the wishes of Lord Liverpool.'

But the man once labelled an apostate had chosen opposition. 'I am a determined Whig,' he wrote to his daughter, Mary Rich. Already in his travels he had held long consultations with the party leaders. He spent a week at Howick, the Northumberland home of Charles Grey, now an earl. At Dropmore, the seat of Lord Grenville near Beaconsfield, he also found Lord Lansdowne, another prominent Whig, and Francis Horner, whose reputation as an MP was rising fast.

Sir James put his own views strongly. He was against the harsh penalties imposed on forgers following the widespread use of paper money, in favour of relaxing the disabilities on Catholics and other dissenters, against continuance of the East India Company's monopoly of trade with the East, suspicious of Russian designs on Poland, supported Wellington's campaign against the French in Portugal and Spain, but opposed the war against America. In a letter to Lord Grey he declared: 'My present politics are vigorous war against the Bank of England, the Protestant ascendancy, allow me to add the French in the Peninsula, and the East India Company—Conciliation with America and a declaration through Russia and Austria of our desire to negotiate a general peace.' It is unlikely this manifesto was to the taste of the earl, particularly as its author wrote from Bath, where he had gone to recuperate after his tour, and might lack the strength to fight on so many fronts at once.

The Mackintoshes went on to Dulwich for a further six weeks of quiet country air in February and March 1813. 'London dinners and parties are so dangerous to an invalid, even though a water-drinker,' he confessed in a letter to his daughters. His wife's brother, Baugh Allen, was Master of Dulwich College, or the College of God's Gift to give its ancient title, although the bequest came from Edward Alleyn, a distinctly earthy contemporary of Shakespeare. The duties were not onerous, and a critic called it a palace of drones. Perhaps P. G. Wodehouse, a distinguished old boy and inventor of the Drones Club, knew of that comment.

James became an Edinburgh Reviewer, having met the editor, Francis Jeffrey, during his tour. His first article was on a book by Edward Wakefield entitled *Account of Ireland, Statistical and Political*. Its opening showed a conscious effort to write in the rather 'flash' style which made the magazine famous:

> Mr Wakefield, the collector of the information contained in the large volumes before us, appears to be a sensible, industrious, liberal minded and well informed man, whose attention has been chiefly directed towards those details which of late years have been thrown together under the newly naturalized, and not very exactly defined name of Statistics. His chief failing is a desire to make a show of reading, and to give an unnecessary air of science and system to the collections of a traveller. An account of the Irish climate does not require twenty references to Roman historians and poets, to prove that Burgundy and the Crimea are now warmer than they were in the time of Pliny and Ovid.

Mackintosh wrote several articles for the review in the next fourteen years, but he confessed he had little relish for flogging authors, and his pieces were weighty rather than sprightly. Jeffrey urged him to be more self-indulgent: 'You are too fastidious as to ornaments, and disdain brilliant images and reflections that come now and then across you, because you think there are persons in the King of Clubs who would boggle at them . . . This comes from ever keeping choice company—I want to vulgarize you a little you see.' He did not succeed. Whishaw once commented of an article in *The Edinburgh Review*: 'It is written with great spirit and vigour and exhibits all Jeffrey's talents, but is wholly deficient in judgment.'

This deficiency was demonstrated when Jeffrey, wishing to go to America to marry, asked Mackintosh to edit the review in his absence. Although the editor's voyage was delayed for months, he was unable to extract from his proposed deputy a long-promised article on Burke to begin the next number. He also underestimated the reaction of Henry Brougham, whose unbounded ambition and energy enabled him to combine a career at the bar with excursions into politics, and numerous contributions to the *Edinburgh* and other publications. Jeffrey confessed in June 1813:

> The review is in no forwardness, and Brougham is intractable and provoking—you know that potent associate of ours I believe—and something of his ambition and love of domineering. He is offended because I have not left the sole management of the Review to him—with whom it would be less safe than with any individual that ever wrote in it . . . Brougham will not communicate with you—or at least not communicate cordially with regard to the review—and will take it amiss if you or indeed any one else are publicly or generally thought of or even guessed as the chief editor for the time.

He declared 'this does vex, and will fret me, if I ever permitted anything to fret me', but compromised by appointing no temporary editor and asking contributors to deal directly with minor assistants who would superintend printing. He was afraid to lose a man who wrote so readily as Brougham; but he should have foreseen his reaction before putting James into an awkward situation. Brougham was always suspicious of rivals to himself as a Whig leader, especially one intimate with Lord and Lady Holland.

Mackintosh combined sight-seeing tours with examining historical manuscripts preserved at the mansions he visited. In London the Prince Regent allowed him to see the Stuart archives, recently obtained from Rome. He acknowledged this was a handsome gesture by the Prince 'considering the nature of my late intercourse with him'; he was not pleased when access was later withdrawn because Walter Scott wished to work on the manuscripts. But by then he had made considerable extracts. With his own rebel forebears in mind he was surprised to find letters that 'abound with unexpected proofs of the very wide diffusion of Jacobitism at a period when it was generally supposed to be extinct.'

The pursuit of material for his history, combined with reluctance to start writing it, overshadowed his life. It was the age of the big book, in which Keats and Wordsworth wasted their time on sagas instead of the sonnets and odes by which they are remembered, and novelists were so wordy wags claimed they scarcely had time to finish a work before its sequel was announced. The reading public was small, but well-educated and often rich, idle and terrified of boredom. Publishers knew better than to offer slim volumes. Coleridge dreamed of the big book; when he visited Germany in 1799 he told Jos. Wedgwood he was collecting material for 'the one work to which I hope to dedicate in silence the prime of my life'. Thirteen years later Mackintosh remarked in his journal Coleridge was 'a man whose talents are beneath his understanding and who trusts to his ingenuity to atone for his ignorance . . . Coleridge has either so aimed at objects naturally beyond his reach or, what I rather believe, he has so fluctuated between various objects, that he has never mastered his subjects, and matured his ideas, in such a degree, as to attain the habitual power of expressing himself with order and clearness'. A later entry read: 'What I said two days ago of Coleridge, may with equal truth be said of myself.'

Sociability disrupted his studies. The breach between the Prince Regent and his Princess Caroline had become more open than ever before; when she arranged a supper party at Lady Davy's she asked that Mackintosh should be among the guests. However, John Whishaw reported to Lady Holland on 31 May 1813 that the Princess talked almost exclusively with Lord Byron 'and was observed to be unusually grave'. James was a favoured guest at Holland House dinners, and at Samuel Rogers' breakfasts—the timing and substance of such meals would now make it brunch. He was an emotional man, deeply attached to his family circle, but not demonstrative in his friendships—Sydney Smith described his handshake as the mortmain, while admiring his 'forty-parson power of conversation'. People he entertained at Great George Street felt they had imbibed a good deal from the fountain of knowledge, poured out in many an argument. This was as well, since Lady Mackintosh, handicapped by lack of money and incompetent servants, sometimes failed to provide a good dinner.

But those evenings were not solemn. Mackintosh extracted much fun from an occasion when one of his relatives from Scotland mistook the irreverent Sydney for the heroic Sir Sidney Smith. The clergyman retaliated by insisting the head of the Mackintosh Clan, Sir Aeneas, who also visited London, was related to the hero of Virgil's epic.

Treated as a lion himself on the strength of a book he had yet to write, Sir James was on easy terms with two people who dominated the social seasons in 1813 and 1814, Byron, and Madame de Staël whose opposition to Napoleon and many love affairs attracted as much attention as her books. He wrote to his daughters: 'She treats me as the person she most delights to honour; I am generally ordered with her to dinner, as one orders beans and bacon.' Byron called the Scotsman 'that brightest of Northern constellations' and a 'rare instance of the union of the very transcendent and great good nature'.

Mme de Staël described Sir James as her English Cicerone—among his attractions he could converse fluently in French—but told him enigmatically she was not content in England because it 'held for her no memories'. There is no evidence he offered to remedy this. So chaotic was her private life her entourage included not only a son and daughter, Auguste and Albertine, but the young Swiss-Italian, Albert de Rocca, to whom she was secretly married. Since everyone thought he was her lover, poor Rocca was barred from London society, dissolute as much of it was.

In 1813 the de Staëls took a house by the Thames and Mackintosh went to stay there. He wrote to his wife on 21 August 1813: 'Richmond 8 am Saturday . . . I arrived very unwell in spite of a hard ride and continued so throughout the evening in spite of your predictions. Our only visitors were the Duchess of Devonshire and one of her sons—the Fosters—who prevented speculative conversation without supplying any other.'

He realised belatedly this separation from Catherine might be misunderstood, for in a further note timed 5pm he said:

> I am really obliged by your compliance and now send the horses to bring you here tomorrow. Mme de Staël is extremely urgent for us both staying tomorrow evening to go as early as we please on Monday morning. She was originally prevented from asking you because she had no separate bedroom to offer which to French decorum it seems is indispensable.

In October he spent a week at the Marquis of Lansdowne's Wiltshire home, Bowood, where Mme de Staël was a guest with a number of leading Whigs, including Sir Samuel Romilly. Lord Lansdowne had been a student in Edinburgh with Brougham, Horner and Jeffrey. With his wife he liked to entertain Thomas Moore and other literary and musical figures.

Mackintosh first went to Cheltenham, where he found several

acquaintances from Bombay in a similar convalescent state to his own, and he wrote to Lady Holland: 'I hope that I shall benefit at Bowood (where I am now going) by a few days Staël.' Historical research continued, he obtained access to the collections of the Duke of Marlborough, and said he looked forward to visiting Holland House 'after my return from Blenheim if I survive the perusal of the 40,000 letters which await me at that place'.

His attention to the French woman did not entirely please Lady Holland, who wrote to Lord Lansdowne: 'She is certainly very clever, but also very tiresome.' She insisted on James staying for some time at Holland House, where he slept in Fox's room. He reported to his daughters: 'My residence would have been delightful, if illness had not counteracted the influence of the society and the scene. I passed a few days at the villa of Lord Auckland, called Eden Farm, where I slept in the bed of Mr Pitt twenty-four hours after having slept in that of Mr Fox.' Eden Farm, in Kent, was another source of family archives.

The events of 1813 came under the scrutiny of Lady Mackintosh's sisters, Jessie, Emma, and Fanny, who spent several weeks at Great George Street and at Dulwich. Mingled with their pleasure at being in London society was anxiety about Mackintosh's health and prospects, and the strain these were imposing on his wife. Jessie wrote in November to Bessy at Maer:

> Mackintosh does not seem much better, and I am afraid will not be well enough to cut a figure in Parliament this session, or do anything but chat with the old dowagers. Lady Holland and Mme de Staël have entered the lists together and divide the prize, and terribly does he lose his precious time between them . . . he dines I believe today with the Duchess of Devonshire. I cannot endure that these old Jesabels should make such a property of him.

Fanny was attractive but showed no anxiety to marry. In addition to Boddington, one of her admirers was a family friend, William Clifford. James, having met William and his mother, commented: 'Mrs Clifford is an uncommonly agreeable old lady. I like her odd, clever and gentle son who seems in love with Fanny.' But Clifford remained a bachelor; he once said he had never taken any step he had not regretted. Later Fanny told her oldest sister: 'If he had given me his heart he should have had mine; there is no man out of my own family I love so much.'

During this visit to London she wrote to a friend: 'We have seen a good deal of Mr Brevoort the American and he continues a great favourite, he was my beau of the night at Vauxhall, and I was very well satisfied with him.' Henry Brevoort, of New York, was a close friend of Washington Irving. In a letter she boasted: 'At Mme de Staël's her friend

Rocca who is certainly the handsomest man I ever saw, talked to me a great deal, he told Kitty to bring him up—you do not know what a compliment this was . . . he scarcely speaks to any woman.' She added Byron had been 'moved almost to tears' when Mackintosh defended him in *The Edinburgh Review*:

> He wrote him an excessively interesting letter with the Bride of Abydos saying it had been written in a week, and had been to distract his mind from the realities of an existence that is almost painful and odious to him. Praise has done Lord Byron more good than any blame ever could—Lord Byron is my pet of poets.

Emma was concerned about Catherine's health, although complaining that when playing the role of elder sister she was 'enough to provoke a saint'. She wrote to Maer after a visit to Great George Street: 'I thought Mackintosh looked better and he said he was very much so, he was more gracious to me than he usually is and invited me to walk with him in the park, Kitty came likewise, put him in a passion and then went and left us. He lamented to me the increased irritability of his temper, but for which he thought he stood excused by three years of bodily and mental suffering.' His wife no longer offered the sympathy he craved. Emma was shocked when, Mackintosh having received yet another request for the article on Burke, his wife 'laughed and told us there was nothing written, how she can treat with so much levity her husband's thus forfeiting all dependence laid on him does surprise me'.

On 11 November 1813 Sir James was elected a fellow of the Royal Society as 'a gentleman highly distinguished for his philosophical and literary acquisitions'. But his enemies were still vocal. Robert Southey met him at Holland House and Mme de Staël's, and wrote to a mutual friend, William Taylor at Norwich: 'Mackintosh has brought back from India a diseased liver, and a reputation which I do not think he will be able to support either in Parliament or in his intended historical labours.' Taylor, who knew James in his barrister days on circuit, rebuked his correspondent: 'I think his bad health a public misfortune . . . From your belligerence I seek refuge in his pacific philanthropy.'

When Southey published *Omniana or Horae Otiosores* he included an attack by Coleridge written a dozen years before accusing Mackintosh of turning against his early friends and semi-revolutionary ideals 'with a cold clear determination, formed at one moment, of making £5,000 a year by his apostasy . . . to be thought a man of consequence by his contemporaries, to be admitted into the society of his superiors in artificial rank, to excite the admiration of lords to live in splendour and sensual luxury, have been the objects of his habitual wishes.'

The damage done by Dr Parr's attacks on his absent friend could never be repaired. Walter Scott wrote to an English friend from Edinburgh enclosing an etching of Mme de Staël:

> Dont say you got it from me as I have no wish to commit myself with a Lady of such literary distinction and who besides threatens us with a visit here when I may probably have the curiosity to see her at least though only from curiosity. As for her proneur Sir Jemmy I know him of old—he cannot like many of his countrymen have left his conscience at the Cape of Good Hope in going out to India and forgot it as he came homeward—for I doubt very much if he carried such an encumbrance with him when he first crossed the Tweed for your grand emporium of talents of all kinds.

Self-interest would hardly have led Mackintosh to stand by the Whigs as he did. After losing office in 1807 they were dispirited and disunited, and public opinion was against a party which was, at best, half-hearted in supporting the war. He remarked in a letter to Lady Holland: 'To be a member of opposition during the remaining twenty years of the war is a strong sinecure which wants nothing but a salary.'

Political groupings were not so rigid as they became later, 'crossing the floor' was not such a serious step; MPs attached themselves more to individual leaders than to Whigs or Tories, and many of the latter regarded themselves as ministerial supporters rather than party men. Each side was not so much a broad church as a congress of sects, subject to internal and external pressures to split. The Commons also contained a high proportion of uncommitted voters, mainly country gentlemen with strong 'church and king' sympathies but liable to make up their own minds on particular issues, or not attend at all if the business looked boring. Consequently a government might suffer a shock defeat. But it was not expected to resign unless it could no longer govern. Even if ministers did resign, the Prince Regent was not compelled to ask the opposition to replace them.

Whig strength, and weakness, lay in the peers who led the two wings of the party, Lord Grenville on the right and Lord Grey on the left. John William Ward, later Lord Dudley, characterised the first as 'stout and able, but he ant conciliatory', while the second 'though nobody's manners can be more agreeable towards his friends and towards all those whom he is disposed to like, is not much calculated to captivate and hold together country gentlemen and weak brethren'. Everyone respected Lord Grey, but he conceded he was aristocratic both by position and by nature. Moreover, a reformed rake, he found it more agreeable to remain at home in Northumberland with his ailing wife and many children than fight for lost causes in Parliament. More than once in subsequent years he appeared to have chosen retirement, only to relent as soon as steps were taken to replace him.

He was not pleased when Mackintosh, as the time for his parliamentary debut approached, urged a full turn-out of Whigs. From Howick on 10 October 1813 came a 16-page reply in which the peer said:

> It is impossible that I should not feel the weight of all the motives you urge for an attendance of the opposition in force at the beginning of the session; and if I cannot make up my mind to yield to them, it is perhaps because I may be too much influenced by personal feelings, in which I will not deny that weariness and disgust may have some share.

He had persuaded himself 'neither the public nor the party will suffer . . . There will be nothing remarkable in my absence.'

Absenteeism in the Lords was matched by weakness and disunity in the Commons. The Whig leader was George Ponsonby, who held the post principally because nobody objected to him, whereas many were fearful of his powerful rivals, brewer Samuel Whitbread, and Henry Brougham. Both were on the radical wing of the party, as was another heavyweight, Romilly, dedicated to law reform. They liked to call themselves 'The Mountain', after the Jacobins of revolutionary days in Paris. This was not calculated to reconcile voters in the country or in Parliament to reform. Mackintosh commented they 'weaken us poor Whigs' and felt the party should distance itself from extremists.

As the allied armies moved into France, he wrote to Lord Holland on 3 November 1813:

> Lord Grenville seems immoveably determined on the part which I suggested to Lord Grey a month ago—that of supporting war for the restoration of the balance of power—and of leaving peace upon the responsibility of ministers. I have been too unwell today to feel any other interest in the issues than that which is inspired by my conscientious schedule to hold together the fragments of the party.

At that time the House of Commons met at four, and late night sittings were frequent. Until fire swept away much of the old palace MPs used St Stephen's Chapel which was small, gloomy and badly ventilated, making it unbearably hot when its hard benches were crowded. On 20 December Sir James rose to make his first important speech. The government proposed the Christmas recess should be abnormally prolonged until the beginning of March; he argued that in view of events in Europe MPs should return to work on 24 January..

Two disagreeable facts were quickly brought home to him. It is virtually impossible to persuade members to reject the chance to stop work; and Lord Castlereagh, though an indifferent speaker, was a masterly tactitian. Mackintosh went to the House armed with replies to what he expected the foreign secretary to say in favour of the long adjournment, which left the government free to pursue their policies abroad without supervision by Parliament. Instead Castlereagh stood up, put the motion formally, and said he would reserve the right to reply to any objections. James was left beating the air, and after he had done his best to overcome what he believed to be the government case, MPs trooped through the lobbies against him like schoolboys granted an unexpected half-holiday.

Nowhere are first impressions more important in public life than before the restless, changing audience in the Commons. Few men making their maiden speech, as he did, at forty-eight ever quite master it. He was not a silver-tongued orator, his gestures were sometimes ungainly and, like Burke, he was handicapped by an accent. Hazlitt said of Mackintosh as a debater:

> When he had wound up the charge of treachery or oppression to a climax, he gratuitously suggested a possible plea of necessity, accident, or some other topic, to break the force of his inference; or he anticipated the answers that might be made to it, as if he was afraid he should not be thought to know all that could be said on both sides of the question. This enlarged knowledge of good and evil may be very necessary to a philosopher, but it is very prejudicial to an orator.

On one occasion Sir James promised to be brief—and carried on for thirty columns of Hansard. On another the reporter admitted 'Sir James enlarged on a variety of subjects in which we have not been able to follow him'. Nevertheless MPs on both sides recognised two qualities they always respect—honest conviction and special knowledge in his chosen topics, law and history. He was to enjoy an occasional triumph, and consistently supported the liberal side of politics, from the abolition of slavery and reform of the penal system, to the folly of trying to extract war reparations from defeated foes and the need to encourage the emerging nations of South Africa, Canada and Australia.

He did not confine his crusading speeches to the Commons. *The Champion* Sunday newspaper reported that on 7 April 1814 he addressed a meeting at the Freemasons Tavern to promote a scheme of education among more than 30,000 London children without schools of any kind. On the platform with him were the Duke of Sussex, Whitbread, and the Reverend Alexander Waugh, forefather of Alex and Evelyn, and a popular figure among exiles from his native Scotland. Mackintosh contributed £20 to the subscription, although he was still in debt.

Clubs played an essential role in nineteenth-century politics. Sir James was proud to be elected in July as the 81st member of The Club, founded fifty years before by Sir Joshua Reynolds and Dr Johnson. Members dined once a fortnight when Parliament was sitting, the original venue of the Turk's Head having been changed to the Thatched House in St James's Street. The following year he was admitted to Brooks's, the Whig stronghold in the same street, his sponsors being the Duke of Devonshire and the Marquis of Lansdowne. He also frequented the non-partisan Alfred Club which met at 23 Albemarle Street. Formed by some literary loungers who visited John Murray's premises at No 50, members included Canning, William Gifford, editor of the Tory *Quarterly Review*, and Byron. The Alfred was finally absorbed by the Oriental Club.

In July 1814 Mackintosh spoke out on a subject which is still with us, the freedom of Poland. She was partitioned between her neighbours during the wars, and it was apparent the Congress of Vienna would pay little regard to her rights. His plea for this 'no insignificant member of the civilised world, but in extent and population the fourth state of Christendom', was ignored except for a letter of thanks from 'all the Poles' signed by their leader Thaddeus Kosciusko.

With the rising of Parliament he set out for the Continent, to gather historical material and renew acquaintance with Mme de Staël, and one of her lovers, Benjamin Constant, and other friends from whom he had been separated by war. Travelling with him were Samuel Rogers and his sister Sarah. They arrived at Dieppe from Brighton at half past four on 22 August 1814 'after a passage of thirty-six hours into which were crowded all the evils that the sea can inflict in the form of foul winds, calms, cabins crowded with disagreeable people etc', Mackintosh wrote to his wife.

The fastidious Rogers found his fellow-traveller trying, particularly when he missed his sleeping bag and discovered James had borrowed it to carry his books. For his part the latter described Rogers as 'a disagreeable companion', and they parted after a few weeks.

Paris, in those months before Napoleon's escape from exile on Elba, was full of English sightseers. The Hollands were among them, and Sir James enlisted the help of Lord Holland in persuading Talleyrand, the arch-survivor of every upheaval in France, to let him study the foreign office archives. Lady Holland exerted her usual sovereignty. At the Louvre 'Lady H could not go upstairs and even in the statue rooms was obliged to lean on my arm and to sit down every 50 paces', he recorded.

Meanwhile Lady Mackintosh was trying to manage affairs at home. London life was beyond their means, and letters passed between them on the advisability of letting the house in Great George Street and renting one in Devonshire, where her sister Caroline lived with her husband, the Reverend Edward Drewe. It is doubtful whether Mackintosh took this scheme seriously, as he plunged into Paris life, dividing his time between research and society, of which Wellington was the lion for the English and the villain for the French—even before Waterloo.

In September he moved on to join a house party at Coppet, Swiss home of the de Staëls. James was careful to tell Catherine 'This is a large house with fifteen principal bedrooms', and 'Rocca who has a spitting of blood and is threatened with consumption looks very pale'. Rocca, soon to die, was upset by the attention Mme de Staël paid to Mackintosh and others. She had never been exclusive in her affections and there can be little doubt that, intellectually, her husband bored her. Sir James wrote home:

We found Mme de Staël preparing for her journey to Paris where she goes next Thursday having taken a house at Clichy. She proposed to me to live there during the time that I shall be occupied by the papers at Paris and she warmly invited you and me with any children we pleased to come here for three months of next summer.

But he asked his wife's advice on whether it would be dignified for him to stay at Clichy, adding, 'I begin to feel some scruples at the presence of Rocca.'

From Coppet he went to Basle, where he met his daughter Mary and her husband Rich. They had travelled overland from Bagdad via Turkey, staying two months in Vienna. It seemed a strenuous journey for Claudius, who was on leave to recover from fever and headaches, but the Georgians believed ill-health required a thorough shaking-up of mind and body. Her father took Mary on a short visit to northern Italy and, returning to Switzerland, they encountered the Princess of Wales at Brieg. Princess Caroline, on a scandalous tour of the Continent with a motley entourage, invited them to dinner at her inn. Mackintosh wrote to his wife: 'The Princess was very communicative very foolish very good natured and very undignified. But I rather like her.'

By 18 October he was back in Paris lodging with the Riches, once more working on the archives. Evidently Lady Mackintosh was getting restive at his long absence, leaving her to look after his affairs—including a Highland aunt to whose support he contributed:

I have no motive of pleasure for continuing at Paris. The lodging is cheap but not agreeable and to confess the truth I have almost seen enough of Mme de Staël . . . I approve of your proposition respecting my poor surviving aunt. How few now remain of those who were kind to my childhood or whom my boyish promise filled with hope and pride . . . You see how carefully I have avoided every disagreeable allusion in your letter. I believe that I should practise the same virtue in conversation if the irritability of disease would let me.

Four days later he wrote again emphasising he was spending five to seven hours daily at the foreign office: 'I have already made discoveries of the utmost importance . . . I have three copyists at work.' But he confessed to Lady Holland, 'I had gay evenings as well as laborious mornings during my three months stay at Paris.'

The East India Company, who disapproved of Rich's extended absence in Europe, suddenly informed him his emoluments would be cut from about £4,000 a year to £900. Its officials claimed the Bagdad mission had declined in importance, and brought charges, later dropped, he had misappropriated company funds. Mary was dispatched to London to plead his cause, with the help of her father's influence with Charles Grant, chairman of the company's directors. She was kindly received by Lady Mackintosh and finally restored their income to about half its original figure.

James had lost much of his former admiration for Claudius, though pleased to find he and Mary were devoted to each other. Not being musical himself he was irritated that in such a crisis his son-in-law spent his evenings at the opera. But he endeavoured to promote Rich's claims to be transferred to a healthier post. He wrote home: 'Poor Rich bears his misfortune like a man. But it is a very great calamity. He is as I suspected still perhaps £2,000 in debt if not more. This is a dreadful result at the end of ten years service with his broken health and expensive habits.'

Mackintosh continued his research, reporting regularly to Catherine 'though you have had the good natured civility and politeness to tell me six times over that you have no pleasure in reading what I write'. There were other irritable asides: 'The interval between your letters seems to widen in proportion to the frequency and fullness of mine'; 'I am heartily tired of Paris and feel a warm wish in which you probably will not participate that I were with you never more to be separated'; 'The accumulation of useless violence which makes so large a part of your correspondence . . .'

He told her one of Mme de Staël's sons had remarked 'he thought there was no social gratification in Paris equal to a dinner at Holland House even with the drawback of Lady Holland'. Mackintosh favoured the anecdotal approach to history, not so fashionable then as now. He was amused to learn Napoleon 'had a daily fit of frenzy after reading the translation of the English newspapers. Talleyrand, Bassano and his most respected and favoured ministers always endeavoured to avoid him for an hour or two after this dreadful perusal. It was common to date notes from the Palace one hour, Two hours, Three hours after the reading of the English papers.' Another anecdote he enjoyed was of Napoleon reaching Warsaw after the retreat from Moscow and staying at a poor inn to keep his arrival secret. It was called Hotel d'Angleterre.

Dining out Mackintosh met an American official Jabez Young Jackson 'who knew some of my Edinburgh comrades and my old cousin General Mackintosh in Georgia'. He had a disagreement with Mme de Staël who 'fell foul of me for my desire of pleasing every body and for my too frequent appearances in the character of Mr Harmony'. She did not know that the day before he wrote to Catherine to say he had been ill: 'I am afraid that you would not welcome me cordially at any time but least of all if I should come home unwell . . . As this is poor Robin's birthday I heartily pray for his happiness before I go to bed and I hope that he may have the advantage of parents who live together as they ought.'

He returned to London with his marital and housing problems unsolved, but still enjoyed life. On 22 April 1815 he was at Drury Lane to see a verse tragedy by Mrs Barbarina Wilmot with a prologue by George Lamb, brother of William who became the second Viscount Melbourne. Lord Byron was on the committee of the theatre, and told Thomas Moore: 'I clapped till my hands were skinless, and so did Sir James Mackintosh, who was with me in the box—but it would not do.' The play was damned, in spite of the eminent claque; however Byron immortalised the playwright with his poem She Walks in Beauty like the Night.

Sir James made a number of powerful contributions to Commons debates during the spring of 1815, mainly on the confused situation brought about by peace negotiations and the renewal of war. He told the House:

> I detest and execrate the modern doctrine of rounding territory, and melting down small states into masses, and substituting lines of defence, and right and left flanks, instead of justice and the law of nations . . . To destroy independent nations in order to strengthen the balance of power, is a most extravagant sacrifice of the end to the means.

He declared:

> All the rights of all governors exist only to make the governed happy. It may be disputed among some, whether the rights of government be *from* the people; but no man can doubt they are *for* the people.

Commenting on the treaty which ended the Anglo-American war of 1812–14, he confessed his 'partiality to America, because she was not only bound to us by the ties of common origin, but by the closer fellowship of civil and religious liberty', and protested against the punitive expedition that destroyed public buildings in Washington.

When news reached London Napoleon was back in Paris, Mary rejoined her husband there, and they made the return journey overland to Bagdad. Their reduced income and the glimpse they had enjoyed of European society made them anxious to seek a new posting. Another of Mackintosh's daughters, Kitty, arrived in England, with her husband Sir William Wiseman. Her father wrote to Mary lamenting there seemed little prospect of William getting command of a ship, while 'poor Kitty is about to bring another child into the world which with their income and prospects is a melancholy event'. He was similarly worried that 'Maitland was going on increasing and multiplying her family without rhyme or reason'.

In the October issue of *The Edinburgh Review* Mackintosh made some amends for his previous treatment of William Godwin, with a double-edged compliment: 'He has thus, in our humble opinion, deserved the respect of all those, whatever may be their opinions, who still wish that some men in England may think for themselves, even at the risk of thinking wrong.'

Although the house in Great George Street had not been disposed of the furniture was auctioned, and James tried to sell his law books. The family moved to Weedon Lodge, near Aylesbury, at the end of the summer in 1815. He told correspondents its attractions included low rent and economy in fuel, and seclusion, their only fashionable neighbours being a fellow-MP Baron Nugent and his wife 'who are very kind and amiable'. He hoped to make progress with his history.

But he could not escape so easily. On 8 November Lord Nugent's brother, the Marquis of Buckingham, wrote:

> If you come and live in our County you cannot expect to be left quiet, or that we shall not show our sense of the honour you do us, but by endeavouring to derive some advantage from the circumstance. I have directed your name to be inserted in the Commission of the Peace for Bucks. In so doing, however I may have taken an unwarrantable liberty, I feel I have done my duty to the County. If I could hope that you would act as Magistrate, it is not necessary for me to say how important an advantage it would be to us all.

His victim could not refuse the irksome duties, since the marquis, the head of the Grenville family, was a political intriguer as well as generous host, who achieved a dukedom before falling into financial distress. Lady Holland disapproved of Mackintosh living so far from her influence, and referred to the neighbourhood as 'a cold boggy country infested by Grenvilles'.

Francis Horner called at Weedon and reported:

> He is living comfortably, and I should think very happily; free from the hectic fever of London idleness, and working just enough to keep him in

regular spirits. He told me, he expected before the meeting of Parliament in February, to have nearly finished the reign of King William; but it rather surprised me, when he added, that this would not form more than between a fourth and a third of his first volume.

On the reassembly of Parliament at the beginning of February 1816, as a further economy Weedon Lodge was shut while Catherine and her daughters visited the Wedgwoods in Staffordshire. Her husband stayed at the Hollands' town house in Mayfair. He reported despondently on the pre-session meeting of Whig MPs:

> Our numbers were twenty-eight of whom about four enemies—we were a pleasant union of the numbers of a Privy Council with the disorder of a mob. After three hours vexatious squabble we ended in no decision but an inclination to open the session by a display of our formidable minority of five and twenty . . . I came home sick and weary of the state of politics.

Poverty increased his gloom; one day he did not attend the House because it was too far to walk 'and I dont like to pay for a coach without a reason'.

Before Parliament were the terms of peace to follow Waterloo and the restoration of the Bourbon monarch. Mackintosh was asked to draft an amendment to the Speech from the Throne for George Tierney, who played a more influential role than the nominal leader, Ponsonby, in coordinating party tactics in the Commons, and later succeeded him. Sir James told his wife: 'It is a difficult species of composition especially as mine is to pass as Tierney's in order to soften Brougham's jealousy or rather his hostility.'

Of the debate he said Lord Castlereagh, who played an important part in the post-war settlement of Europe, 'spoke with his usual prolixity, art, confusion and bad English but with considerable conciliation for four mortal hours'. His own spirits had drooped by the time he rose to speak at eleven at night. He was not satisfied with his hour-long speech, but after returning to the Hollands' house in Savile Row at two 'I took a little sherry and water and slept better than I generally do after debates. Rose after eleven and found in the *Morning Chronicle* that my speech was called eloquent and not reported which was friendly.'

In fact he offered the treaty-makers advice that would have been valuable at Versailles a century later. Discussing a proposal to levy monetary reparations on France he declared:

> Cession of territory is the usual misfortune of the vanquished; tribute has rarely been imposed upon a state of the first class in the modern world; it is ignominious, it is a protracted irritation, it is a remembrance of defeat and

disgrace; it keeps up and exasperates the vindictive spirit of the French against the conquerors, and against the sovereign whom these conquerors established. The king of France was for five years, to appear to his subjects as a tax-gatherer for foreign conquerors.

Life as an MP rarely rose to such heights. On another occasion he could only chronicle: 'Thence to a meeting of the Highland members about the distilleries where the Duke of Athol was dull and tiresome beyond the privilege of ducal dignity.' Social life was more entertaining, with the scandal over Byron's separation from his wife Annabella Milbanke, and his continued pursuit by his discarded lover, Lady Caroline Lamb. There was also the story that Margaret Mercer had told him she would have managed him better:

> Lady Holland asked Miss Mercer whether the report was true of Lord Byron's having proposed to her. She said never—but that he had spoken a good deal to her, that he threatened the lady who then persecuted him that if she did not let him alone by G - - he would marry Miss Mercer or Miss Milbanke to get rid of her. He once told Miss Mercer, 'Some people praise me and many abuse me. The latter are in the right—my mind is as deformed as my body.'

When Lady Holland called on Caroline's father-in-law, the first Viscount Melbourne, and asked him how he did he answered 'as well as one can be who lives in Bedlam'. One of the girl's indiscretions was to write a novel, *Glenarvon*, a thinly disguised version of her affair with Byron in which Lady Holland was dubbed the Princess of Madagascar. Mackintosh described an encounter with his witty friend Ward:

> I told him I had a message to him from the Princess of Madagascar. He took off his hat and said 'A message from the Throne' as the Speaker does in such cases in the House of Commons.. But he desired me to throw him at her Highness's feet.

Another scandal was the relationship between Lady Frances Webster and the Duke of Wellington:

> Talked of the £2,000 damages which Mr Webster has recovered from the St James Chronicle for having with some truth asserted that Lady Frances had been vanquished by the Great Captain. Lady Holland said she understood that Webster had received £50,000 from the duke.

Following his speech opposing reparations on France James was invited to dine with the Duke of Orleans, living in a mansion by the Thames near Twickenham:

The Duke told me that he had many years ago translated the greater part of my book against Burke. He presented me to the Duchess who is plain with red eyes and white eyebrows and at present very big with child.

Robert Mackintosh was an amiable and spirited nine-year-old. His father reported Lord and Lady Holland's daughter Georgina 'renewed her courtship of poor Robert who is a great favourite here and will I hope by the same good and agreeable qualities make friends for himself when he loses my frail support'. Georgina was delicate and died three years later when she herself was nine. If the boy showed his father's and grandfather's good nature, there were signs of their failings too: 'Carried Robin to school where he has done nothing since his return because *his class* is not returned. I fear he does little at any time.'

Continued stomach upsets and headaches meant frequent visits to watering places for Mackintosh, and consultations with a variety of medical men. Among them was Dr George Darling, who treated many poets, authors and artists. His advice generally amounted to common sense prevention, and it was unfortunate his patient would not take the recommended cure of giving up the Commons and the late nights and social life that went with it.

When Darling published *An Essay on Medical Economy* he dedicated it to Sir James:

> I can think of no one to whom I can address what I have written with so much propriety as to you, who to a complete store of literary knowledge, and the most eminent attainments in the science of political economy and law, add a more than ordinary acquaintance with the philosophy of medicine and the condition of its professors.

Several minor writers dedicated works to Mackintosh, a measure both of their affection for him and trust in the attraction of his name on the title pages.

Among sensible proposals in the book was a reduction in the standard fee of a guinea for every visit or prescription by a physician. Dr Darling said this led people to consult unlicensed apothecaries who charged much less. This would have made wry reading for his patient, who wrote to Catherine: 'Darling asked me yesterday for money and I was obliged to give him £50.'

Another patient of the doctor and an acquaintance of Sir James was John Scott, Aberdeen-born editor of *The Champion* and author of two popular books, *A Visit to Paris* and *Paris Revisited*. Both Scott and his wife, Caroline, daughter of printseller Paul Colnaghi, were ill in the spring of 1816, and Scott believed Darling saved Caroline's life. Early in May Mackintosh wrote to his wife: 'Darling, Scott and Robert breakfasted with me. Scott looks and is very ill. Both his liver and lungs alarm Darling. He and his wife talk of going to Italy in a month.'

Lady Mackintosh wrote to John Scott seeking details of

> where the medical people have advised you to go at this season with any other particulars about accommodation and expense . . . I am unfortunately very much interested to obtain these on account of a sister of mine who is advised to take her eldest boy immediately abroad for a very similar complaint in his lungs.

This sister was Caroline Drewe, having lost her husband, she found two of her children were consumptive.

Scott's foreign trip was a tragic one, for although it benefited him and his wife, their eight-year-old son died in Paris. In her note to the newspaper editor Catherine enclosed an open letter to John Nash, published in *The Champion* on 2 June 1816:

> Sir—From the professsional situation you hold near the person of his Royal Highness the Regent, it is probable that the erection of the intended Monument, that is to commemorate the great victories of Trafalgar and Waterloo, will be chiefly committed to your direction . . . To the pillar or the column I think there is an insuperable objection in its obvious inutility, and its ostentatious air of antiquity, so much affected in their buildings by the modern French.

Her choice was the arch:

> Its form is peculiarly susceptible of beauty, both as to outline and decoration, and it possesses in its natural application as a gateway, that obvious utility which good taste will always seek in works of art.

She suggested one commemorating Waterloo should be placed by Hyde Park at the entrance into Piccadilly, while 'the gate of Trafalgar' should be erected at Westminster Bridge. Having reminded Nash of his career in Wales, the open letter ended: 'You will, I believe, Sir, recognise an old acquaintance under the name of FENONIE.' Among Nash's early works was a Pembrokeshire house called Ffynone. London did get its Nash Marble Arch, matched by Decimus Burton's Constitution Arch. But modern traffic made their inutility as obvious as that of Nelson's Column.

In the summer of 1816 Oxford, which can be grudging with its honours, made Sir James a doctor of civil law. The suggestion came from his friend, Dr Edward Copleston, provost of Oriel, and later a bishop. Their friendship transcended political differences, for Dr Copleston was a

Tory, although of the tolerant school of Canning rather than that of Castlereagh.

Mackintosh's money troubles were overshadowed suddenly by a crisis in Davison and Co., the bank in which John Wedgwood was a partner. He had very little grasp of its affairs; his brother Jos. tried to extricate him, but he was more a country squire than a businessman. They accused two other partners, Alexander Davison and Sir Gerard Noel Noel, of trying to save themselves at the expense of John. Eventually the bank was taken over by Coutts. Bessy Wedgwood wrote to her unmarried sisters, who were in Switzerland, from London on 22 August 1816: 'Your balance and everybody else's is now at Coutts, and everybody must be very glad to find their money there . . . The definitive deeds were not signed till 4 o'clock this morning, and the partners of both houses were here up all night.'

John emerged a poor man, dependent on a fund raised by his relatives. Nor did Sir Gerard escape; the contents of his home, Exton Park, near Stamford, including '108 portraits of nobility' were auctioned for more than £10,000 and he told a meeting of tenants his embarrassments arose 'from propping up a tottering bank'. Mackintosh's own balance was only about £40, but no doubt he was thankful to preserve it. His spirits were already depressed by a visit to Buckingham's estate at Stowe and having to carry out his duties as a Grand Juryman at the assizes.

Perhaps this crisis persuaded him to insure his life. It proved a valuable introduction, for he later became a director of two assurance companies. He still found time to give a helping hand to his fellow-countrymen, promising the owners he would promote *The Scotsman* by bringing the prospectus of this new publication to the attention of parliamentary friends.

In January 1817 James took lodgings at 35 St James's Place, the street in which Rogers lived. The little banker-poet occupied a strange place in society. His breakfasts were famous, and he could be a generous friend. But his literary pretensions were derided and his sharp tongue was feared. Mackintosh told his wife of a meeting of the Fox Club, where conversation turned to Lord Erskine who, after briefly tasting power as lord chancellor in 1806 and 1807, was ruined by extravagance and an unfortunate second marriage:

> Rogers represented Erskine as mad, supposing himself to be haunted everywhere by a quizzing spirit which he could render visible by touching, and having lately touched it he describes it as the ugliest and most hideous little wretch ever seen—I was tempted to ask whether it was not Rogers himself.

For once the Whigs were in good heart as the opening of Parliament approached: 'I went to call on Lady Spencer whom I found alone in high spirits and expecting an almost immediate change of ministers.' But dissension again clouded this rosy dawn, compounded by unrest in the country. Peace had not brought prosperity, and the extremists were busy; the Radicals in the Commons called the opposition front bench 'Rotten Row'. Sir James with Whishaw and another colleague, James Abercromby,

> laboured to dissuade Lord Holland from precipitating a breach with the Grenvilles—so essentially necessary as a pledge to the public of the safety of our measures and as a counterpoise to the democratical tendency of the present circumstances.

Leadership remained weak. Tierney's health was failing, and respect for Brougham's oratory was tempered by distrust of his ambition. His principal rival, Francis Horner, was desperately ill, and went to Italy with his brother, Leonard, to ease his chest complaint. Lady Holland had been particularly kind to Horner, and he wrote from Pisa: 'I find there are some acquaintances of mine here, but I have not seen any of them yet, as going upstairs still incommodes me.' For some reason—perhaps fearing her ladyship's love of gossip—he did not tell her the acquaintances were Caroline Drewe and her unmarried sisters, who travelled there on a similar quest for the health of the young Drewes.

On 4 February 1817 Francis wrote to Holland House: 'The use of opium is still but an experiment.' Four days later he died. His brother Leonard reported:

> I derived the greatest comfort from the more than friendly attentions of Mrs Drewe (the sister of Lady Mackintosh), her daughters and the Miss Allens, her sisters . . . they stood by my side when I laid the mortal remains of my dear brother in his grave at the Protestant cemetery at Leghorn.

Among his medical attendants was Dr John William Polidori, who originally went to Italy with Byron. The poet informed Thomas Moore: 'Dr Polidori has, just now, no more patients, because his patients are no more.' The two sick Drewe children died, and the sisters returned to England.

The political news Mackintosh sent his wife was still mixed with scandal. Lady Caroline Lamb was not the only member of the family to cause gossip. Her husband's brother George was troubled by a relationship between his wife, also named Caroline, and Brougham. Lord Auckland, James reported, 'narrowly escaped an elopement with Cleopatra Lamb', and went on:

The report of Brougham's elopment with her was told by the Regent with
some glee to Sir Walter Farquhar who with officious haste carried it to
Lady Melbourne. Cleopatra's venerable mother on hearing the other day of
George Lamb having the gout wrote to say 'that Caroline must come over
to nurse her dear Curly Pate'. Curly Pate had it seems consulted Scarlett
about the legal means of getting rid of Cleopatra. Scarlett got out of the
scrape.

Such attempts to amuse Lady Mackintosh were interspersed with acid
exchanges concerning his feeble health, lack of success in his various
ambitions, and the difficulty of finding somewhere to live cheaply. There
was friction of another kind over the education of their daughters,
Catherine wanting them to share her own musical taste, Sir James more
concerned they should learn to sketch.

She suggested taking separate lodgings in London so the girls' music
practice would not disturb their father, which drew the reply: 'I will do
everything to contribute to their accomplishment but consent to our
having separate lodgings at a distance of a few paces. So disreputable a
step would injure them in more desirous matters than music.'

The 1817 session of Parliament did not bring triumph to the Whigs,
and two incidents caused embarrassment to Mackintosh. Caroline
Drewe's eldest daughter Harriet had married barrister Robert Gifford, a
Tory appointed solicitor-general in May. There was surprise a barrister
who had not yet 'taken silk' as a king's counsel should be given the post.
Mackintosh, who himself became a judge without such distinction,
recorded: 'Westminster Hall is I fear in a state of perfect rebellion against
the appointment of Gifford. All the ministerial lawyers of high standing
are in a phrenzy. The novelty of a *worsted gown* made solicitor-general is
the general talk.'

It was not so easy to make fun of the situation when his old friend
Canning came under fire for having undertaken a special mission to
Lisbon from 1814 to 1816, with handsome emoluments. It was assumed
the government found it convenient to remove him temporarily from
the Commons, where he and Castlereagh were rivals; they had fought a
duel without serious consequences. On his return Canning took over the
board of control, while Castlereagh remained foreign secretary and
leader of the Commons.

On 6 May 1817 John Lambton, an influential Whig destined to
become Lord Durham, introduced a motion charging the government
with criminal misapplication of public money, claiming Canning's
appointment as ambassador extraordinary had cost £18,800. Mackintosh
faced an unenviable choice. A general election could not be far off, and
he had received no offer of a constituency in the next Parliament. He
explained to his wife:

At the moment of seeking an opposition seat my absence on such an occasion will be ill-thought of by our party. On the other hand to vote against Canning is disagreeable to myself, and if I do not get a seat I forfeit by such a vote the right to small acts of service to which I might in that case pretend from him.

Maria Graham and her husband were in London at the time. Women were not only barred from voting and becoming MPs, they were not allowed in the public gallery to watch debates. His letter continued: 'I happened to step into Graham's lodgings about three and to my amusement found Mrs G. dressed as a young gentleman for the gallery. Her attendant was to be a huge and coarse Scotchman, a Captain Fyfe of the Navy and Murray was to join her.'

In the debate he said of Castlereagh, who defended the government, his 'speech was so faint and confused that if he had not been protected by indisposition he might have been suspected of treachery', whereas 'Canning's speech was the best I ever heard him make'. Mackintosh, Abercromby and Richard Sharp squared their consciences by voting for Lambton's motion while adding the rider they approved 'the resolution as censuring the government for the appointment but not Canning for the acceptance'. They justified this by saying although the cabinet knew the special mission was unnecessary, it was possible Canning did not.

The House showed little interest in their quibbles before rejecting the motion: 'When we rose to make our explanations we were saluted by cries of Question . . . Murray sat next to Mrs Graham who was placed in a corner of the front seat and saw all without being much seen . . . Mrs Graham said she had more pleasure than in any other day of her life.'

Mackintosh's reputation remained high in America in spite of failure to produce his history. Alexander H. Everett, diplomat and author, met him in London, and wrote on 6 June from Boston: 'If the advantage of a correspondence in the New World will be any compensation for the trouble of it I hardly need say, how much I should be gratified by that of one of the first statesmen and philosophers of Europe.'

Mackintosh told Catherine he received a visit from 'the poor travelling philosopher of America', James Ogilvie. 'He seems to have an unbounded reverence for me and indeed my fame seems to have found a refuge in America.'

He was less happy with his standing at home, particularly in the eyes of the party leader: 'Dinner at Lord Grey's. On the way Lady Holland tried to convince me that Lord G. was warmly my friend though the clique by whom he is governed were my enemies.' She was working hard to secure a seat for him in the next Parliament; but Lady Holland required some return. At her suggestion Mackintosh wrote an obituary notice for *The*

Morning Chronicle on Mme de Staël who died in Paris. 'I have obeyed your commands,' he told her, but added: 'I have said too much which is the sin that most easily besets me.'

To distract him from the uncertain future, she took him on excursions in her carriage. On 4 December 1817 he wrote to his wife:

> Lady Holland carried me yesterday to see the orang-outang who is certainly our cousin. He is in every respect perfectly human. The likeness was at first shocking but a moment after he seemed no longer an ape but a pigmy Chinese or Malay. His shake of the hand is complete. Baugh it seems had a kiss with which I was not favoured.

It was a curious description from the uncle of Charles Darwin ten years before the voyage of the *Beagle*.

As the year drew to a close Sir James considered retiring from politics and settling in Scotland. But he moved only into Hertfordshire.

Chapter Six

Family Scandal

The move to Hertfordshire followed the appointment of Sir James in February 1818 as professor of law and general politics at the East India Company's college, now Haileybury public school, near Ware. It was established to train young men for the service, as suggested by Lord Wellesley in Calcutta eighteen years before. Mackintosh told William Adam negotiations had been needed 'to induce the troublesome professor to resign'. This was his predecessor, Edward Christian, of whom *The Dictionary of National Biography* says he was a brother of Fletcher Christian of the mutiny on the *Bounty*, and was 'in the full vigour of his incapacity' when he died five years later.

A salary of £500 a year for part-time duties, with a housing allowance, was important to the newcomer, while his experience in Bombay and as a lecturer on international law qualified him to fill the post, for which he was nominated by influential friends. But, remembering the attacks on him for accepting the recordership, he took his duties seriously and rejected any attempt to fetter him politically.

Before the final decision he wrote to Lord Holland:

> My friends were unexpectedly given to understand that though I was acceptable in other aspects continuance in Parliament after the general election would be an objection. To this I am sure you will not doubt my answer. It was and is that I could have no more of any stipulation about my continuance in Parliament than about my conduct while in it . . . In all possible events I am determined to carry with me through the remains of life an assurance that if I am not again in Parliament I have not quitted my post and my connections from any prospect of advantage.

On the contrary it sometimes happened parliamentary duties, combined with ill-health, disrupted his work at Haileybury. But he did his best for his young students, and according to his son: 'It was no mean gratification to him to receive occasional communications from the very heart of Asia, from some who had most profited by his instructions.'

He was welcomed warmly by a fellow-professor, the Reverend Thomas Robert Malthus, whose manner contrasted with the chilling message of his writings on population and political economy. Lady Mackintosh was reluctant to move to Hertfordshire, which was interpreted by some professors' wives as snobbishness but was more a symptom of growing estrangement between the couple. They were too poor to keep up a London home, when Parliament was sitting James either took lodgings or stayed with the Hollands while his family remained in the country. Writing to his wife from 35 St James's Place on 27 February he said: 'I am as heartily disposed as you can be to forget the coolness of the few last years or to impute them to my own fault and to receive forgiveness from you. My labour at the college is moderate consisting only of two lectures on two days following in each week for 8 months.'

She was exasperated by his chronic ill-health, and lack of the faculty for getting on, either as politician or historian. She was herself active in social reform, and her support for the Wellington and Nelson memorials was only one of several topics on which she wrote to newspapers. When *The Edinburgh Review* published what she considered flippant remarks about the work of Mrs Elizabeth Fry among women in jail, Lady Mackintosh wrote a pamphlet rebuking the anonymous writer. As this was Francis Jeffrey, her husband may have winced at the intervention.

To propitiate his 'dread goddess' Mackintosh continued to send her the current gossip: 'The Duke of Wellington was brought to Murray's two days ago by that mad wicked trollop Lady Caroline Lamb'; 'Lord Abercorn is dead. Yesterday morning he was apprised he had not many hours to live on which he ordered his coach and took an airing along the New Road for half an hour'; 'Sir Walter Farquhar has been for some time in danger. During the whole of one night he showed fear of instant death and roared out "Oh I'm going to see Mr Rose' taking George Rose naturally enough for the Devil.' Rose, patronage secretary to Pitt, had been unpopular with the Whigs. Sir Walter was a doctor; when the fifth Duke of Devonshire died in 1811, Ward said he added another to Farquhar's victims.

For an invalid who sometimes brooded on his own possible early death, James adopted a cavalier attitude to the mortality of others. On Lady Melbourne's death he commented: 'Lord Melbourne they say will either mope to death or marry his mistress, Mrs Elliott who thirty years ago was the mistress of the Duke of Orleans.'

Toothache as well as his recurring liver complaint figured largely in these letters—the Georgians were fascinated by their ailments and imagined others shared that interest, not always the case with Catherine. On one occasion he informed her: 'Worst day of my life. Perpetual agony. Laudanum and ether almost constantly in my mouth, allaying pain for moments but producing lethargy, headache and sickness.' the next day he felt even worse.

Mackintosh admired William Wilberforce, and supported his long
fight to suppress slavery, but showed little sympathy for his opium-
induced vagueness: 'Wilberforce came to me at twelve by appointment
to talk of the Slave and West Indies motions in the House. He was as
usual on such occasions vexatiously loose and desultory—as unfit for
business as a woman.' It was an unfortunate comparison to make to his
wife.

He had the grace to direct some mockery at himself. After
encountering Amelia Sloper, now married to Charles Warren, at a dinner
party he reported: 'Mrs Warren was to me almost a new acquaintance.
She is extremely improved in the last fifteen years—having thrown off
affectation and juvenility and behaving like a modest serious and sensible
woman. I presume that I have degenerated in nearly the same proportion
during the same time.' Sir James also admitted Lord Holland 'says I am
the only Scotchman he ever knew who feels the delight of lounging'.

On February 20 he attended a lecture given by Coleridge on
Cervantes, but was not impressed:

> It was an amplification of two hours length in the cloudiest language of
> German metaphysicians of an opinion which you have often heard from me
> that Don Quixote was a representative not of knights errant only but of
> benevolent heroic and eloquent madmen and in less degree of all who seek
> to serve mankind without wisdom to discover the right means.

This criticism was echoed by Henry Crabb Robinson who, while
noting in his diary disapprovingly that Sir James seemed to be in a party
who were 'in a satirical mood', added: 'Indeed Coleridge was not in one
of his happiest moods . . . His digressions on the nature of insanity were
carried too far, and his remarks on the book but old, and by him often
repeated.'

Mackintosh gave the Whigs something to cheer when he persuaded
the Commons to set up a committee to investigate the great increase in
forgery, especially of banknotes. 'Although the crime was always visited
with the utmost severity of punishment, they had not yet been able to
repress it,' he told the House, 'but on the contrary, the more the
promotors of capital punishment cried hang! hang! the more the offence
was committed, and the more numerous were the offenders executed.'
This was in spite of the reluctance of shopkeepers to prosecute in cases
involving small notes.

He accused Bank of England directors of complacency because
although it was easy to engrave a note that would deceive the public, few
forgeries deceived their own officials, and they spent large sums
prosecuting anyone caught with the notes. Sir James said he had
interviewed artists and scientists who thought it would be possible to

devise notes more difficult to counterfeit than those in use. The crime was not a capital offence in America and he pointed out that 'the banks in that country, not having the assistance of the gibbet to depend on, had employed the utmost ingenuity in the fabrication of their notes'. Later he wrote to his wife: 'Lady Spencer told me that she heard I had made one of the finest speeches ever made in Parliament and that it had converted the House and overawed the Ministers. The Governor etc of the Bank are incensed against me.' Lady Mackintosh still showed reluctance to moving, so his note ended 'Pack. Pack. Pack.'

In spite of this success his future was uncertain. The seat provided by Lord Cawdor would not be available at the forthcoming general election and his health and poverty prevented him contesting any seat except one where the Whig interest made the result a formality. It was an odd situation for an advocate of parliamentary reform: '*The Times* represents me as saying that I abhor close boroughs—an inconvenient imputation when a close borough is my only chance of a seat.'

Although the aristocratic party leaders enjoyed the company of Sir James over dinner, and listened at least with patience to his views on political tactics—he had slipped into the role of elder statesman without ever being a young one—they did not treat him as an equal. After a call on Lord Lansdowne he commented: 'He is very civil but reserved on politics—as indeed befits my insignificance.' Mutual mistrust marked his relations with Lord Grey. He recounted with relish an anecdote from Lord Holland about the 1812 negotiations with the Prince Regent, in which the Whigs felt they had been excluded from power through Sheridan's influence on the Prince: 'Lord Grey besides his natural dislike of Sheridan's meanness and artifice had at that time a very unjust source of hatred against him. His Lordship had just then been a successful lover of Mrs Sheridan and it seems to be his principle to hate all those husbands whose rights he usurps.' The second Mrs Sheridan was a cousin of the earl.

Nor was Mackintosh always at ease with fellow-lawyers. Of a meeting about the abolition of slavery, he told his wife: 'It was not one of Brougham's days of civility to me. Nor one of Romilly's winters for the same purpose.' He felt better after a call on Earl Spencer and his family in their mansion overlooking Green Park. From there he went to the temporary residence of Lord and Lady Holland in Clifford Street 'where my spirits foresook me as they often do I know not why unless it be that they are not so easily pleased as my less clever friends at Spencer House'. It is fair to add that although the Hollands kept late hours and liked to be entertained by brilliant talk, Lady Holland would arrange for James to go straight to his room with a cold supper when he had taxed his health with special exertions in the Commons.

Even Haileybury did not provide a quiet haven. The students, their minds chiefly on the riotous and profitable days they hoped to enjoy in India, grumbled when one was reprimanded for breaking a lamp outside the residence of a professor. 'I found matters in a most confused and disagreeable state,' Mackintosh wrote from the college on 8 April.

> The students espoused his quarrel on Monday evening, had recourse to horrid noises in the evening etc. But last night they not only threw stones at the chapel windows but actually fired a pistol loaded with slugs through a window when all the professors were in chapel and all the students ought to have been there. They fired detonator balls etc. This morning the council have rusticated six suspected of being ringleaders.

Sydney Smith wrote to Lady Holland he thought academic life suited Mackintosh's talents, but advised her to keep him quiet at Holland House till 'the season for lapidating the professors' was over: 'He is a very great and a very delightful man, and with a few bad qualities added to his character would have acted a very conspicuous part in life.'

Maitland Erskine made a trip to Britain for her health and that of her children, leaving her husband William in Bombay. She spent some time with the Wisemans and Grahams in Scotland, and late in April 1818 saw her father in London before returning to India. Both Wiseman and Graham were waiting for command of ships. Mackintosh wrote to his wife that Kitty, who was at Dundee, 'will now be left entirely alone for Mrs Graham is at Edinburgh dangerously ill of a complaint in the chest and if she recovers she is ordered to live as far south as she can'. He went on: 'Graham is soaked in whisky. He rises only to get drunk and goes to bed only when he is so.' Maitland told Sir James Maria was most intemperately jealous of her husband and of his friendship with a young cousin.

Religious enthusiasm was fashionable, and Maitland was introduced to the Clapham Sect by a Bombay friend, the wife of William Taylor Money. Mackintosh was sceptical of Mrs Money's beliefs:

> She goes on Fridays to Lady Emily Barry's religious conversaziones where among other singularities the Bishop of Gloucester preaches a sermon. They have introduced a new language in which they never say A.B. is good or virtuous or even religious—but that he is 'an advanced Christian'. Dear Mr Wilberforce is the most advanced. Mrs Money has a sister named Mrs Chatfield who has lost three children without a pang and who is so advanced a Christian that she could see the remaining ten 'with poor dear Mr Chatfield' removed with perfect tranquillity.

The professor and his wife at last moved into Mardocks, a large house by the river Ash, about four miles from Haileybury. It was demolished in the middle of the nineteenth century. Opinions about Mardocks differed. Lady Holland disliked it, probably because she once called there unexpectedly when the family were out; she was sensitive about not being admitted to any house, since sometimes she was not welcome because of her scandalous early life. Young Elizabeth Mackintosh found the location cold.

At least the Mackintoshes had a settled base near enough to London to entertain friends, although this meant slow progress on the writing of history. The unmarried Allen sisters returned from Italy, and Fanny went to Hertfordshire, where she remarked Mackintosh was so 'affectionate and tender as made me very sorry to quit him'.

One of his last interventions in the outgoing House was a skirmish with Lord Palmerston, then among the young men around Canning. A Select Committee on the Copyright Act recommended that publishers should provide a free copy of new publications only to the library of the British Museum. The existing Act extended the privilege to university and other libraries, a burden on publishers of expensive editions.

When a member complained the committee was evenly split on the recommendation passing it only by the chairman's casting vote, Sir James drily pointed out the opposition came almost exclusively from MPs for Oxford and Cambridge, two universities affected, who could not be impartial. Lord Palmerston, MP for Cambridge, rose and ssaid he treated the insinuation he had not acted with candour and fairness with contempt.

This was dangerous language in those duelling days. Sir James retorted he was not imputing improper motives to anyone, merely partiality for constituents, which the right honourable gentleman had a right to exercise. But he objected to the word contempt, and begged leave to say he did not consider any member who applied such language on such an occasion as qualified to give him lessons as to his conduct in the House or in committee. According to *Hansard*, Lord Palmerston expressed regret he had misconceived his opponent's meaning.

Palmerston took his revenge when he cooperated with others in a pamphlet, The New Whig Guide, full of satirical verses on the party leadership, including the lines:

> On the other hand Mackintosh strives to unite
> The grave and the gay, the profound and polite:
> And piques himself much that the ladies should say,
> How well Scottish strength softens down in Bombay;
> Frequents the assembly, the supper, the ball,
> The philosopher-beau of unloveable Staël;
> Affects to talk French in his hoarse Highland note,
> And gargles Italian half down his throat;

His gait is a shuffle, his smile is a leer;
His converse is quaint, his civility queer;
In short—to all grace and deportment a rebel—
At best, he is but a half-polished Scotch pebble.

John Wilson Croker, a Tory, claimed he heard James himself quote the
lines at a dinner party; he may have thought it preferable to others doing
so behind his back. The squib was taken up in a malicious review of the
pamphlet in *Blackwood's Magazine*. This article, probably by John Wilson,
praised the skill with which the rhymer

> plants some of his blows in the many weak sides of the learned knight's
> character. No man enjoys at the moment a greater reputation, built upon a
> more slender and inadequate foundation of merit, than Sir James
> Mackintosh. We well remember when he chose to desert his friends, the
> Whigs, for the sake of a snug appointment . . . We think there is no harm in
> saying that Sir James has really lived quite long enough upon the
> remembered sweet sayings of Madame de Staël, and the eternal
> advertisement of that eternal work, his history of Great Britain.

He at last found a parliamentary seat, Knaresborough in the West
Riding of Yorkshire, a handsome town rising beside the river Nidd like a
Rhineland village. Its population was less than 5,000 and only 50 to 100
had votes, yet it returned two members, the other being George Tierney,
Whig leader in the Commons following the death of Ponsonby. The
result of the election, held in June, was never in doubt since nearly all the
voters were tenants of the sixth Duke of Devonshire, and the returning
officer was ready to challenge any choosing the wrong candidate. The
reformer told his wife with surprise; 'We have been elected very quietly,
to the apparent satisfaction and almost with the applause of the people.'

At the end of December, before the 1819 session of Parliament began,
Mackintosh gathered with other Whigs at Bowood. They were joined by
Tom Moore, who confided to his diary:

> Music in the evening; all but Mackintosh and elder Macdonald attentive.
> They talked the whole time; I did not mind Macdonald; but I was very
> sorry for Mackintosh. I said, when I got up from singing 'I see these two
> gentlemen like to talk to accompanient', which brought the rest of the
> company upon them, and they were put to the blush. Mackintosh soon
> atoned by the agreeableness of his conversation and I was too selfish to
> follow the example of his *not listening*.

Even for Moore it seems Mackintosh had charms equal to those of
music. The politician liked the diminutive musician and poet, and when
he got into financial difficulties James advised him to take sanctuary from

creditors in the precincts of Holyrood Abbey, Edinburgh, telling him: 'The Continent is best for pleasure, Holyrood for study, composition, present income, and lasting fame.' Moore chose Paris.

The visit to Lord Lansdowne's estate was one of a number combining historical research with political and literary talk. Some idea of the industry with which he pursued his divergent careers was conveyed in a letter from Fanny Mackintosh to her sister Mary from Mardocks on 30 December 1818:

> Father returned from a visit to Lord Hardwicke at Wimpole . . . on Christmas day he went down to Lord Lansdowne's where he spent a week very agreeably. After leaving Bowood my father went to Middleton, Lord Jersey's, where he fell among a large party of Dandies which company as you may suppose was not the most suitable in the world to him and after staying two days and discussing the most approved style of drinking coffee and deciding the point that in the evening it was best without milk or sugar . . . at last he took himself off. Her Ladyship was however most gracious to him and gave him a heap of pamphlets she had brought from Paris.

He then, wrote Fanny, passed a week at Althorp, the Northampton-shire home of Lord Spencer famous for its library. He found many friends there, but the week's stay was marred by Samuel Rogers who had just published his long announced poem, *Human Life*. The poet was

> so irritable and fretful that he completely destroyed the pleasure of everybody and they were all very glad when he went away . . . to go on with the history of father's peregrination, from Althorp he was to have proceeded to Woburn for a few days but he was frightened away by meeting on the road Lord Wellington and a large party of barbarians who were going there to shoot so he put off his visit and returned here.

In spite of the quietness of the Knaresborough election, James wrote approvingly in *The Edinburgh Review* of the rough and tumble of the hustings in contested constituencies, and against polling in secret: 'The advocates of the ballot tell us, indeed, that it would destroy canvass and tumult. But after the destruction of the canvass, elections would no longer teach humility to the great, nor self-esteem to the humble.' Although he wanted a wider franchise, he did not believe in a vote for every man, or even in uniform qualification for it. He preferred a mixed system, in which the voice of the majority would be heard, but the middle classes would predominate.

Enemies complained this moderation differed from his views nearly thirty years before in *Vindiciae Gallicae*. Of the change of inconsistency, James said: 'This will indeed be the judgment only of the vulgar, but on the vulgar the success of a politician depends.'

His next major speech in the Commons concerned criminal law reform, which he undertook after the death of Sir Samuel Romilly. On 2 March 1819 he called for a committee of inquiry with particular reference to crimes punished by death. He told MPs there were some 200 capital felonies on the statute book: 'Every Member of Parliament has had it in his power to indulge his whims and caprices on that subject; and if he could not do anything else, he could create a capital felony.' The result was reluctance to prosecute anyone committing trivial offences and, when transgressors were convicted, the likelihood they would be reprieved. Sir James quoted a former Master of the Rolls, Sir William Grant, as saying 'during the last century, there had been a general confederacy of prosecutors, witnesses, counsel, juries, judges and the advisers of the Crown to prevent the execution of the Criminal Law'.

Mackintosh knew he was addressing men fearful the slightest relaxation in a largely unpoliced society might lead to them being murdered in their beds: he stressed he was not proposing abolition of hanging:

> My object is, to bring the letter of the law more near to its practice, to make the execution of the law form the rule, and remission of its penalties the exception. I hope to see an effect produced on the vicious, by the steady manner in which the law shall be enforced.

Even Lord Castlereagh, for the government, praised the temperate manner in which the question had been brought forward, but still opposed it. So did Canning. James got his committee by 147 votes to 128, applauded by his friends. However William Cobbett, in his *Rural Rides* pointed out with justice that the member for the Duke of Devonshire's borough of Knaresborough had not discussed the savage laws against poaching. Mackintosh once said: 'Cobbett is like a typhoon. He runs in an instant round every point of the compass and blows with equal violence from all.'

The journalist, unlike the politician, did not have to exercise the art of the possible. Getting any kind of law reform past the country gentlemen required tact, and to link it with something that would interfere with their sports when they dispersed to their estates would have been fatal. Even the setting up of the committee was only a first step, important as it was; years passed, in which government and Lords fought grimly against any amelioration, before the battle was won. In a subsequent debate James commented the conduct of ministers reminded him of the man who was a great friend to general principles, but had an exception for every particular case. Nevertheless, the seeds of the great reforms eventually carried out by Robert Peel as home secretary were sown by

Whig reformers led by the ex-recorder of Bombay; their persistence
made change inevitable.

Mackintosh's sentimental attachment to the hustings was put to the test
at a by-election in the Westminster constituency in March 1819; George
Lamb won for the Whigs after a disorderly contest, against two
candidates, one of them Byron's friend, John Cam Hobhouse, a
determined Radical. Reporting to his family, James said:

> Hobhouse's mob have been very outrageous. A great party of Whigs sallied
> from Brooks's on horseback to attend Lamb's triumph. If I could have got a
> horse I should have been with them. It was lucky I was not for they were
> driven back with mud stones and brickbats. Some of the gentlemen were
> hurt.

He was still at heart the young man who paraded with Horne Tooke's
colours in his hat.

The party needed cheering news. After a visit to Holland House on 27
April Sir James reported:

> Found Lady H. with a sprained ankle. The Duke of Bedford with blue eyes.
> Lord Grey blowing one of the coldest and bitterest of his Northumbrian
> winds. Lady Jersey in merry romps. Lady Grey rather melancholy, her
> daughter showing how ugly Ld G's face is on female shoulders, Adair sad
> and sentimental, Adam very ill . . . a very bad evening.

Robert Adair was a veteran Foxite.

His own health remained poor, in spite of unending consultations with
both orthodox and unorthodox physicians:

> On going to the galvanist who is tomorrow to try his battery against my
> stomach I met a man in a palsy who having heard my name introduced
> himself as Wilson the accoucheur at Stoke in 1799. Mrs Diggle was there to
> have her little frame excited.

If Catherine did have triplets evidently Mr Wilson delivered them and
was not ashamed to say so. Sir James felt his shock treatment did him
good: 'Tierney seems to be in a very bad way. I wish I could prevail on
him to try galvanism. Brougham has recovered all his health, insolence
and malice.'

But 1819 brought family happiness. Young Robert was accepted by
Winchester College. Handsome Jessie Allen, who was forty-two, married
ugly historian Sismondi and went to live in Switzerland. Baugh Allen,
Lady Mackintosh's younger brother, resigned the mastership of Dulwich
College and married Caroline Romilly, niece of Sir Samuel.

As the parliamentary session closed Mackintosh felt he could look back 'with the satisfaction of having done some service and placed my own reputation on quite a different footing'. He relaxed a little socially. One of the quirks of Georgian society was that while tradesmen were looked down on, nobody disdained the hospitality offered by the ancient City of London guilds.

On 2 August 1819 Sir James recorded:

> Most scrumptious dinner by the Fishmongers Company at their hall. So much turtle, venison and champagne with such profusion of fruit of the finest sorts I never before saw . . . A speech after every health was a great drawback on the splendid feast. The Duke of Kent spoke neatly. The Duke of Sussex more vulgarly than can easily be conceived . . . I was well received though towards the end interrupted by a man who had got drunk and whom it was found necessary to turn out . . . The Duke of Sussex compelled me to drink three glasses of champagne to his three bottles.

He woke the next morning with a sharp headache. But he attended one of his legal clients, he still engaged from time to time in constitutional proceedings. Then he went to the Palace of St James to take notes from the Stuart papers: 'My little key let me into the vast drawing room where I was a good deal interested by the contents of the papers and the singular residence.'

After spending the rest of the summer and autumn at Mardocks he returned to his London lodgings. Hopes of better relations with his wife did not bear fruit. On 25 November he wrote: 'I shall be very happy to receive you all at St James's Place—but you must excuse me for not doing anything so ridiculous as asking a bed from Lady Holland as soon as my wife and children come to town.' A few days later he added: 'If you can come to this lodging without absolutely turning me out of doors, I shall most heartily rejoice to see you. I may well go farther and say that I never wished more for your company.'

Brougham surprised friends and enemies by announcing he had married Mrs Mary Anne Spalding, described by John Whishaw as 'a handsome and rather dashing widow with three children, a good jointure and a house in Hill Street'. Mackintosh reported: 'Mrs Brougham is brought to bed of a daughter. He says the child is come a month too soon. It is certain that somebody was a month too soon.' Brougham remained as ebullient as ever. He called Lord Wellesley 'Old Morality' after a speech in the Lords considered too pious to be good.

James wrote to Jos Wedgwood: 'Brougham last night made an attack which was I hear unprovoked and coarse on our Welsh nephew Gifford.' Young Harriet Drewe's husband, now Sir Robert Gifford, was promoted to attorney-general in 1819; he was accused by Brougham of endeavouring to subvert the free constitution of the country. In particular he claimed to have overheard the minister say, in relation to the Seditious Meetings Prevention Bill, that it did not matter whether reporters were allowed to attend public meetings or not. Sir Robert retorted he had 'not said a syllable on the subject of reporters'.

The Whigs were conscious government moves to curb the press might end in muzzling all opposition, at a time when unrest among the poor was widespread. Two days after Brougham's outburst Lord Castlereagh moved the second reading of the Blasphemous and Seditious Libel Bill on 21 December 1819. The next day he moved the third reading of the Newspaper Stamp Duties Bill. The effect of these measures was to extend the tax on newspapers to periodicals and pamphlets, and impose stiffer penalties, including transportation, on anyone found guilty of seditious libel, which for ministers meant outspoken opposition to their measures.

These moves provoked a passionate defence of the freedom of the press from Sir James. He warned MPs attempts to reverse the growing power of newspapers would fail: 'This power they might exasperate or they might conciliate but not annihilate.' As sometimes happened when deeply moved, he pushed his argument too far for safety in an essentially conservative assembly. Canning, speaking for the government, complimented his opponent, saying he always listened to him with great pleasure because, even when he could not come to the same conclusion, he heard much to delight and much to inform him. But he asked the House whether the freedom of Parliament was to yield to the freedom of the press. The Bills were passed by large majorities.

Early in January 1820 Lady Mackintosh and Fanny made a hurried journey to Dundee, where Kitty Wiseman and her daughter Mary were dangerously ill. Kitty survived but the child died. Sir James wrote to Catherine in Scotland, mentioning the marriage of Walter Scott's daughter, Sophia, to John Gibson Lockhart, who collaborated with John Wilson on *Blackwood's Magazine*:

> 'I am sorry that Miss Scott a lady of noble family in the Republic of Letters should make a mesalliance. Whatever Lockhart's talents may be there is a taint of blackguardism both in the object and manner of his writings which renders it a disparaging union. Dont quote these phrases of mine as they might make a clever blackguard more my enemy than he is already. Cobbett is enough for me.

George III's approaching death cast its shadow over politicians, for a new King meant a new Parliament. The Whigs were in their usual disarray. It seemed ill-health would force Tierney to give up leadership in the Commons. Lord John Russell, who frequently consulted Mackintosh about his special interest, parliamentary reform, travelled from his family's home Woburn Abbey, in Bedfordshire, to call at Mardocks on 15 February. Mackintosh told his wife:

> Lord John says he never saw Brougham in higher spirits or more agreeable than at Woburn. Being a candidate for the immediate succession to our leadership he has put on his campaigning manners and his most conciliatory humour. Lord John however thinks that his succession will occasion much ill-humour and probably an open division among us. Lord John had hinted it as probable in the summer to Lord Lansdowne who altogether rejected the idea and said Mackintosh was the only leader with whom he could act. Twenty or even ten years ago this would have roused my ambition and not a little disturbed my mind—at present it affords me only a calm and very moderate gratification.

In the following month James was elected again with Tierney for Knaresborough, and they travelled back to London together:

> Tierney in the course of our journey told me that he could no longer attend regularly or even frequently in the hot weather—that as I had the same illness with himself he had no choice but the appointment of Brougham to act in his stead. 'It would,' he said, 'kill you in a year.' . . . In examining the case calmly I cannot pretend to deny to myself that his determination was right. But to be deprived of so great a distinction which to have been brought within reach by a most unexpected concurrence of circumstances must be felt to be painful even while it is acknowledged to be not unreasonable.

In fact hostility to Brougham proved insuperable, and Tierney continued as best he could for a while.

The Highlander was flattered when his chief, Sir Aeneas Mackintosh, who died in 1820 without a son, left instructions to name him among those in line of succession as part of the settlement of the estate. Sir James wrote to his wife, who was visiting Edinburgh after her mission to Dundee, on 20 February:

> My place or rather Robert's in the entail of the Mackintosh estate is little more than honour. It is singular that Sir Aeneas while passing over his sister's children for the sake of mere strangers as heirs male should have placed next in succession my family which is so old a branch as to have many before us in the male line. Robert's chance, little as it is, does not I suppose descend so low as not to be capable of being valued and sold in the money market.

Six days later he asserted: 'If Robert has descendants some of them will have no bad chance of the estate of Mackintosh as a Scotch entail is perpetual.' Within a month optimism was unbounded: 'To Robert the entail may produce a handsome fortune.' The fortune in fact went to a cousin of Sir Aeneas in Canada.

Another death opened prospects for himself. He was invited to apply for the chair of moral philosophy at Edinburgh University in succession to Dr Thomas Brown. 'Circumstances partly connected with my own health and fortune, partly arising out of the state of the country and of our party have of late often made me hold an inclination to steal out of public life,' he wrote to Adam Gillies, a friend since student days, who was a leading lawyer in the Scottish capital. 'There is no retreat for my age which I should like so well as Edinburgh . . . The professorship which six and thirty years ago was an object of my ambition might now afford an eligible retirement and a competent addition to my income.'

As so often before, there followed a period of indecision while he consulted everyone on the choice before him. Scottish friends, including Francis Jeffrey, urged acceptance; London friends rejection. His wife considered the post beneath him, while Holland House raised the spectre of a repetition of the attacks made on him over the retreat to Bombay. Lord Lansdowne spoke flatteringly of

> your present station in society, your future prospects, your power of serving others, and general usefulness to the public, all of them considerations to which I am sure you would allow their true weight, even at the expense of some personal comfort, and without some sacrifice of that, few situations of eminence can be held, or aspired to.

Mackintosh was not unduly impressed. He told his wife his noble friend suggested

> that after having worked up my way in eight years to a very distinguished station in public life it would be thought singular to leave it at the very moment I had reached it. Still however he said nothing explicit about the place which he wished me to fill in the House of Commons. He is the best example of sincerity without frankness of any man I know. His fear of pledging himself and also of encouraging hopes which he may be unable to gratify render it difficult to know his opinion.

James considered lecturing in Edinburgh in winter and attending Parliament in spring and summer, which would have destroyed any chance of improving his health or finances. In the end he refused the offer.

One of his interests was in the welfare of Britain's overseas possessions, where he feared the issue which sparked off the American War of Independence, taxation without representation, would arise again. He met a delegation from Gibraltar, and supported protests to the government over imposts on merchants there. They suggested he might act as agent in London for the territory, an echo of the proposal formerly made to him in India.

He wrote to Lady Mackintosh he had been to a part of London he had never seen before, Whitechapel

> where I found Mr Aaron Cardozo, the great Hebrew merchant of Gibraltar . . . He spoke with warmth yet with caution about his project for me. I asked him whether he remembered a Highland regiment at Gibraltar during the siege. He said perfectly. I asked if he remembered a Captain Mackintosh who was lame from a wound in the Seven Years War. His eyes filled with tears and he said 'Remember Captain Mackintosh, he was the benefactor of me and my family and I revere his memory. During the bombardment he gave me his own tents which were placed in safety and he did all he could to save our house, warehouses etc. He had rented our house.' I then told him that Captain Mackintosh was my father. He took me by the hand and said he had a new motive to labour in my service. He begged permission to send me a pipe of sherry a favour which I granted with ready generosity.

James speculated the post of agent might be worth £600 a year: 'They must also give me an office in London and a clerk. The office will probably offer a humble town residence.' This was another appointment which did not materialise. Apart from appearing before the judicial committee of the Privy Council in a case concerning Cardozo's property, Mackintosh's only business with Gibraltar was to ask for a memorial stone to be placed in the church there to commemorate his mother's death forty years before.

Fanny Allen and her sharp pen visited Mardocks in the summer of 1820, reporting her impressions to her sister Bessy: 'Lord John Russell came here yesterday, and unfortunately stays till Monday . . . His manners are so cold, that he quells us all, yet there is something pleasing in him when he does talk . . . He takes not the slightest notice of the two girls, as if he had never seen them, and very little more of Kitty.' Shyness was Lord John's handicap. At the end of his long career he is said to have remarked: 'I have seemed cold to my friends, but it was not in my heart.'

Lady Wiseman was also at Mardocks, but her illness had not reconciled her to Catherine. Fanny called her 'the funniest goon I ever saw', adding: 'She is going to town on Friday for a week, which will be very well as her perpetual bristling up, and making ready for combat, with Kitty on every subject indisposes Kitty more and more towards her, and a little absence may disperse the ill-humour that is growing against her. She has a nice little boy Jimmy.' The Wisemans continued to be improvident, but Sir William had got a ship, and he and his lady finally went to Jamaica, leaving the children with their grandparents.

Samuel Rogers liked to repair breaches between his friends. In July 1820 he invited Mackintosh to dinner to make up his quarrel with Dr

Parr, who told the banker 'I want to shake hands with Jemmy Mackintosh before I die'. Rogers wrote to James: 'That you can forgive, I know full well. That you will forgive in this instance—much as you have to forgive—I hope fervently.' He accepted.

Both James Perry and Dr Parr gave him written statements withdrawing their allegations over the subscription for Joseph Gerrald. The doctor later offered to go into court to testify, if Mackintosh decided to prosecute any of those who, from time to time, revived the old libel. Typically he marred his retraction by hinting in the same letter he suspected James Scarlett of attempting to curry favour with ministers, and by classing nephew Gifford among several 'patriotic lawyers' guilty of apostasy.

This long-delayed reparation had little effect. Three years later Hobhouse wrote in his diary:

> Creevey entertained me all dinner-time by laughing at Mackintosh's mean-looking face and figure. He told me that the story of Mackintosh appropriating to himself the money collected for a poor fellow, who was transported for his political conduct in the beginning of the French war, was quite true.

In these circumstances James showed courage in continuing to lend his name to fund-raising. With John Murray, Dr Darling, Dr Waugh and others he joined the appeal committee for the family of his friend John Scott. Scott was editor of *The London Magazine*, notable for its essays by Charles Lamb and Hazlitt, and for his own contributions. But he also used his columns to engage in a literary brawl with *Blackwood's Magazine*. This ended in a duel in which Jonathan Henry Christie, a friend of Lockhart, fatally wounded Scott.

Christie's friends complained the appeal for Caroline Scott and her children might prejudice his trial. Legally a duel death was murder, although the law rarely took its course, affairs of honour being looked on as a necessary hazard in a gentleman's life. This one caused a sensation in London and Edinburgh, and it was considered unwise for Lockhart or any one else connected with *Blackwood's* to take an active part in the defence of Christie; Walter Scott, now a baronet, had business in the south and acted as adviser to his son-in-law's friend. When Sir James wrote to Constable to ask him to collect money for John Scott's widow, the Edinburgh publisher at first demurred because of 'a peculiar situation in our intimate connection with Sir Walter Scott'. Constable, who had himself suffered at the hands of *Blackwood's*, later agreed to help.

The peculiar situation was not allowed to interfere with the social round. Early in April 1821 Lord Holland's sister, Caroline Fox, wrote of 'a delightful dinner' at Holland House at which Sir Walter 'told us many a Highland tale', with encouragement from Lord Lauderdale and Mackintosh. Little more than a week later Christie and his second were tried at the Old Bailey, and acquitted.

In June James had another victory over the government when he carried a Bill through the Commons to mitigate punishments for forgery. In doing so he again demonstrated the art of the possible by agreeing to retain the death penalty for forging notes issued by the Bank of England. It was argued this was essential to protect poor people who trusted the notes.

He told MPs he regretted having to make exceptions, he would have preferred to substitute transportation or prison in all cases. He felt however it was not for him to discard the opinion of those willing to cooperate with him to a certain extent, particularly where such cooperation was essential to the attainment of any portion of success. Sir Robert Gifford immediately replied that far from the amendments removing his objections to the Bill, they had confirmed them. However, Sir James got his Bill by 117 votes to 111, the narrow majority showing he was right to conciliate waverers.

It was an achievement for a man noted more for his table talk than the steady application needed to drive the Commons to take action in the face of ministerial inertia. It is difficult to judge how much his reputation owed to charm and how much to intellect. There were plenty of gossips writing diaries and letters then, but no Boswell to draw a rounded portrait. In any case James was not a master of pithy sayings, and too courteous to act the boor in company. He discouraged any attempt to report his conversation; judging from books compiled about some of his contemporaries he was wise.

Perhaps the shrewdest picture of Mackintosh at this time was sketched by George Ticknor, from Harvard University. He met the great talker first at Holland House, where he found him 'a little too precise, a little too much made up in his manners and conversation . . . a little given to affect universal learning', while admitting 'he discourses most eloquent music'. He noted a difference when invited to Mardocks, to a party attended by Sismondi and his bride, Jessie Allen, and by Lord Russell and Malthus.

Ticknor wrote:

> It was therefore, a party well calculated to call out each other's faculties and to interest a stranger. Lord John was more amusing than I had known him in London or at Woburn. Sismondi, with his new-born gallantry, very gracious but not very graceful, undoubtedly did his best, for he was brought into direct contact with Malthus, from whose doctrines he had

differed in his own treatise on the same subject, recently published; while Sir James, who delights in the stir and excitement of intellectual discussion, seemed to amuse himself by beating round on all sides, now answering Lord John with a story of the last century, now repeating poetry to Mrs Sismondi, and now troubling the discussion of the eminent political economists with his ponderous knowledge of history, statistics, and government, in short the subjects on which all three were most familiar and oftenest differed . . .

Sir James led in everything, and seemed more interested and agreeable than I had seen him in London society. I suppose that, on the whole, I have never met with an Englishman whose conversation was more richly nourished with knowledge, at once elegant and profound, if I ever met with one who was his equal. What is best in modern letters and culture seems to have passed through his mind and given a peculiar raciness to what he says. His allusions to his reading are almost as abundant as Scott's, and, if they are not poured out so rapidly or with such wasteful carelessness, it is, perhaps because he has an extraordinary grace in his manner of introducting them, and a sort of skilful finish in all he says.

The reference to Lord John confirms what others said of Mackintosh; while he talked brilliantly, he encouraged others to do so too. Not everyone fell under his spell. James Mill, one of Bentham's closest disciples, accused Sir James of living only for social display. Mill was a leading official of the East India Company in London, appointed on the strength of his monumental *The History of British India*. He may, wrongly, have attributed to Mackintosh an article on this in *The Edinburgh Review* which, although generally favourable, did point out Mill had never been in India, and said his style was careless and sometimes tasteless.

Lord Holland's son, Henry Edward Fox, a precocious young man to judge from his *Journal*, took a detached view of the orator's family. He referred to Lady Mackintosh on one occasion as 'a great gig—hat and feathers, plaited cord, and very quizzical indeed', mocking her passionate devotion to various causes. Henry described Fanny Mackintosh as 'pleasant and clever, though with vulgar manners, and like her mother, she is brusque and not ladylike'. But he did record a rare example of one of her father's *bon mots*, concerning a notorious dandy and a house of ill-fame in the West End: 'Lord Alvanley saw a hearse stopping in St James Street opposite one of the *Hells*. He went up and said gravely to the driver, "Pray, Sir, is the Devil dead?" Sir James Mac says he supposes he had a strong reversionary interest.'

Mardocks was the nearest the Mackintoshes came to a settled home. When Maria Edgeworth visited it, the Irish writer told her mother: 'We arrived here in our usual happy time—firelight, an hour before dinner; most cordially received both by Sir James and Lady Mackintosh; house pretty, library comfortable, hall and staircase beautiful: house filled with books.' She added cameos of two of the youngsters: 'Robert, a very intelligent boy of fifteen, little for his age; like his father, but handsomer, and he listens to his conversation with a delight which proves him worthy to be the son of such a father.' Fanny Mackintosh she considered 'one of the best informed and most unaffected girls I ever knew, with a sweet voice and agreeable conversation'.

Her description of handsome Robert was confirmed many years later by Henry Wadsworth Longfellow, who said he was exactly like the Lawrence portrait of James. The painter was known to flatter his sitters. Longfellow and Robert Mackintosh married two sisters, of the wealthy Appleton family of Boston. But at this time Robert was still a schoolboy, and a typical one to judge from a letter he wrote from Winchester to his sister Elizabeth, dated March 1821: 'We had the pleasure of seeing the Duke of Wellington today. There was a ball and dinner given to him on account of his being made Lord Lieutenant of the County. Ask the higher powers to send me a £1 note, as I had the misfortune to lose the only one I had in my posession, by return of post.' The importunate ending echoes his father's unhappy demands on Bailie John in the previous century.

The social event of the summer was the coronation of George IV, the interest heightened for the Whigs by the former Prince Regent having dismissed his favourite, Lady Hertford, and replaced her with Lady Conyngham, whose husband was a Marquis. She was friendly to the opposition. Mackintosh attended the coronation and watched the subsequent banquet in Westminster Hall. He wrote to Lady Holland:

> By the goodness of Lord Gwydyr I had tickets for his box and was seated by the railing which enclosed the part of it where all the exquisite and superfine ladies were assembled with their due retinue of dandies . . . You have heard of course much more than I have to tell you of the state of the court. There seems to be no doubt of the new marchioness's intrigues to remove the ministers and of the king's consequent quarrels with them. It seems to be certain that he or rather she wish and even design to call in the Whigs . . .
>
> Some of our friends are indignant at those who listen to the voice of a marchioness . . . even though she should have the power and the will to make a change. I am vulgar enough to wish that the Whigs were in power by any means, if it were only for a few months and to do two or three things.

To his wife he added a little scandal about the royal favourite: 'Lady Conyngham has it seems the modesty to call her diamonds "old family jewels" which it is true they are though not of her family.' In the end the King proved more faithful to his ministers than his mistress.

In the East both Claudius Rich and William Erskine were having an uncomfortable time, partly because Sir Evan Nepean, the spy master eager to track down Jacobins thirty years before, was governor of Bombay for seven years. He disliked both of them. James was still trying to get Rich a transfer to Bombay, and prospects brightened when Lord Moira became governor-general at Calcutta, with the title Marquis of Hastings, in 1821, while another acquaintance, Mountstuart Elphinstone, took over in Bombay. Lord Hastings wrote to Mackintosh to say Rich was likely to be given a new post at the port, superintending the trade in opium. But before Claudius received permission to leave the Gulf he died of cholera on 5 October 1821, still only thirty-five.

The year closed with Mackintosh negotiating with the firm of Longman's for publication of the first volume of his history, on which he hoped to receive one third of the total payment of £6,000. But in a letter from Mardocks to Holland House he said: 'History occupies every hour and I often have painful misgivings that after all I only collect materials for some man of greater powers who will begin the arduous work in a season of more leisure, cheerfulness and strength.' His prophecy proved right; his research papers were finally passed to Thomas Babington Macaulay.

James never lost his interest in American affairs, and enjoyed meeting anyone from the republic. On 7 March 1822 he wrote to his wife from London:

> Whishaw carried me to the Hollands where I met Mr Washington Irving the author of the Sketch Book whom I thought not only clever but agreeable though it be high treason to allow agreeableness to an American. It was a brother of his who visited us in George Street in 1813.

He also reported meeting John Randolph, Virginian orator and diplomat, and was friendly with the American ambassador, Richard Rush.

It was presumably through the influence of George Ticknor that he received an honorary doctor of laws degree from Harvard University in the summer of 1822. At that time recipients did not have to travel to Boston. His friend Edward Copleston also received an honorary degree.

In July Coleridge came close to apologising for his attacks on Sir James. The poet was lobbying for support for a Bill, promoted by the governors of what is now Highgate School, to allow them to pull down its old chapel and erect a new one. At the suggestion of Basil Montagu, Coleridge wrote to Mackintosh for his help 'as a personal favor or honor to me', and assuring him of 'unfeigned admiration and true respect'. When he received a courteous reply, he wrote again:

I should be ashamed of myself if I had not been gratified, and highly gratified, by your letter; but I can truly say that (though far from insensible to praise of less worth than yours) it was more endeared to me by its kindness, beyond what I have merited from you, than by the too favourable opinion which it expresses of my intellectual powers.

If the recipient exerted himself in the matter he failed, for the Bill did not pass Third Reading. However, the chapel was eventually demolished.

Unfeigned admiration and respect quickly wore off. Less than a year later Coleridge's *Table Talk* included the comment:

'I doubt if Mackintosh ever heartily appreciated an eminently original man. He is uncommonly powerful in his own line; but it is not the line of a first rate man. After all his fluency and brilliant erudition, you can rarely carry off anything worth preserving. You might not improperly write on his forehead 'warehouse to let'. He always dealt too much in generalities.

When Sir James became a vice-president of the Royal Society of Literature he gave whole-hearted support to seeing Coleridge was awarded a privy purse pension of 100 guineas a year.

He travelled to Glasgow in January 1823 to be installed as rector of the university, an honorary post filled by popular votes of staff and students. He addressed them at length, though much of what he said was beyond their grasp, for Scottish undergraduates then were boys rather than young men. He ran into something like barracking when he expressed satisfaction that in Scotland, as elsewhere, religious intolerance was fading: 'Catholic chapels are now erected at Amsterdam and Geneva; I have seen a catholic bishop at Boston; and even in Glasgow I have been delighted to see erected, within these few years, a catholic chapel, probably the most beautiful in the island.' New England first had a bishop, based in Boston, in 1808.

He was not a vindictive man, but he surely derived pleasure from the yelp of pain that rose from Edinburgh on his election. Bessy Wedgwood told her sister Jessie in a letter: '*Blackwood's Magazine* is always running at the *E. Review* and at all the authors with a malignity that I dont know how to account for. A number is regularly sent to Mackintosh at Brooks's, he does not know from whom, and it generally contains some abuse of himself.'

In the election for rector of the university the losing candidate was Sir Walter Scott. Lockhart, his son-in-law, hastened to offer to readers of the magazine an explanation of the 'real nature and character of the affair . . . occupying two or three pages with a very brief and plain statement of the true facts of the case'. He was anxious readers of Whig newspapers in London should not be suffered to nourish the exquisitely absurd notion that Sir James Mackintosh, Knight, has been here to receive a compliment resembling, even in *genus*, any of those high marks of distinction for which the first noblemen and statesmen of England, are accustomed to be competitors on the Cam and the Isis.

The agitated writer went on to stress many of the electors were aged twelve to seventeen—they became progressively 'children' and 'illiterate urchins' as the article went on, its promised two or three pages stretching to six. Sir Walter, who did not publicly acknowledge his novels for another four years, presumably winced at the passage in which his champion turned his pen on Jeffrey, the previous rector, who made an introductory speech at the inauguration: 'He dared to speak of Sir James Mackintosh as being superior to Sir Walter Scott "in what is properly called *learning*". Did he ever read Ivanhoe ÷' Lockhart went on to refer to 'little Mr Francis Jeffrey, when seated in his little library'. He sneered: 'Sir James Mackintosh is, no doubt, a man of very considerable talents. The origin from which he has raised himself is so humble that it must be so.'

Ironically, Mackintosh had refused an offer from Glasgow Whigs to have a public dinner in his honour, wishing to keep the occasion non-pol-itical. In any case he received another offer he could not refuse, to preside over a great Fox dinner in Edinburgh at Oman's hotel on 14 January. A solemn dirge was performed by the band as he proposed the toast to 'the immortal memory of the Right Honourable Charles James Fox'.

On his way back to London James, accompanied by his daughter Fanny, called on Sydney Smith, who now had the living of Foston, Yorkshire. The clergyman described the visit in a letter to Lady Grey:

> About half after five in the evening (3 feet of snow on the ground and all communication with Christendom utterly cut off) a chaise and four drove up to the parsonage and from it issued Sir James and his appendages. His letter of annunciation arriving the following morning . . .
>
> Mackintosh had 70 volumes in his carriage; none of the glasses would draw up or let down but one. He left his hat behind in our house.

Dr Robert Darwin had predicted frail Elizabeth Mackintosh would die young. She was buried in the churchyard of St John's, Hampstead, in April 1823, in the grave where her baby brother had lain for twenty years. A tablet in the church commemorates her virtues fulsomely. More poignant was the inscription on the table memorial in the churchyard:

> Here also within the tomb of her dear child hopes to rest and through the mercy of the Redeemer to rise with her to that life everlasting in which they shall no more be separated her afflicted mother.

During the rites at the graveside, Sir James leant in agony of grief against the yew tree which still throws its shade over the spot.

His distress was described by the clergyman who officiated, to Mrs Katharine Thomson, daughter of Thomas Byerley, a partner in the Wedgwood pottery firm. She was another young bluestocking who fell under the spell of the man she said was 'tall, cold in aspect, kindly at heart'. In her *Recollections* published thirty years later she wrote:

> I had the happiness of knowing Mackintosh. Our dawning acquaintance was heightened into something less close than friendship, more intimate than ordinary acquaintance, by an illness with which I was afflicted. It resembled at first the fatal disease of which a favourite daughter had recently died, and the sensitive feelings of the most amiable of men were touched by the detail of symptoms which recalled the anguish which he had endured. He called almost daily to enquire after my health, and supplied me with books, admirably chosen for the diversion of an invalid.

In spite of his sorrows, James did not neglect his Commons duty, where he missed no opportunity to sound warnings about Russian expansionism, which had first alarmed him when in India. After Spanish liberals extorted a constitution from their king, Ferdinand VII, the so-called Holy Alliance of Russia, Austria and Prussia, whose rulers thought it their duty to suppress freedom anywhere in Europe, threatened to intervene. The Whigs protested at the reluctance of British ministers to support the Spanish liberals. Addressing the House on 4 February 1823 Mackintosh raised the spectre of 'a Muscovite army lining the shores of the continent, from Amsterdam to Cadiz'. Three months later he referred to Russian claims on the north-west coast of America and Canada, and over the approaches to it—'doubtless as a preliminary step to that universal dominion by land and sea, which the recent plans and views of the Russian emperor seemed to contemplate'. In the end the reformers in Spain were crushed by a French army, and Russian designs on American and Canadian territory were ignored.

Whigs were always harrying the government to encourage freedom fighters everywhere, yet they were also the apostles of peace, and suspicious of expenditure on a standing army. It is a dilemma not unknown in modern politics. Mackintosh realised the problem while managing, as reported by *Hansard*, to crack one of his rare parliamentary jokes:

> He admitted, that on going to war, a government should found itself not only on what was the interest of the people, but also on the justice of the case. The case of a government in this respect might be compared to that of the guardian of a minor, who, in getting into chancery, should consider,

not only whether he had a just cause, but whether at the end of twenty years, he might not come off with a decree in his favour which would have the effect of involving his ward in ruin. He admitted, that in mentioning only twenty years, he might be derogating from the solemn dignity of that court, and allowing, perhaps, too limited a period for the grave and mature deliberation which was there exercised; but twenty years would be sufficient for his illustration.

It was a time when Lord Chancellor Eldon's court was known as that of *Oyer sans Terminer*; Dicken's *Bleak House* was nearly thirty years in the future.

James found time for benevolent lobbying. On 13 July 1823 with the younger Charles Grant, his cousin and MP for Inverness-shire, he visited the prime minister, Lord Liverpool, to plead for Mary Kennedy, widow of an Inverness Doctor. Their memorandum stated:

> Her husband who had originally served in medical offices in the Army and was for thirty years the principal physician at Inverness where he lately died and from his disinterestedness and generosity has left his widow with little provision for three children and two grandchildren. Amost all those who could now have supplied the place of a husband to her have fallen in the service of their country. Major Scott her brother was killed at Albuera. One of her sons was killed at Waterloo. Major-General Mackenzie her nearest relation was killed at Talavera.

The memorandum added Sir James had been her intimate friend from childhood. Perhaps she was the beautiful Miss Scott who was his first love. Lord Liverpool granted a pension of £100.

Next day another literary pilgrimage began. He wrote to Lady Mackintosh: 'Set off from the Saracen's Head in the Rockingham Coach with Sir E. Alderson, a vulgar civil little man.' Sir Edward, who became a judge, had just married their niece Georgina Drewe. The destination was Welbeck Abbey, Nottinghamshire, seat of the Duke of Portland: 'Dined at half past seven—with the Duchess, who never uttered a word, Lord Titchfield, Lord Henry the youngest son and the Ladies Harriet, Caroline and Charlotte . . . the duke returned from Nottingham Races at three in the morning.' On the following day: 'The duke showed me two boxes of papers. He is the coldest, most dry, and most substantially civil man in the world—a Cavendish grafted on a Dutchman.'

Later he noted:

> The duke has attended me with packets of papers with all the diligence of an excellent waiter . . . the dumb duchess speaks, the proud duke is quite thawed and the good-natured girls have so far conquered their fears of an old political bore as to laugh very heartily at threadbare stories and sorry jests.

In between his labours Mackintosh went riding through Sherwood Forest with the duke's eldest son, but lamented: 'Lord Titchfield is I am afraid almost a Tory and altogether a Puppy—perfectly unworthy of his excellent father.'

He had reason to be mordant, and out of town, in mid-July. It was his custom, in his letters, to refer to his children as 'poor Robin' and 'poor Fanny'. But one of them, Kitty, suddenly became 'my wretched daughter'. Lady Wiseman had eloped from Jamaica with John Turnbull. This greatly upset her eldest sister, Mary Rich, who returned from India deeply distressed by the loss of her husband, and sought consolation in religion. Mary asked her father to find a house for her and the delinquent, then pursued Kitty to her refuge in Bordeaux, and brought her back to London, where the Mackintoshes had moved into 42 Cadogan Place. From there Fanny Allen wrote to her sister Jessie in Switzerland:

> When Mrs Rich returned from abroad, she was obliged to come here first to know where the house was taken, her poor sister was in the carriage, and by accident Sir William Wiseman dined here with the boys that day, and just the moment before the boys were playing on the balcony. Mrs Rich walked in quietly, and was a good deal affected by seeing him and the children.

Lady Mackintosh had barely time to warn Sir William to keep the children from the window as Mary hastily drove off with her sister. Kitty refused to give up Turnbull, and Wiseman began divorce proceedings. This was a protracted business. It required a civil action in which the husband sought damages against the seducer, and an ecclesiastical lawsuit to obtain a separation. Finally, if the parties wished to remarry, a private Act of Parliament was necessary.

Fanny Allen provided a commentary on the civil action:

> Scarlett was for the prosecution and Sir J. Copley for the defendant, and nothing could be more decent than the trial was . . . Scarlett made so affecting a speech that the judge as well as counsel burst into tears. Scarlett said he had known Lady Wiseman from her childhood. The damages were £150.

The trial was too decent. When the Bill to sanction divorce was presented in the House of Lords they decided the evidence was insufficient. It could not be passed until their lordships had gravely considered the evidence of a chambermaid to Turnbull and Lady Wiseman sharing a bedroom at the George Hotel, in Rye, Sussex. It was 1825 before they could marry; Sir William also married again.

His enthusiasm for the freedom of the press did not prevent Mackintosh protecting his own privacy from that freedom. In spite of his many enemies the divorce proceedings were not reported. This was partly due to the efforts of Brougham, a constant contributor to the London newspapers with considerable influence over their editors. In *The Times* archives is a letter from Sir James to editor Thomas Barnes thanking him and the owner, John Walter, for the consideration they had shown 'for the feelings of a father'.

When Rich died he was virtually penniless, still arguing with the authorities over the allowances lost when he visited Europe. On Mary's return to England her father busied himself on her behalf, and finally extracted a pension of £200 a year from the East India Company. Rich had been a discriminating collector of eastern manuscripts and artefacts. Again through Sir James the House of Commons voted £7,500 to purchase the bulk of the collection for the British Museum. It included manuscripts of great rarity, some previously unknown, in the words of a museum official.

With the purchase went a portrait of Claudius; whether the handsome painting is a good likeness is uncertain for the artist, Thomas Phillips, grumbled he had to work from a faded miniature. This was buried with the widow in 1876. Mrs Jos. Wedgwood wrote from Maer to her daughter Elizabeth who was on a visit to London: 'Your brothers are all in a ferment at the idea of Mrs Rich's giving Sir Walter Scott her Turkish dagger.' Whether this indignation arose from the baronet's strong Tory politics, or a boyish wish to have the dagger themselves was not revealed.

Another blow fell on the family. In May 1823 Sir Edward West, chief justice in Bombay, dismissed William Erskine from his office of master in equity and clerk of the small causes court. He accused Erskine of fraud, oppression, extortion and corruption, and alleged his 'robberies on the public exceeded 2,000 rupees monthly'. Erskine was undoubtedly a muddler—he once noted in his diary with satisfaction his financial position was 'much improved my debt being nearly rupees 22,000 less'. However many in that venal city felt he had been harshly treated; he was widely respected both as a man and a Persian scholar, and for his work as secretary of the literary society and for charity.

He had been promoted beyond his capabilities by his father-in-law. Bur Sir Edward West was not above a little nepotism himself, since his nephew was given two legal posts at his own court. Erskine, Maitland and their large family were forced to retire to Europe, although more than one son became an Indian civil servant. James Claudius Erskine followed in his grandfather's footsteps as a judge in Bombay.

Mackintosh agreed to serve on the committee setting up the

Athenaeum early in 1824, together with Thomas Moore, Rogers, Earl Spencer, Lord Lansdowne and Lord Palmerston. He was not deterred by his political opponent, John Wilson Croker, being the prime mover in founding it. He was already an active member of The Travellers, in which Lord Castlereagh had played a leading role. Asked to canvass Lord Holland to join the Athenaeum, James replied the peer was 'already overclubbed, and I certainly might plead the same exemption. But I am desirous of promoting the new club.'

Overclubbing probably played a part in his continued ill-health, combined with family sorrows, commuting to Haileybury, and parliamentary late nights. Often his important speeches in the House were preceded by bilious attacks, and followed by sleepless nights. His letters referred to taking opium pills, and their antidote, calomel, and excursions to Cheltenham, Harrogate and other health resorts. His many doctors included Henry Holland, and the experiments with the galvanic machine were supplemented with vinegar baths, and the application of the flesh brush.

In June 1824 he wrote to Lady Holland: 'Dr Holland . . . yesterday permitted me to resume the ancient practice of eating—totally suspended in my case for about 80 hours—by a roasted apple for dinner.' That same month he resigned his professorship on health grounds. Fortified with a further pension of £200 a year the Mackintoshes again made London their home.

Chapter Seven

Bitter Fruits of Office

One legacy of the Napoleonic era was protracted turmoil in Latin America, where Spain's colonies declared themselves independent, partly in protest at the appointment of the puppet king, Joseph Bonaparte. The principal territories concerned were Buenos Aires, now Argentina, and Gran Colombia, where Simon Bolivar held sway over an area which included modern Venezuela. American and British merchants began trading with these newly-opened markets. During the 1820s investors provided millions of pounds for loans raised by the rebel governments, and for speculative ventures, usually in mining companies. It was hoped these, once freed from Spanish bureaucracy, would prove so many El Doradoes. When France invaded Spain to restore power to the Bourbon dynasty there bankers, and merchants in London and Liverpool feared an attempt might be made to re-establish the colonial regime and wipe out their investments.

Mackintosh had always disliked the reactionary Ferdinand VII and distrusted his protectors in the Holy Alliance, and he supported the rights of colonial communities, both inside and outside the British Empire. On 15 June 1824 he presented in the Commons a petition from the merchants of London seeking 'recognition of the Independent States established in the countries of America formerly subject to Spain'. He told MPs:

> When Great Britain (I hope very soon) recognises the States of Spanish America, it will not be as a concession to them, for they need no such recognition; but it will be for her own sake,—to promote her own interest,—to protect the trade and navigation of her subjects,—to acquire the best means of cultivating friendly relations with important countries, and of composing by immediate negotiation those differences which might otherwise terminate in war.

He called for an appointment of consuls in some territories, and reminded his hearers of the Monroe doctrine on non-interference in the American continent proclaimed by the United States the previous year. Sir James looked forward to the time when 'a single communication cut through these territories between the Atlantic and Pacific would bring

China six thousand miles nearer to Europe . . . that new road for the commerce of the world'. He added it was important 'to prevent the dictators of Europe from becoming masters of the new world, to re-establish some balance of opinions and force, by placing the republics of America, with the wealth and maritime power of the world, in the scale opposite to that of the European allies'.

Canning had been foreign secretary since Castlereagh's suicide in 1822. Some six months after listening to Mackintosh's plea he granted recognition to Mexico, Buenos Aires and Colombia. In doing so he borrowed his friend's sentiments but put them more memorably: 'I called the New World into existence to redress the balance of the Old.'

At the time however he declined to be rushed into recognition, hinting those with investments in Latin America might be over-anxious to see such a step. Mackintosh retorted:

> With regard to the influence of what may be said here upon the loans to the independent states, I can only say, that I have not the slightest interest in them. I find ample employment for the whole of my capital at home; and, however I may speculate in other matters, I am certainly not a speculator of that sort.

Catherine's charitable interests extended to animals, and she was particularly concerned at conditions in London's Smithfield meat market. Her husband supported her and when what is now the Royal Society for the Prevention of Cruelty to Animals was founded he joined its committee, with William Wilberforce and Basil Montagu. He called attention to the conditions in which animals were slaughtered when addressing the first meeting on 16 June—at Old Slaughter's coffee house in St Martin's Lane.

Another committee member was Richard Martin, an Irish MP who campaigned in the Commons against ill-treatment of horses and cattle. Martin introduced a Bill to abolish bear-baiting and other practices, including the beating of domestic animals, but was opposed on behalf of the government by Robert Peel. Just as Cobbett criticised Mackintosh's legal reforms because they left the game laws alone, opponents of this Bill taunted Martin with failing to seek abolition of all cruel sports, from coursing to fishing. Such a measure would not pass the Commons even 160 years later.

James derided the suggestion that because the Bill would not protect all animals, no attempt should be made to save any. However, he defended the use of animals, where necessary, in medical vivisection, remembering the body-snatching scandals associated with the dissecting lessons for student doctors he attended in his Edinburgh days. The Bill was thrown out by 50 votes to 32.

Two days after the RSPCA meeting he went with Jos. Wedgwood to Freemasons Tavern to support a subscription for a monument to the potter's friend, inventor James Watt. Lord Liverpool took the chair, and other ministers attended. Mackintosh took a prominent part in the proceedings; his readiness to cooperate with Tories in non-political activities must have scandalised some of the Whigs.

Inviting American ambassador Richard Rush to dinner in July, James added in his letter: 'I am ready at any time to do all that depends on me to promote the views of Mr Jefferson and the other respectable trustees of the Virginian University.' The establishment of this non-sectarian university, a year later at Charlottesville, was one of the last ambitions of Thomas Jefferson. Professors were recruited from Britain.

While Parliament was in recess Mackintosh embarked on a rapid tour of the Low Countries and Rhineland. From Rotterdam in mid-August, 1824, he reported to his wife: 'I bowed with due reverence to the statue of Erasmus.' He took the precaution of travelling with a doctor, but ill-health made him testy. From Bonn he wrote: 'Dr Somerville is loquacious forward, not very considerate towards others and neither a speedy, a pliant nor economical traveller.'

By 15 September he reached Brussels on the return journey where he mused on his visit thirty-five years before with his young bride and Dr Alexander:

> I immediately recognised the Park, the Place Royale and the Hotel Belle Vue where I stopped . . . The part of my early life which was spent at Brussels was according to the humble measure of so unimportant a person, eventful. Those who accompanied me were the objects of my warm affection. It is many years since all of them are dead. Such has been the effects of the many changes through which I have since passed that all the circumstances of that time seemed like a painful dream of a pre-existent state. They fluctuated between reality and fancy. Though I knew them to be true I scarcely felt as if they were events that now concerned me more than any other being. I cannot describe my feelings otherwise than by saying that they were attended by an uneasy sentiment of separation of my past from my present existence, a sort of apprehension that part of my former life was vanishing into nothing; and a melancholy consciousness that our best affections may sometimes be mortal.

A short excursion to Antwerp by diligence brought less ethereal reflections: 'I was forced to sit backward in a division of the carriage which contained four Flemish dames of comely faces but of ultra Rubensian dimensions.' He should have been making for home, but the death of Louis XVIII tempted him to take one more look at Paris.

There he attended the coronation of Charles X in Notre Dame: 'Talleyrand appeared as grand chamberlain, after having figured in almost all the public ceremonials of the last thirtyfour years, since he officiated as bishop at the federation of 1790.' A Frenchman who sat next to Mackintosh held Talleyrand to be a model of a good citizen for supporting every government in succession.

One of the few issues on which the Whigs were broadly united was Catholic emancipation. Even Tory ministers, Castlereagh, Canning and Peel, realised the absurdity of a great Catholic landlord like the Duke of Norfolk being able to choose six MPs for constituencies under his control, while barred himself from serving as a local justice of the peace. In Ireland there was little hope of peace while the bulk of the inhabitants were treated as second class citizens; many were qualified to vote, but they could do so only for candidates who subscribed, however nominally, to the established church. Restrictions were imposed on non-Catholic dissenters too but annual Acts of Indemnity removed most disabilities. Radical reform was blocked in the House of Lords by the royal Dukes, loyally supported by bishops who feared for their revenues as well as their status.

Mackintosh backed every attempt at amelioration. In 1825 he told the House he rose to protest against an attempt to silence the complaints of the people of Ireland, without redressing their wrongs. While he venerated the Reformation, 'and gloried in the name of Protestant', he believed freedom of opinion, and security from persecution were the only real basis of civil and religious liberty.

He underlined his tolerant attitude to politicians who disagreed with him by quoting Dr Johnson as saying one of his friends was a 'good hater'—he hated a Whig, and he hated a Scotchman. Sir James told MPs he himself had the honour to appear in both these characters, and was a member of an institution (The Club) which the doctor founded. But he did not believe Johnson had ever meant hatred to a party implied anything like hatred to the individuals who composed that party.

Another good hater, Dr Parr, died in March 1825, leaving Mackintosh a mourning ring and an assurance of his 'unfeigned respect', an echo of Coleridge's half-apology to him. Presumably their abuse of him was feigned. Their victim probably derived more satisfaction from being invited to a great dinner held in his honour in Glasgow the following month. James went there at the conclusion of his two-year term as rector of the university, a post he handed on to Brougham. Local Whigs insisted on the kind of party display he declined two years before.

But nervous sickness turned what should have been a triumph, gratifying to him as an expression of confidence from fellow-countrymen, into a disaster. He became ill while preparing for the dinner. As he told his wife, Dr Richard Millar stopped the retching by a grain of opium. I took some minced collops and madeira, dressed myself and went over about 8 with Millar in his carriage . . . On entering the room I was received with deafening shouts . . . in about ten minutes I was compelled (in spite of brandy and water) to rush out into an adjoining room where I retched and vomited for twenty minutes . . . I was carried home in a chair and put to bed.

Robert James, only eighteen, had to reply to the compliments paid to his father. He acquitted himself well and rose next morning to go on to Edinburgh although as his father said: 'Robert had a very sick headache in consequence of his efforts to supply my place.' Mackintosh recovered on the sea journey back to London.

His son was gliding comfortably into the role of man-of-the-world, but his attitude to academic work remained a worry. As a Winchester boy he went to New College, Oxford, with which his school was linked. Even by the relaxed standards of the day, New College was known for gentlemanly idleness. But a new broom in the shape of Dr Philip Nicholas Shuttleworth had been appointed warden three years before and on 18 December 1825 he wrote to Sir James:

> It is very seldom that we find our junior members apply themselves to their studies with proper diligence till the first sensation of becoming their own masters is in some degree gone off. I hope therefore what I have to say respecting your son will be received rather as a caution than a formal complaint. His conduct in a moral point of view, and as a gentleman, has been, as far as my own knowledge extends, unexceptionable; but there is an apparent systematic indifference about improving his mind and a general indolence of character, with what appears rather a contemptuous disregard of advice which if not soon checked must shortly lead him into serious dif-ficulty. I have reminded him in decided language that he is at present only on a two years probation and that his final attainment of a fellowship will absolutely depend upon his conduct, and his diligence during that interval.

His fellowship carried a stipend, and Robert must have heeded the warning, for he remained at New College until his marriage fifteen years later. The year 1825, when the Wiseman divorce completed its progress through the Lords, was not a good one for his father: much of it was summed up in the diary entry for 27 December 'Indisposition and Despondency'.

In the following month Mackintosh wrote his will. It is a moving document in which for once he combined deep emotion with brevity:

> Being of a perfectly sound mind but infirm health and believing the duration of my life to be now unusually uncertain do make this my last will and testament deposing of five thousand pounds sterling insured on my life

in the London Life and Rock Insurance Offices of my books and manuscripts which last are of very considerable value of my furniture and of shares in the Economic and Asylum Insurance Offices and all other property of which I may be possessed to Lady Mackintosh well knowing her affection for her children and believing that she will assist Robert to complete his education, and leave the residue after her own death to my daughter Frances . . .

My eldest daughter has a provision sufficient for her moderate wishes and my second daughter well knows my inability to contribute to her comfort. I desire that each of them may have a book out of my library as a memorial of my tender and constant attachment. I wish my unfortunate third daughter to be assured that I die with kindest wishes and prayers for her. I wish Robert to keep my Cicero which is one of my favourite books in remembrance of me. I hope he will remember the fond hopes which I have always cherished that he would far surpass his father in every respect. If he should inherit the estate in Scotland to which he is one of the heirs entail I earnestly exhort him to do as much for his Mother and sisters as I should have done if that inheritance had fallen to me. My most deserving children will not be surprised or displeased at a preference for my dear Daughter Frances which has lasted for twenty six years and beg her to keep my Milton and my Bacon for my sake. I beseech Lady Mackintosh to forgive my many faults . . . written and signed in Cadogan Place near London.

The international jurist failed to have his signature witnessed and when the will came to be administered the signature and his soundness of mind had to be attested by a manservant, and brother-in-law Baugh Allen. Mackintosh's continued hope his son might benefit from the entail was bolstered by the death of the chief, Alexander Mackintosh, unmarried in 1827. But he was succeeded by a brother Angus, living in Canada.

More than thirty years later Robert had the chance to buy the Kyllachy estate his father inherited and sold. He wrote to his sister Fanny he was glad to have the chance to show his son, Ronald, 'the paternal acres', adding: 'It is in the market and probably in the present rage for Highland places will go very dear. I could just manage the purchase, but then I should be halving my income, which in these days wont do at all. I was well pleased to have a good look at the place before it goes.'

It is to be hoped Robert respected his father's wish to preserve 'my Cicero'. His later career as a minor diplomat had some parallels with Marcus, son of that most likeable Roman of them all, who appears to have been indolent, of mediocre talents, but with an aptitude for administration.

Sir James was not alone in finding the times depressing, with great City business houses going bankrupt and industry and agriculture stagnating. On 18 February 1826 he wrote to Lady Holland: 'The discussions in Parliament are all on the distress and only show how little can be done to relieve it. The failure of Goldschmidt was for £1,700,000. He is one of the best of Hebrews. There are no books except on political economy—the favourite science of a season of commercial ruin.'

Among firms to fall was the publishing empire of Archibald Constable, owner of *The Edinburgh Review*. Apart from concern at the misfortune of a friend—'You have done more to promote the interest of literature than any man who was ever engaged in the commerce of books' he wrote—Mackintosh was agitated by the knowledge he owed the house £350 advanced to him years before. His note for this amount was presented to the Bank of Scotland, adding to his financial embarrassments.

Sir Walter Scott faced the abyss as well as his publisher, although he was rescued from bankruptcy by the kindness of friends and by working himself to death in trying to meet his commitments. James wrote the novelist a letter of condolence which was rather effusive in view of their spasmodic acquaintance. The baronet sent a polite reply assuring his correspondent neither he nor his family was ruined, and 'round as a neep I come toddling home'. In his journal he indicated he found the letter offensive, an attempt to welcome hin into the club of the perpetually insolvent, of which his fellow-countryman had been a member for so long.

This year at least saw a lifting of the burden on James of trying to drive penal reforms through a bored House of Commons and hostile House of Lords. Peel, as home secretary, was applying his great talents to the obvious abuses. How much he owed to the groundwork by Mackintosh and his colleagues is shown by a note from Whitehall on 9 February 1826 about a measure on laws dealing with theft:

> Should Sir James take the trouble of looking over the Bill and should any suggestions seem to him as to the details, to which Sir James may think it useful that maturer consideration should be given—that perhaps could be given in a Committee of the House of Commons—Mr Peel will direct his best attention to them.

Peel's reforms, sweeping as they proved to be, did not meet some of Mackintosh's wishes for more humane justice, but they had the merit of reaching the statute book instead of sinking in the pages of *Hansard*, as the most admirable of opposition proposals often do. He still found time for the latest novels commending *The Last of the Mohicans* and others by James Fenimore Cooper to his wife and to Lady Holland. Another distraction was the visit in May to Cadogan Place of Sismondi and his wife from their Swiss home. Fanny Allen and her brother John travelled from Wales to join the party, and the lawyer nephews, Gifford and

Alderson, were among the callers. Fanny wrote that Sismondi was fired with enthusiasm for the Greek struggle for independence from the Turks, a cause which Lady Mackintosh also adopted: 'Mack is very well and I think enjoys having Sis here and certainly Jessie's company.'

In June he was re-elected for Knaresborough, although ill-health prevented him attending the poll. Among the new MPs was his old barrister colleague, Robert Fergusson, home with a fortune gained from practice in Calcutta. James told Catherine Fergusson 'looked as pert as he did at Broadstairs' nearly thirty years before.

Robert Southey was another elected in 1826. Mackintosh, who met his detractor while visiting the Lake District the previous year, hastened to congratulate him, though admitting their votes were likely to differ. He added: 'When I saw you I envied so much the wisdom and happiness of your plan of life that I was on the point of asking you the probable expense of a family at Keswick who did not entertain and kept a man and boy with a gig and saddle horse.'

The congratulations were misplaced, since Southey had been nominated for Parliament without his knowledge and he declined the honour, saying his pension as poet laureate would in any case debar him from taking his seat. But he provided his correspondent with a letter of introduction to a Dutch contact who could help with material for the never-ending history research, in which he said:

> Sir James Mackintosh, whom I introduce not merely as one of the most distinguished Members of the British Parliament, but as one who ranks as high in the world of letters as in politics, who in his political character has more especially the interests of literature and of humanity at heart, and who is equally to be admired for the amenity of his public conduct and of his private life.

Retiring to Keswick was one of several unlikely schemes considered by the family. While it was true, as James told the House in 1824, he had not speculated in Colombian bonds, he did not escape the general crash of 1826, fuelled partly by the collapse of investments in Latin America. At the centre of some scandals was John Diston Powles, of the City company of J and A Powles, which had related companies in newly-recognised countries. When doubts were cast on the viability of their activities, Powles employed young Benjamin Disraeli to write encouraging pamphlets on the enterprises. Disraeli advised publisher John Murray to speculate, and both of them, with Powles, lost heavily when the price of shares in the Colombian Mining Association and similar concerns fell sharply.

Mackintosh's own involvement was with another Powles company which at least had a worthy aim. For some time he had urged emigration as a solution to unemployment and overcrowding in Britain, a view vindicated later in the century. Sir James became chairman of the Colombian Association for Agriculture and other purposes, with a share capital of £1,300,000. It proposed settling British migrants on land provided by the Colombian government, and later improving the country's transport system with roads, a railway, and river steamboats. The first shipload of settlers, some 250 men, women and children from Scotland, arrived at the end of 1825 and were allocated land at Topo, about nine miles from Caracas, now the capital of Venezuela. The experiment proved a disaster.

Sir Robert Ker Porter, British consul in Caracas, assumed the ambivalent attitude generally adopted by officialdom to innocents abroad. At times he sympathised with the settlers, who claimed they were misled about the suitability of the land for growing the crops and raising the cattle with which they were familiar. But he grumbled they included 'several drunken and idle persons . . . likely to become troublesome to me when turned loose in the country'. Among these he included the Reverend I Ross, pastor at Topo. By the end of 1826 the intended colony was almost deserted, many of its people having gone to America or Canada; before disbanding they sent home a petition setting out their grievances.

Mackintosh came under fire from both the Topo Scots and shareholders. On 6 December 1826 he wrote to Lady Holland: 'I am obliged to go to London to be present at a meeting of the Colombian Association of which I have the misfortune to be chairman. I begin however to hope I shall get out without being burnt to death.' Later he interviewed the surgeon to the settlement, J Williamson, on his return to Britain. He confirmed the migrants felt they had been deceived. He agreed about a third of the men were unsuitable through intemperance, indolence or lack of agricultural experience, but defended Ross, saying he had 'been drunk twice or thrice but these faults did not in any degree contribute to the failure of the settlement'.

Topo was not the only ill-chosen venture by this least commercial of men. He was chairman of the improbably named Promoter Benefit Society. This again proved to be ahead of its time, a white collar benevolent fund for employees in the higher posts in the Civil Service, banks and public companies, to protect them in old age and sickness, and meet the expense of launching their sons on careers. It was hoped employers would join staff in contributing. When a general meeting was held on 5 April 1826 it appeared from the comments of an angry shareholder the only person to benefit had been the original promoter, George Farren.

An entry in Mackintosh's diary read: 'Anxiety about Derbyshire Association which looked the best and has turned out to be (hitherto) the worst of my speculations.' It seems he was rescued from the more pressing of his embarrassments by drawing on the money paid to his daughter for the Rich collection, since another entry said: 'Paid into Coutts poor Mary's £1,000.' Even his bookbinder, John Macdonald, was involved in the juggling of cash: 'Gave Macdonald a note for £25 at six months of which I owe him 12 or 13 the rest he promised to pay Coutts at three months.'

At least he received fees for his connection with the Promoter Society, as he did for the chairmanship of another company with which it was associated, the Economic Life Assurance Society, a less innovative concern that survived until merged with others to become the present Sun Alliance Insurance Group. In addition to Keswick he considered retirement to Switzerland where the Sismondis advised him living was cheap, or Tenby, scene of that happy holiday before embarking for India. James wrote to Lord Holland:

> I have a project of at least twelve months retirement for health, history and economy. I find it impossible to preserve in London the quiet which is thought essential to the decisive improvement of health or that perfectly undisturbed leisure which would give me the best chance of shortly bringing out my first volume . . . By leaving London or its immediate neighbourhood I shall lose an income of about £400 per annum which I draw for weekly attendance for two days at two insurance offices and which would last for life or at least as long as I have health to attend.

He indicated his preference was Switzerland, but he was reluctant to abandon Parliament: 'I should be glad to hear your opinion of my project in general but more particularly on the degree in which going abroad might affect the propriety of continuing to hold my seat.' It was not unprecedented for an MP to spend several months abroad returning, if at all, only for debates of personal interest to him.

Predictably, the advice from Holland House was against weakening the Whigs by withdrawing a weighty orator, and the loss to Lady Holland of a favoured guest. This was mitigated by the offer of the Hollands' Bedfordshire mansion in Ampthill Park as a temporary refuge. This stately home was bequeathed to Lord Holland, but the family rarely lived there, since it was large and expensive to run in the manner to which his wife was accustomed. Writing to her on 29 August 1826 Mackintosh said: 'If the long library should prove too cold for winter work I can easily keep my books there and write in another room, for instance in the other library. I had indeed an ambitious fancy of writing history in one room and using another for the shabbier part of my labour.'

He was not a jealous man, indeed he frequently found consolation for his own setbacks in the success of friends. But he may have mused on the strangeness of fate when he joined a small company in the Rolls Chapel, whose site is now occupied by the Public Record Office, in September. They were there to bury Robert Gifford, son of a Bristol tradesman who progressed rapidly to solicitor-general, attorney-general, lord chief justice, and finally master of the rolls, whose duties included presiding over appeals and privy council cases. He was on course to be the next lord chancellor when struck down by cholera at forty-seven. His obituarist in *The Gentleman's Magazine* said this rapid advance was 'the more remarkable when it is considered that his powers, though respectable, were not splendid,—though solid, not profound'.

In spite of rearrangement of the publishing agreement, 1826 ended with no sign of the first history volume. Longman's wrote to another firm interested in the project, R Cadell & Co, to say the original agreement with the author dated from 1812 but 'we have not received a sheet of copy, though we have been urging him on from time to time . . . Sir James now intimates to us that his circumstances do not admit of his devoting his time fully to the history, unless we would make him advances . . .

'As we fear there is no chance of getting him forward without making this advance, we are disposed to agree to it.' The letter ended with a reference to 'this unfortunate concern, upon which we have already made heavy advances'.

Even at Ampthill the author was easily diverted from study. Bessy Wedgwood wrote to her husband on 24 November to say she and her daughter, Charlotte, were enjoying their visit. After dinner, while Catherine wrote letters to newspapers about good causes, and Fanny Mackintosh played the piano,

> Charlotte and I smuggle an hour's conversation with Sir James . . . he seems to enjoy conversation, and he is so wise and luminous in all his views, that I feel I have made a step towards wisdom in listening to him . . . Kitty has been getting a man convicted of cruelty to his ass, and he is sent to prison, but Kitty has been visiting his wife and supplying her with money and blankets while he is away, and Kitty told me that the wife seemed not displeased that the man was gone.

In a further letter Bessy said of her brother-in-law:

> He is now, he says, obliged to toil like a labourer because he would not work when he was so much better able to do it, but if he can but live to get his history through the press, of which he now seems to doubt, he will compound for all the rest. He is working very hard, and at the same time takes as much care as he can of his health, but he looks ill, and I never saw anyone's hand shake as his does.

Fanny became friendly with a large family of girls at the country home of Sir Robert Inglis, the Manor House at Milton Bryant in Bedfordshire. In addition to his own daughters he had assumed responsibility for the orphaned children of banker Henry Thornton, including six girls. The eldest, Marianne, described her new friend as everything a daughter of Mackintosh should be—'and more, much more, than anyone would expect her to be—very clever, full of information, yet loving fun as well as any child, and abounding in life and spirits. Yet as pious and devoted as if she had been a Miss Wilberforce.' This last qualification was important; the Inglises and Thorntons were enthusiasts of the Clapham Sect, where they lived when in London, and she was writing to the devout Hannah More.

When fever struck Ampthill, Mackintosh turned doctor once more. On 30 March 1827 he wrote to Lady Holland: 'This neighbourhood is altogether occupied with the war between ague and quinine pills . . . I have cured two patients at the Lodge. The younger of the two labourers behind the house is under Lady Mackintosh's care. Fanny has several patients . . . there are many hungry not entitled to parish relief.'

Lord Liverpool, prime minister for fifteen years, was forced to retire through ill-health and in April George IV reluctantly called in Canning to form a government. This caused a split in the Tory party, many of whom distrusted him and his liberal views on Catholic emancipation and foreign policy. He was forced to seek Whig support and began negotiations with Lord Lansdowne. Lord Grey held aloof, partly through personal dislike of the new prime minister, partly because he judged, rightly, Canning was not prepared to make real concessions in power-sharing.

As a veteran opposition front-bencher James hoped for cabinet office in a coalition government. On 28 April 1827 *The Times* published a provisional list of the new ministry that included James Scarlett as attorney-general and Mackintosh as judge-advocate. Although not of cabinet rank this was an office of distinction. James received letters of congratulation; it was humiliating when he discovered he was not to receive any post at all.

Why this happened is not clear. Scarlett, who became Sir James on his promotion, said later:

> I can state, upon my knowledge, the surprise and concern Mr Canning expressed, that the name of Sir James Mackintosh was not amongst those who were proposed to form a coalition with him; he had certainly thought him, not in merit only, but in estimation, one of the foremost of his party, and he was aware of the sacrifices he had made to it.

Lord Lansdowne, on the other hand, said Canning did not put this view to him, and when it was suggested Sir James should be judge-advocate, the prime minister said he must have someone in the post who could guarantee constant attendance in the Commons. Mackintosh was in the invidious position of having long complained public duties were ruining his health and keeping him from his history, and suddenly being taken at his word.

Both party leaders were disingenuous in their afterthoughts. To retain what support he could among the Tories, Canning kept in place those colleagues loyal to him. This reduced the number of cabinet posts for coalition partners to three, of which Lansdowne and Tierney took two and the third went to Lord Carlisle. Lord Lansdowne appears to have acquiesced too readily in Mackintosh's exclusion from even minor office. He brushed aside an offer from Sir James Macdonald, appointed a commissioner on the board of control, to stand down in the ex-recorder's favour. There was much in the comment of Lord John Russell: 'Whilst honest as the purest virgin, Lansdowne was too yielding, too mild, and most unfit to deal with men in important political transactions.'

Mackintosh complained to his friends he felt not only the lack of salary office could bring but the public snub his enemies were quick to exploit. He sought an interview with Canning. But his only consolation was to be made a privy councillor, unpaid, with the prospect of early appointment to the board of control. This would be worth £1,500 a year, but carried little prestige since most decisions were taken by the minister who was the board's president. James wrote to Lady Holland: 'I refused it thirteen years ago on political grounds and when it was offered me by McMahon at Bath with a message from the King.' In the event even this failed to materialise because, as he told her, the man he was to succeed, Lord Stowell, 'intimated his resolution not to resign without a pension. This is certainly a shameless proposal from a man of 82 with a fortune of near half a million'.

He extracted wry humour from the problems of those who failed him. Lord Holland had backed Grey in holding out against the coalition—the group were dubbed the Malignants by Canning's supporters. Writing from Holland House in July 1827 Mackintosh said:

> Lord Lansdowne very much wearied . . . in answering the thousand applications made to the Whig of the cabinet who has yet not an atom of patronage. The evening was hot. Lady Holland indulged herself as usual in abrupt and incessant opening of windows etc with no very amiable disregard to the opposite feelings of Lord Holland.

Mackintosh managed also to laugh at himself, recounting that Jeffrey 'is very much afraid of a bad promotion to the Scotch bench in the person of Sir John Connell. He begs me who could not make or unmake a corporal to prevent it!'

Even Lord Lyndhurst, the American-born lord chancellor who opposed the penal reforms advocated by James, sympathised with him and considered finding him a legal post. But one of his Wedgwood nephews, Henry, himself a barrister, wrote home with the cruelty of youth that his uncle becoming a judge was 'out of the question, for though the work in London is nothing, and therefore he might easily do that, neither his health nor his legal knowledge can be fit for circuit'.

James took a day off from politics in July to accompany Mary Rich to the British Museum where rebuilding had taken place in Bloomsbury, although he had ingenuously suggested the royal family might like to provide a site in what is now the garden of Buckingham Palace:

> Went with Mary to see the walls of the Lond: Univ: which in one place have already risen 8 feet above the ground. Thence to the museum where we admired the new building for the library, particularly the interior in which are four columns each of a single block of Aberdeen granite, the finest I have ever seen. The Rich collection in its new dress looks magnificent and the librarians repeat the assurances that the Mss especially of the Syriac Version are the most valuable ever brought to Europe. It is satisfactory to find that Mary and I cannot be charged with giving the public a bad bargain.

Politics again became all-absorbing when Canning died on August 8. James contributed a shrewd assessment of his friend to an annual called *The Keepsake*, saying that if he had a love of fame he also passionately loved the glory of his country. He added Canning was delightful company in private life but

> he was liable to be discomposed, or even silenced, by the presence of anyone whom he did not like . . . nor could he conceal that senstiveness to public attacks, which their frequent recurrence wears out in most English statesmen . . . It was said of him at one time that no man had so little popularity and such affectionate friends . . . No speaker used the keen and brilliant weapon of wit so long, so often, or so effectually, as Mr Canning. He gained more triumphs, and incurred more enmity by it, than any other.

Meanwhile the family took up residence for several months with Jos and Bessy Wedgwood at their Staffordshire home, Maer. There Fanny fell in love with cousin Hensleigh, three years her junior, and James, having moved great quantities of books from Ampthill, made sporadic efforts to write his history by day, and played whist in the evenings. Bessy told her sister Emma: 'We play a rubber every night, which he enjoys very much, and considering he is a genius, he plays very decently.'

Another guest at Maer was Charles Darwin, who studied medicine in

Edinburgh but was still undecided about his career. All his life he remembered his autumn shooting trips to the old house and society of his relatives:

> Life there was perfectly free; the country was very pleasant for walking or riding; and in the evening there was much very agreeable conversation, not so personal as it usually is in large family parties, together with music. In the summer the whole family used often to sit on the steps of the old portico, with the flower garden in front, and with the steep wooded bank, opposite the house, reflected in the lake.

Darwin, who later met Carlyle, Macaulay, Huxley, and other great talkers, said his 1827 visit was

> memorable from meeting there Sir J Mackintosh who was the best converser I ever listened to. I heard afterwards with a glow of pride that he had said 'There is something in that young man that interests me'. This must have been chiefly due to his perceiving that I listened with much interest to everything he said, for I was as ignorant as a pig about his subjects of history, politics and moral philosophy.

One man who benefited from the ministerial changes of 1827 was Mackintosh's Oxford friend, Edward Copleston. He became Bishop of Llandaff and acquired the country residence of Llansantffraed, where Catherine and James first met. Copleston was a Tory, if a moderate one, yet his promotion underwent some scrutiny. George IV wrote to Viscount Goderich, the new prime minister: 'I think you would do well to take the new Bishop from Oxford. If you can, therefore, get from Copleston under *his own hand* that he is *thoroughly Protestant upon the Catholic question,* I will appoint him the new Bishop.' Within eighteen months even the reactionary Duke of Wellington, heading a Tory government, was forced to concede emancipation to the Catholics, and his monarch, whose family also ruled Hanover, is said to have told him: 'Arthur this will send you to Hell and me to Hanover.'

When James attended his first privy council meeting in November he expressed himself cynically on the proceedings:

> The King is said to be in good humour with his ministers—the contrast between his deeply flawed and lacerated face with the youthful arrangements of his wig, gave him to me a great resemblance to Blake the hairdresser. He kept us standing or walking in the anteroom three hours which perhaps made me look on him with a less good-humoured eye ...
>
> After going through some common business on the proposition of the home secretary we were directed to withdraw when the recorder's report was to be made at which none are present but the cabinet ministers, lord president and the blackguard little recorder himself.

This report was on prisoners condemned to death, and recommendations for mercy. The recorder of London, Newman Knowlys, was not noted for being merciful.

Late in December the new privy councillor paid what he described as 'my 11th and probably last Christmas visit to Althorp' where he was 'busy taking notes from books elsewhere inaccessible to me'. He found his host, Lord Spencer, in decline: 'Lady Spencer apprehends immediate overthrow and though I do not say "the wish is father to the thought" yet neither can I think the fears are those of anxious kindness.' There was family anxiety because 'Young Spencer the Rector is becoming mildly Evangelical'. The Reverend George Spencer, youngest son of the earl, later resigned and became a Catholic monk.

Mackintosh's last evening at Althorp was enlivened by a visitor:

> Brougham came from Nottingham for dinner and the night. I went to my bedroom early to prepare by a good night for my journey. But I was persuaded into going down by the mighty monster, who kept me up two hours and excited me so completely by severe judgments, alarming secrets and daring projects that I did not sleep a wink for the whole night.

Like James, Brougham had shares in the new university in London and they served on its council with other leading reformers. Later known as university college, it opened in 1828. As with Jefferson's establishment in Virginia, it was non-denominational and became know as 'The Godless Institution in Gower Street'. The names of the founding council were engraved on a copper place placed in a cavity of the foundation stone.

Brougham also sought to involve the man he had robbed of sleep in another of his schemes, the Society for the Diffusion of Useful Knowledge, publishing educational books for working men. James promised an introductory volume on history, but in spite of urgent reminders from Brougham, nothing appeared. At least he acted as a spur to another historian. Macaulay wrote to his father on 19 January 1828 that he was writing an article for the *Edinburgh Review*: 'Jeffrey put me on my mettle by telling me that he wished to compare it with the paper on the same subject which Mackintosh is writing for the Library of Useful Knowledge.'

James continued to defend in Parliament the interests of the citizens of overseas territories. As early as 1816 he had told MPs there was no colony which united more sources of prosperity than the Cape of Good Hope, which became the nucleus of South Africa. He added: 'Canada is a possession which either must be held by the attachment of the inhabitants, or never can be worth holding.' The American War of Independence left that territory in a dangerously exposed position. It was divided into two provinces. Lower Canada, now Quebec, down the St Lawrence river was the home of early settlers of largely French Catholic stock, with a sprinkling of British merchants based on Montreal; upriver, in what is now Ontario, were the Protestant communities of immigrants from the home country, joined by American loyalists who did not wish to stay in the United States. At first few British ministers believed Canada would remain independent from its larger neighbour for long, and it is doubtful whether some even cared.

However, when the country survived the 1812–14 war serious thought had to be given to its future. The provinces of Upper and Lower Canada each had an elected assembly, but nearly all power rested with the executive bodies. These comprised a lieutenant-governor and nominated council, all appointed by the authorities in London. When it was proposed to unite the provinces a storm arose among French Canadians, who feared their laws and culture would be abolished.

On 2 May 1828 Mackintosh presented a petition said to be signed by 87,000 inhabitants of Lower Canada, and declared: 'We should leave the regulation of the internal affairs of the colonies to the colonists, except in the cases of the most urgent and manifest necessity.' Emphasising the danger of appearing to favour British Protestants at the expense of French Catholics, he added: 'Are we to have an English colony in Canada separated from the rest of the inhabitants—a favoured body, with peculiar privileges . . . shall we deal out to Canada six hundred years of such miseries as we have to Ireland?'

William Huskisson, minister in charge of colonial affairs in Wellington's government, referred the question to a select committee of the House of Commons, on which James served. Among those who gave evidence to it was fur trader Simon MacGillivray, born a few miles from Mackintosh's own home in Inverness-shire of a family which belonged to the Clan Chattan. He favoured union of the two provinces, as did most of the commercial community. The final report said:

> The committee cannot too strongly express its opinion that the Canadians of French extraction should be as little troubled as possible in their peaceful enjoyment of their religion, laws and privileges, as guaranteed by Acts of the British Parliament.

Another recommendation was that public revenue and expenditure should be put under the control of a popularly-elected assembly. Several years passed, marred by half-hearted rebellion, before Canada received this degree of democracy, but it eventually became the pattern for other developing nations of the empire. In gratitude to Mackintosh the assembly of Lower Canada proposed he be appointed the province's

London agent with a salary of £1,000 year, a large sum in Canadian terms then. This was blocked by the all-powerful executive.

In June he turned his attention to Australia. But he failed in an attempt to get the Commons to introduce trial by jury and to have one-third elected representatives in the legislative assemblies of New South Wales, and Van Diemen's Land (later Tasmania). In the same year Henry Hellyer, surveyor of the Van Diemen's Land Company named one of his discoveries in the northwest of the island the Mackintosh river. This has since given its name to a hydroelectric scheme there. Hellyer was impartial in honouring politicians—he named other rivers Huskisson, Brougham, and Canning.

That summer the Mackintoshes moved to Clapham where their neighbours included Sir Robert and Lady Inglis. Mary Rich accompanied them, and her interest in the Clapham Sect probably played a part in the choice of home. Lady Mackintosh was impressed by two fashionable preachers, Thomas Chalmers and Edward Irving. The house was a solid Georgian mansion, now named Western Lodge, overlooking the Common. Although twenty-eight Fanny Mackintosh was still something of a tomboy. She would scramble over the wall to visit the Thorntons, and they did the same to listen to her father talk. Clapham was then a rural district, but in reach of Westminster by a short carriage drive.

In a family sketchbook preserved among the Thornton Papers in Cambridge University Library is a cartoon of Sir James with Marianne Thornton. Believed to be the work of her sister Henrietta, it depicts him looking rather straighter and slimmer than he probably was at that time. He has his back to Marianne—'he always turns his back on the people he is talking to'—is the artist's explanation, while Marianne has her back to the world, and appears as an ample seated figure with an elaborate hairdo. His caption is: 'It's an established fact that all ladies are deficient in geometry, grammar, and justice. Do you agree with me?' She replies: 'No. I should be deficient in the last quality if I did.' Mackintosh was evidently enjoying spirited female company once more. Marianne considered him and William Wilberforce the best talkers she knew, but having spent a morning taking down their conversation she burned her notes the next day as unworthy of them.

By August 1828 another excuse to defer the writing of history was available, and gratefully accepted. Macvey Napier, editor of the seventh edition of the *Encyclopaedia Britannica*, invited James to contribute a history of ethical philosophy. Knowing time spent on this, which greatly appealed to him, would have to be filched from his history, Mackintosh pledged the editor to secrecy and began.

Over the next twelve months he wrote a series of letters to Napier, either enclosing portions of the manuscript, corrected proofs or, too often, explanations of his failure to do so because of ill-health and parliamentary duties. Apart from missing deadlines, the work overran the allotted space, and never received the scholarly revision it required. Nevertheless, when published separately as *Dissertation on the Progress of Ethical Philosophy* it became his most considerable work since the introductory lecture to the Lincoln's Inn lectures on international law. Once again it showed the great stores of knowledge he acquired in a life of intensive reading.

Sydney Smith said of Mackintosh: 'He had looked into every moral and metaphysical question from Plato to Paley, and had waded through morasses of international law, where the step of no living man could follow him.' But the author had lighter moments, as when he said of David Hume that his 'theory of causation is used as an answer to arguments for the existence of the Deity, without warning the reader that it would equally lead him not to expect that the sun will rise tomorrow'. On David Hartley: 'Even in the single passage in which he shows a glimpse of the truth, he begins with confusion, advances with hesitation, and after holding in his grasp for an instant the principle which shed so strong a light around it, suddenly drops it from his hand.'

He put forward his view of ethics as resting solidly on the primacy of conscience, and in doing so attacked the theories of Jeremy Bentham and the so-called Utilitarians. This brought forth *A Fragment on Mackintosh* by Bentham's admirer, James Mill, almost as long as the book it attacked. While it contained legitimate criticism, the vein of personal vituperation running through it distressed even Mill's own son. It would be interesting to know whether the author remembered the Benthamite principle of weighing the pleasure it gave him to assail his opponent against the pain it might inflict. Perhaps he did—the work was not published in the lifetime of Sir James.

A wittier appraisal of the philosopher was published in *The Athenaeum* before his book appeared, possibly the work of John Sterling:

> His mind is made up of the shreds and parings of other thinkers. The body of his philosophic garment is half taken from the gown of Locke, and half from the cassock of Butler; the sleeves are torn from the robe of Leibnitz, and the cape is of the ermine of Shaftesbury; and wearing the cowl of Aquinas, and shod in the sandals of Aristotle, he comes out before the world with the trumpet of Cicero at his lips, the club of Hobbes in one hand, and the mace of Bacon in the other.

But the writer acknowledged: 'Sir James is one of a small and neglected class, the lovers of wisdom . . . rich in all recorded knowledge and an honest and eloquent teacher.'

8 Mary Rich (artist unknown).

9 Maria Graham by Sir Thomas Lawrence.

10 Fanny Allen by James Leakey.

11 Mme de Staël. An engraving.

Lady Holland's friendship was not retained without demands on his time. In November 1828 Mackintosh sent her a brief manuscript history of Holland House down to 1753, asking her to correct and return it for him to add an account of later events: 'I think it best to be very brief in the last sixty or seventy years.' This was probably the reverse of what she desired, for a month later he repeated: 'I should think that the latter period of Holland House shall be touched rather shortly. Your list rather frightens me.' Whatever the reason, this was yet another task that was not completed.

Undeterred, in 1829 he took on a popular *History of England* for a series called *The Cabinet Cyclopaedia* published by Longman's under the supervision of Dr Dionysius Lardner. He hoped to receive £1,500 for this, drawing on notes intended originally for an introduction to his history of the revolution of 1688 and after. Companion volumes were provided on Ireland by Thomas Moore and on Scotland by Sir Walter Scott.

Through it all James kept Lady Holland supplied with political gossip. The Duke of Wellington's administration suffered a split in Tory support after he conceded Catholic emancipation. On 30 April Mackintosh wrote to his benefactor: 'I presume King Arthur means to make no change in his Round Table.' Apparently there was a rumour he himself might be solicited for support, since five weeks later he told her: 'I have seen no symptoms of the approach if I must not number amongst them a shake of the hand with unwonted kindness which I had in St James's Park from the great Captain.'

Although he complained of 'incessant drudgery', Clapham Common was also the scene of convivial dinner parties. On 6 June 1829 Moore visited the Mackintoshes with several others and noted in his diary: 'The conversation very delightful, at least Mackintosh's part of it.'

But another visitor Bessy Wedgwood, detected stresses under the surface: 'I have now and then a nameless fear about Kitty which makes me wish she should be soothed by her family as much as possible.' In the autumn Catherine went abroad, travelling first to Paris, and on to the Sismondis at their house in Chene, near Geneva. At some stage in this journey her widowed sister Harriet joined her. Daughter Fanny declined to go with her mother, preferring to join her father when he accepted an invitation to visit Mme de Staël's daughter Albertine. She was married to the Duc de Broglie, one of the leading liberals in French politics, and they lived in Normandy some thirty-five miles from Rouen. James wrote to Lady Holland: 'I was very much gratified in finding Albertine grown into so amiable and respectable a woman.' He enjoyed talking to her husband and was impressed with his abilities. Back in London he took Fanny Allen to the Lord Mayor's dinner to show her 'the best sight and worst dinner in the world'.

It seems Lady Mackintosh did not keep in touch with her husband after leaving England. On 12 November 1829 she wrote a cheerful letter from Switzerland to their friend Whishaw, gossiping about the time she spent in Paris; however when she reached Chene her sister Jessie noted symptoms which made her uneasy. On 6 May 1830 this troubled woman died, after suffering a stroke.

Chapter Eight

Opium and Disenchantment

The circumstances of Kitty Mackintosh's death, and its effect on the family at Clapham were the subject of letters between the Allen sisterhood. Jessie Sismondi wrote to Bessy on 25 May 1830 to say she had received letters showing 'my dear Mackintosh had not been made ill by the shock' while

> Robert indeed was far more shocked than I had expected from his previous hardness and the coldness of his reception of the first news. I pity him poor fellow from my heart and partake a little of his suffering, for remorse alas! is the most general ingredient in the sorrow felt for her loss. Her unfortunate susceptibility of wrong made it impossible to all but yourself and John to go an hour with her without offending. She was, too, so little demonstrative herself that one could never show her the little caressing tenderness that others are continually exciting and which she seemed to disdain . . .
>
> Her faults of temperament were redeemed by many great and noble virtues, and I cannot but think her death, thus sudden and without suffering, is a merciful dispensation. She could neither make herself or others happy, and I dreaded the future (which must necessarily have darkened more and more on her as she advanced) so much, that it seems to me as if a great evil was withdrawn from me in its being denied to her. If she had got Fanny out to her I think she had some vague notion of never returning. The suspicion of this, that the pains in her limbs were exaggerated for this purpose, made me slow to perceive her real ails, and hard in my feelings towards her. The event has shown how unjust I was in my suspicions, and I now belive she made very light of the fore-running symptoms of her terrible disorder . . . The disorder had been creeping on all winter and was clearly no one stroke.

Jessie went on to refer to her sister as 'a person so little loved, of so proud a spirit and so irritable a temper', and said one night she had told Harriet 'if I am imbecile, I never never will return home'. Her letter added: 'Her husband and children will be easily enough reconciled to her loss alas! She had been long lost to them; I shall not therefore give them or others the particulars that I now give you, it would seem a treachery to her memory. I wish them to grieve a little for her.'

In reply Bessy expressed similar remorse:

> I go back to think over what I could have done to have made her happier,
> and I am sad when I think that she was less cordial to me the last year, and I
> might have done more for her . . . I grieve now at having burnt her last
> letter, because it was written in so cheerful a mood that I should now derive
> comfort in reading it, perfectly collected and expressing but one regret, that
> Fanny had not joined her.

After speculating this might have been an attempt to detach her from
Hensleigh Wedgwood, his mother continued:

> I was not at all sorry that Robert suffered for I hoped that his heart would
> be softened but I fear that it was only for the moment for he is now as
> rough and unfeeling in his manner to his father and sister as ever—Mrs
> Rich says that there lies a tender heart under that rough outside, I wish it
> may be so. I believe his first idea when he heard of his poor Mother's
> sudden death was a *dreadful* one, and I must confess that a vague fear of the
> same kind crossed my private thoughts, for that, or insanity have long been
> a dread with me . . . that troubled heart is now at peace.

For twenty years the relationship between James and his wife had been
one of growing disenchantment. As early as 1811 he wrote from
Bombay: 'Nothing is more remarkable in your *undisturbed* understanding
than the good sense of your determinations.' But he added 'persons of
warm temper must be cautious not to mistake the hasty suggestions of
passion for the rapid tact of good sense', and she should not reject
suggestions 'because they come from one whom you have insensibly
learned not to respect'. Replying to her complaints he was not working
on his history, or on a life of Burke which he also contemplated, he said:
'Your correspondence might have produced a better prudential effect if it
had contained less rebuke and more amusement for I dare not expect
declarations of affection.'

Their life in England was punctuated by periods when they lived apart.
The extent of these may be exaggerated, since they are chiefly known by
his letters to her, and the evidence of correspondence is naturally lacking
when they were together in London, or at Weedon and Mardocks. But
he sometimes expressed irritation, not just about her absence, but at
learning her whereabouts only from other members of the family. When
the Whig–Tory alliance of 1827–8 broke up, he wrote: 'I heartily regret
your absence at this critical moment.' On another occasion he
commented she had told John Whishaw not to visit them at Mardocks
because the house was damp, without apparently considering her
husband must live there.

Catherine was not always to blame for these separations. His parliamentary duties meant he had to spend time in London, and they rarely had the money to maintain two homes, while the health of the children benefited from country air. James made frequent excursions to aristocratic estates in pursuit of historical material. His similar visits to the Continent were taken alone, although he sometimes urged her to accompany him.

Her life compels sympathy. She married at thirty-two and bore four children in eight years; one she lost as an infant after a desperate attempt to nurse him back to health, while her younger daughter, Elizabeth, was always delicate and died at nineteen. In addition Kitty Mackintosh suffered a miscarriage at thirty-nine and the references to triplets and her illness in 1799 seem to indicate the delivery of still-born children. Through it all she had the care of three rebellious step-daughters, partly in the inhospitable climate of India.

But the darkest shadow over her life seems to have been chagrin at the failure of her husband to achieve the distinction as author, lawyer or politician, predicted for him. Certainly early in their marriage she was loyal to his interests; when the treachery of Dr Parr became apparent she wrote him a letter of such pointed recrimination the couple's friends in England refused to deliver it. Her regret was intensified because she was herself a woman of marked talent, as can be seen from her private and public letters. In correspondence James treated her, not perhaps as his intellectual equal, few people were that, but as one capable of sharing his philosophical speculations and literary tastes. Whishaw, a level-headed man, addressed her as a woman whose mind he respected. Another barrister, Charles Marsh, called her the bluest of blues.

Catherine made little attempt to disguise her disgust when she saw her brilliant groom sink into a prematurely-aged invalid, dissipating his gifts in gossip with Lady Holland and dancing attendance on Mme de Staël and Maria Graham, deferring to peers who finally treated him with contempt, and reluctant to deal firmly with the Riches and Erskine when they quarrelled with his wife. She might have preferred a man like Brougham, who rarely reined in his energy and ambition out of respect for others.

The question arises why Mackintosh failed to fulfil his potential. Modern commentators have suggested opium, basing the charge partly on guilt by association. Some of his best friends were known addicts, Wilberforce, Robert Hall, and Dr Brown; then there was Coleridge, while Mme de Staël and Tom Wedgwood at least used opium. While there is no indication his friendship for these people was drug-oriented, James undoubtedly took opium, both in pills and laudanum. He mentions them frequently in letters to his wife. Once he told her: 'I am well if a man can be called so who owes the suspension of a most vexatious complaint to the daily use of calomel and opium.' He suffered the hypochondria common in those dependent on drugs. There were references in his letters to strange maladies, such as 'brow ague'.

Sometimes he mentioned alarming dreams, but was principally worried by one which was quite rational in which 'I have of late often fancied myself to be returned to Bombay as recorder'. Perhaps significance can be read into a letter he sent to John Taylor, publisher of *The London Magazine* after publication of Thomas De Quincey's *Confessions*:

> I have just read the second part of the 'Opium Eater' with more delight than I know how to express . . . I had not the soreness which your writer on Madame de Staël supposed I should feel at some passages of his criticism, and I read of parliamentary debates being 'the rinsings of the human understanding' without abating or embittering my admiration of the 'Opium Eater'.

In one of his innumerable volumes of reminiscences, Cyrus Redding said of Mackintosh: 'He latterly carried in his waistcoat pocket a small bottle with, I presume, some kind of medicine, which he occasionally tasted.' This sounds like laudanum or ether. Then there was his confession to Parr on the death of his first wife that she 'rescued me from the dominion of a degrading and ruinous vice'. His daughter Fanny spoke of him 'trying different remedies, to a degree we sometimes lamented'. However, it should be noted she spoke of different remedies, not dependence on one.

In the *Memoirs* Robert Mackintosh referred to his father's indolence and self-indulgence, often codewords for addiction. James himself liked to dwell on the hours he spent on a sofa with the latest novel or a book of French reminiscences. But nineteenth-century ideas of sloth were not quite our own. In 1808 he wrote 'in the latter part of February and the first few days of March' his time was divided between his court 'and the idle business of thirtysix letters' to friends and relatives at home. Those letters were rarely formal notes.

On another occasion he referred sarcastically to 'my report on the police, which is only 70 folio pages'. This document became the basis for reform of the Bombay force following the imprisonment of its chief; it had been preceded by a dissertation drawn up for Governor Duncan on the proper tribunal for the trial of non-military crimes committed by natives in the subsidiary levies. His known works—books, pamphlets, articles, speeches, letters, journals, would fill many fat volumes. In the shadows are the unknown writings—untraced articles, lost letters, manuscripts his son destroyed, and fifty or more volumes of source

material for his historical project, which he either transcribed or super-
vised as the work of copyists.

His life was not that of a recluse hugging a secret vice. Much of it was
spent in the public eye, as barrister, lecturer, judge, orator. True,
Wilberforce managed to combine addiction with a career as a reforming
MP, but he seems to have been a man of iron discipline, which
Mackintosh was not. Even when he had no duties to perform the latter
was an inveterate diner-out; should ill-health or country residence
prevent this, he gathered friends and relations at his own table. If opium
addiction had been a problem it is unlikely he would have enjoyed the
affection of several of his sisters-in-law or that Bessy and Jos. Wedgwood
could have been happy to let their daughters visit the Mackintoshes. Nor
would he have been a welcome guest at so many stately homes.

His days were often too full of business. Writing to Lady Holland
from Brooks's in March 1821 he said: 'Tonight I must attend Newport
on the Catholics. Tomorrow I dine at Lansdowne House. Friday at
Hallam's—Saturday and Sunday I must be at Haileybury. Monday is the
third reading of the Catholic Bill.' Sir John Newport was an Irish MP, a
staunch Whig and supporter of Catholic emancipation. Henry Hallam,
historian, was the father of the young man who inspired Tennyson's *In
Memoriam*.

Throughout life Mackintosh had enemies only too willing to strike.
Yet none seem to have hinted at opium. We all know, but only half
believe, that in Georgian England opiates, whether pills or laudanum,
were the general pain-killer. Few went through life without recourse to
them. In 1813 Lord Grey excused a brief letter to Sir James with the
remark 'I have written with a very confused head from the affects of
laudanum'. Fanny Allen once wrote to her younger brother: 'I am now
physically well but one day this week I thought I was nearly demolished
by an overdose of opium.' Robert Hall, whose addiction began through
suffering from stone in a kidney, told a medical friend: 'What a merciful
provision laudanum is, sir! I could not exist without it.' Sydney Smith,
like other country parsons, had the care of the bodies as well as souls of
his parishioners. The free use of opium and its antidote is shown in two
couplets from his *The Poetical Medicine Chest*:

> Laurel-born camphor, opiate drugs prepare,
> They banish pain, and calm consuming care . . .
> When with black bile hepatic regions swell,
> With subtle calomel the plague expel.

As a student in Edinburgh in 1786 Mackintosh submitted a paper on
intermittent fever to the Royal Medical Society showing the use of

opium had been common since the days of classical Greece. He recounted the experience of an eighteenth-century doctor who 'gave his patients about thirty drops of laudanum, an hour before he expected a paroxysm, which generally stopped it'.

He returned from India with malarial 'intermittent fever' as well as a damaged liver, perhaps already affected by heavy drinking in his youth. The doctors he consulted, including Darling, prescribed opium. This combined with his ailments to depress him. In 1827 after he had been overlooked for office he told Lady Holland: 'I know that the few who will think of me when I am dead will call me a hypochondriac. If they knew my whole condition in mind, body and estate they would rather wonder at my cheerfulness.'

As a doctor himself he knew the dangers of opium and dreaded the fact it had frequently to be followed in his case by the purgative calomel. In February 1822 he wrote to Catherine: 'My complaint continues—but I am unwilling to venture even on a slight opiate.' He experimented with mild medicines, such as Dover's powder which included ipecacuanha as well as opium diluted with lactose, and with a French preparation called morphium 'which pretends to have all the good and none of the bad qualities of opium'. When Mrs Ashburner, one of their Bombay friends, arrived in London, desperately ill, he reported she was emaciated and weak: 'A magnesia draught with laudanum is her almost hourly resource and she shows that union of feebleness with disturbed excitement which is its natural effect.'

If it is difficult to believe that the man who wrote the ethical philosophy dissertation at sixty-four was a slave to opium, it is still a fact he looked on himself as a failure and the world was not slow to agree. Diarist Charles Greville said after a house party in 1829:

> I never was in Mackintosh's society for so long before, and never was more filled with admiration. His prodigious memory and the variety and extent of his information remind me of all I have heard and read of Burke and Johnson, but his amiable, modest and unassuming character makes him far more agreeable than they could either of them (particularly Johnson) have been, while he is probably equally instructive and amusing. Not a subject could be mentioned of which he did not treat with equal facility and abundance, from the Council of Trent to Voltaire's epistles . . . I could not help reflecting what an extraordinary thing success is in this world, when a man so gifted as Mackintosh has failed completely in public life, never attained honours, reputation or wealth.

Nearly a century later Mrs Humphry Ward wrote that he 'was so near to greatness and so near to happiness, and never achieved either'. It was because he aimed too high, and at too many targets, and because he pined for the devotion of the lost Catharine Stuart that he never sustained the bright promise of the *Vindiciae Gallicae* days at Little Ealing. The desultory nature of his education and the uncritical admiration his gifts aroused left him without the discipline and analytical power required by the historian or the thick skin essential for a statesman.

The scars left by the old charges of apostasy kept him loyal to the Whigs and their dinner tables, when he would have been wise to withdraw from public life. Truly it might be said of him he gave up to party—and to parties—what was meant for mankind. He missed his true vocation when he did not take the post offered by the University of Edinburgh in 1820; later he was heard to say, 'I sigh for the professorship.' Oliver Elton put it neatly: 'He would have been a great professor, but it is hard to say of what.' Mackintosh wrote of Dugald Stewart 'his disciples were his best works', words applicable to himself.

He never attempted to form a coterie of young MPs personally devoted to him, the general power base of the period. But he influenced and guided some, among them Francis Horner, who spoke warmly of 'the stimulus to which he excited to great undertakings and good hopes everyone's mind that approached him'. From 1819 on Mackintosh was the steady counsellor of Lord John Russell in the battle for electoral reform.

Francis Jeffrey called James 'the wisest and most accomplished person I have ever seen or heard of', and dismissed the idea he should be judged by the failure to write the projected history:

> We know of no code of morality which makes it imperative on every man of extraordinary talent or learning to write a large book, and could readily point to instances where such persons have gone with unquestioned honour to their graves, without leaving any such memorial—and been judged to have acted up to the last article of their duty, merely by enlightening society by their lives and conversation and discharging with ability and integrity the offices of magistracy or legislation, to which they may have been called.

His philosophical writings were respected in his day. When Ralph Waldo Emerson read the *Dissertation on Ethics* he called it 'the most important book on the most important science', and referred to the author as 'this Oracle', though he later conceded the work was likely to be superseded. William Ewart Gladstone, who was to become an MP in 1832, made notes on the work, comparing some of its sentiments with those of Cicero. At one point he wrote: 'Did Sir James Mackintosh ever read or remark the following passage: A reproof too strong for him, yet in substance very applicable perhaps to his theory—de Fin V. 25.' It is safe to assume no passage in Cicero was unread by James, and few went unremarked. But the passage to which Gladstone referred, about pleasure, motive and habit, seems more applicable to the Benthamites Mackintosh was attacking than to himself.

Although he thought of himself as a detached philosopher, he was really most effective in tackling practical problems, as during his years in Bombay. At home every project for a more just society had his active support. On becoming a vice-president of the Society for the Improvement of Prison Development and for the Reformation of Juvenile Offenders, he made a point of visiting jails to study conditions. Few who joined in the anti-slavery movement could say, as he could, they had actually secured the release of a slave.

Undoubtedly he dissipated too much time on social intercourse. Samuel Rogers charged him with rehearing these dinner-table displays, as many Regency wits did. But it seems unlikely a man who lectured on international law with only the sketchiest of notes to guide him would bother to polish up his repartee. In any case, those who heard him recalled not pungent epigrams but his wide knowledge and pleasure in sharing it.

James was conscious his fame might die with him, and quoted Dryden's lines *To Mr Congreve*:

> Be kind to my remains; and O defend
> Against your judgment, your departed friend.

In an early *Edinburgh Review* he replied to those who sneered at what were known as 'conversation men', putting forward

> a theory of the talent—if we must not say of the art—of conversation, which affords so considerable a part of the most liberal enjoyments of refined life. Those, indeed, who affect a Spartan or monastic severity in their estimate of the society of capitals may almost condemn a talent, which in their opinion only adorns vice. But that must have a moral tendency which raises society from slander or intoxication, to any contest and rivalry of mental power. Wit and grace are perhaps the only means which could allure the thoughtless into the neighbourhood of reflection, and inspire them with some admiration for superiority of mind. Society is the only school in which the indolence of the great will submit to learn. Refined conversation is at least sprinkled with literature, and directed, more often than the talk of the vulgar, to objects of general interest. That talent cannot really be frivolous which affords the channel through which some knowledge, or even some respect for knowledge, may be insinuated into minds incapable of labour, and whose tastes so materially influence the community.

While nobody seems to have referred to James taking opium unwisely, there is a hint Catherine was suspected of it. Fanny Allen, writing to her sister Emma from Cadogan Place on 27 June 1823 said: 'You were quite wrong I knew about Kitty taking ✶✶✶✶✶.' But this isolated statement is itself ambiguous, and since Lady Mackintosh's own health suffered from the Indian climate she probably required the same treatment as her husband. It seems likely James was referring to his wife when he wrote to Lady Holland on 23 January 1829: 'I was not in spirits on Saturday nor indeed at all well however I might look. If I could tell you all you would give me some indulgence on the other subject.'

Whatever the reason, there was something cold and aloof about Catherine, the woman who wrote to her lonely husband in India telling him she would not reveal the address of his erring sister, Anne, to prevent him writing to her. When his wife died James described her as 'an upright and pious woman, formed for devoted affection who employed a strong understanding and a resolute spirit in unwearied attempts to relieve every suffering under her view'. It was not, somehow, an attractive picture, an echo of his reference to her as a dread goddess, and a contrast with the warm tribute he poured out to his first wife. Partly he was reacting to Lady Mackintosh's marked reluctance to relieve his own bodily and mental sufferings. It is possible, of course, though there appears to be no record of her saying so, she attributed those sufferings to opium.

Catherine seems to have been a little out of her depth in the narrow society of Bombay. On one occasion James referred to a Bombay doctor as 'a very worthy man one of the few Indian acquaintances whom I should wish to convert into an English friend. This number is small with me but you must allow me to say it is too small with you.' He also accused her of having 'a mania for gentility', and hinted she was too conscious of her rank as a Lady. Yet when writing to relations and close friends, he always referred to her as Lady Mackintosh or Lady M, even addressing her formally when seeking her forgiveness in his will.

Her quarrels with stepdaughters could be discounted as customary in the case of a father's second marriage. But her own children treated her with scant respect. Fanny refused to accompany her abroad in her final flight, while it appears from Bessy's account that Robert suspected suicide when news of his mother's death arrived. They were evidently unobservant of the real nature of her illness.

Fanny Allen was a prejudiced witness, her own suppressed emotional involvement with her brother-in-law was apparent, but there was presumably truth in this account of her sister's opposition to her daughter's romance with Bessy's son written on 1 August 1829:

> . . . my dear tender Hensleigh with his love for Fanny Mack which I believe
> was begun in pity, and cemented by her mother's crossness and tyranny,

and while that lasts Fanny will always have her 'Glendower' at hand. Hensleigh's love for Fanny is the prettiest thing I ever saw, every act of unkindness of K's is noticed and he redoubles his attentions to make F's burthern light, and if it were not for it her life would be wearisome enough and with it she is an enviable woman.

It is the opinions of Bessy and Jessie, the most affectionate of Kitty's sisters, which tilt the scales against her; she must at least share the blame for the unhappy decline in the marriage. When Sismondi's wife fell ill in Switzerland she wrote to James:

> We are bound to you not only by our own obligations to you for long years of unbroken affection and many hospitalities when a less generous man might have found it a charge, but by your forbearance and long suffering and unwearied love for one who if she would but have accepted it might have saved you as well as herself much misery, a mind not exactly in equilibrium alone can account for her conduct. Your patient and unresentful nature has beyond words endeared you to me.

While ready to pity Mackintosh, Jessie did not absolve him from blame for the wasted years. In a letter to Bessy she commented:

> He had an understanding to comprehend all the beauties of the high moral feelings and those of affection, but not the heart ever to feel them, so that he knew their heaven, sighed for it, yet, as if a curse was on him, could never put his foot into it. He loved passionately and fondly only one person in the world, and she never could love him, though he was the only person in the world that truly loved her.

Chapter Nine

A Majority of One

When news of Catherine's death reached London, her youngest sister was there. Mackintosh reported to Lady Holland on 18 May 1830: 'Fanny is recovering by the extreme tenderness of her aunt and namesake whose presence here has been a Godsend. Poor Lady Mackintosh mentioned some alarming symptoms such as numbness and pains in the arms and legs during our stay at Denman's last September. But she had always a disbelief and dislike of physicians.' Even at such a moment he referred to his wife formally by her title.

Work on his history for Lardner and duty as an MP dulled whatever sorrow he felt. The previous month he had participated in the kind of parliamentary occasion he enjoyed. Rising to support his cousin, Robert Grant, who introduced a Bill to repeal the civil disabilities on Jews, he gave way to Thomas Babington Macaulay, making his maiden speech. When Mackintosh finally spoke he complimented his new colleague, and poured scorn on his Clapham neighbour, Sir Robert Inglis, who opposed the Bill because 'the object was to obtain the admission of Jews into Parliament'. James suggested that having emancipated seven million Catholics, the House should extend the same principle to 40,000 Jews. It was some years before the Commons could bring themselves to do so.

He was similarly ahead of his time in championing the natives in British India; early in May, he backed a petition in support of half-castes living in Calcutta who protested they were excluded from superior offices in the civil and military service of the East India Company. He told MPs he had heard much of 'the natural inferiority of particular races—that there was one race born to command and another to obey'. But he knew there was no foundation for it in any part of India. This, he declared, he spoke upon due consideration because he had observed boys of all races in places of public education. Remembering no doubt some MPs were men who had lived in India, made their fortunes there, and followed the custom of taking local mistresses, he suggested rejection of the half-castes 'had the odious appearance of disenfranchisement by fathers against their children . . . they had done as public men, what as private individuals they would have recoiled from with horror'.

Although Sir Robert Peel, who succeeded to a baronetcy on the death of his father, introduced measures of penal reform, Sir James urged him to go further. Having failed in May to substitute imprisonment or transportation for capital punishment in cases of forgery, he reached a compromise in June by reintroducing his proposed amelioration of the law, bowing only to retention of hanging for forging wills. In spite of government opposition, this was carried by 151 votes to 138. The cabinet was prepared to accept this defeat, but the Lords threw out the clause. However, this proved more than a moral victory, for no one was executed for forgery after the Commons vote, those convicted were reprieved. Mackintosh wrote to Lady Holland with grim satisfaction: 'The judges behave very ill resenting the pardon of the convicts left for execution as lowering their judicial character. They are angry that men are not hanged to keep up their dignity.'

About this time the first volume of the *History of England* appeared in Dr Lardner's Cabinet Cyclopaedia. It was followed by a second, and Mackintosh carried the story down to the sixteenth century in a third, which was completed by another hand. In spite of occasional forays into legalistic byways, its style was more popular than earlier histories. The print order of 10,000 copies had soon to be reinforced, and sales continued for more than thirty years. It would have amused him to know that five years later Maria Graham would publish *Little Arthur's History of England*, running to seventy editions and more than a million copies.

Longman's must have abandoned hope of extracting *The History of England since the Revolution of 1688* from their author, since they asked him to contribute a *Life of Sir Thomas More* to Lardner's series. Mackintosh welcomed the chance to write on this lawyer-saint of Lincoln's Inn who, like himself, suggested hanging was not a deterrent to starving men. But somehow the book wandered between its subject's domestic virtues and the legal niceties which enmeshed him in public life without throwing much light on either. But then reticence was the hallmark of this reluctant martyr.

George IV's death meant a general election. Mackintosh's medical advisers forbade him travelling to Knaresborough, so he wrote to Brougham, who was standing for the county of Yorkshire, on 31 July 1830: 'As you find time for every thing I hope you may pass two or three hours at Knaresborough next Tuesday and say something for me without laying too much stress on the indisposition. I count upon your Yorkshire election being carried without substantial resistance.' The man who had written *Vindiciae Gallicae* referred to events in Paris, where the government of Charles X, whose coronation he had seen, suspended the constitution: 'We have no particulars yet from Paris. It is certain street fighting took place on Wednesday with serious bloodshed. The rumour of a regiment going over to the people is believed. The beginning is hopeful.' The skirmishes proved sufficient to instal Louis Philippe as a constitutional monarch, which influenced agitation for reform in Britain.

Ill-health and the need to reduce his literary arrears, led him to offer his resignation as chairman of the Economic Life Assurance Society. Anxious to preserve the family income, he suggested Robert should become a director; the offer was not accepted, and he remained chairman, surviving some anxious meetings of directors when it was discovered the company's actuary had engaged in large-scale fraud.

Mackintosh and daughter Fanny spent September and October at Cresselly, where Fanny Allen, now forty-nine, and her sister Emma, were living with their widower brother John. For the weary philosopher it proved, if not an Indian summer, at least an autumn idyll. After a few weeks of country life he confided to his sister-in-law: 'I thought it was impossible for me ever to feel as I do now—as if I could go back to 25—I am better than I have been any time these two years. I find I can work well here too, the quiet and regularity of life are favourable to me.'

Historian Sir Archibald Alison, who married a niece of Lord Woodhouselee, said Mackintosh only wanted 'a biographer like Boswell to have equalled Johnson in the fame of his conversation'. During this visit Fanny Allen tried to keep a record of their daily life for the benefit of Jessie. But she was terrified of 'the sage himself' finding this out, as she had heard him say 'taking down what one said would be an almost insufferable habit and would entirely prevent any pleasure in conversation or indeed any conversation at all'. He once told Macaulay the last time he saw Boswell the biographer was sitting drunk at a tavern table.

Fanny's journal noted some candid coments: 'M said Lady Lansdowne was a cleverer person than her husband—yet she was much afraid of him.'—'M talked of the evils of lay patronage with respect to the church . . . Bishops and dignitaries belong to the Devildom and not to Christendom.'—'Sir R Inglis he thought was one of the most benevolent men he knew, but he was a little absurd and he thought the Thorntons might laugh at him without encroaching much on their respect and affection for him.'—'He had met George IV—once at Lord Thanet's, he thought him rather pleasant. He had too much manner, to be really well-mannered, he had some cleverness, though it was not much, altogether a poor creature.'

The talk turned often to literature, on which James had some eccentric ideas, he once referred to Mme de Staël as the first woman of her age. But as he grew older he became increasingly fonder of the novels of Jane Austen, particularly *Emma*. He was probably conscious enough of his own foibles to realise he had much in common with Mr Woodhouse, the sociable valetudinarian who liked to speak of 'poor Isabella' and 'poor Miss Taylor', an indulgent father who dreaded the thought of his daugher leaving home.

One evening, Fanny wrote:

> After dinner he said John was the greatest John Bull he ever knew, he thought him now the only man who believed that one Englishman could beat 3 Frenchmen—I observed, that he was one of the many to whom it was painful to displace opinions, that have been long settled in one's mind. M it is not uncommon, there are many such—but in reality we must be beyond measure wise, or a fool, not to have frequently changed one's opinions, since we were 25.

He was that age when he wrote *Vindiciae Gallicae*.

Her delight in the company of her brother-in-law was clear: 'One of those lovely days that are now rare in autumn. We walked after breakfast in the court to bask a little in the sun.'—'The day was so fine I tempted Mackintosh to take the brown mare, and take a little ride.'—'At one I went into his study to persuade him to ride again on the brown mare, he is easy to be entreated in every thing, and he agreed. I endeavoured to persuade him to remain here over the month of November but he says in spite of his getting so well here, he must go on account of the questions coming on in Parliament.'

'I was very much struck and pleased by M's appearance, as he sat, listening to our reading, in his great chair . . . I should like to have had his picture taken in this attitude, which is very natural to him, rather than as Sir T Lawrence took him which is an attitude not suited to his character.'

'Took a walk in the woods with M. I can recollect nothing of this conversation so I must pass on.'—Even his card playing improved: 'We played whist in the evening, Mackintosh and I beating John and Caroline every rubber.'

But these golden weeks were only an interlude. Fanny noted: 'M received a letter from Lady Holland very peremptory respecting the necessity of his return to town, to be in the ranks of opposition by the 2nd of November.' Later she wrote: 'I was grieved to see Mackintosh's preparations for quitting this place, though I was myself going some part of the way with him for the sake of being with him a couple of days longer.' On 28 October she parted from him 'with the deepest regret' at Llansantffraed, the Monmouthshire residence of Bishop Copleston. Thirty-three years before a happy Catherine Allen had written to Fanny of meeting 'ye celebrated Mr Mackintosh' at that house.

In London James resumed history writing. In a letter to Cresselly he said: 'I must now, my dear Fanny, turn to Queen Mary's persecutions, not so agreeable an object in my eyes as you, whom I like better at the end of thirty years than I even did at the beginning of them.' To John Allen he lamented his lack of will in not quitting the Commons, knowing attendance would soon undermine his restored health: 'But courage never was a good quality of mine and at my present age it is one of my privileges to be timid and irresolute.'

He could not turn his back on his own reputation, which was international as well as national. A fellow-MP, George Agar-Ellis, wrote to him: 'I enclose you an anxious note I have just received from Stockmar, Prince Leopold's confidential agent and friend—Can and will you be so very amiable as to furnish the Prince with your view (for that is what he writes) of what you consider would be the faithful execution of the treaty of the 6th of July.' Prince Leopold of Saxe-Coburg was George IV's son-in-law. The treaty concerned the liberation of Greece, whose throne had been offered to Leopold. He finally declined, and became King of the Belgians.

Lady Holland did not exaggerate the importance of a full muster by the Whigs. On 15 November the government headed by the Duke of Wellington fell. At last Lord Grey was called on to form an administration. Mackintosh again glimpsed a prospect of office, although aware it might be no more than that. As in 1827 it was rumoured he would be judge-advocate.

It would have intrigued him to know of a report current across the Atlantic. Alexander Hill Everett, writing in Boston's *The North American Review*, said:

> He was generally styled in the newspapers whenever he was mentioned, the friend of America. A report, which was spread soon after the entrance into power of the present ministry, that he was coming out to reside among us as British minister, was heard with much satisfaction, and there cannot be a doubt that his reception would have been of the most gratifying kind.

Everett, who met Mackintosh in London in 1817, compared him, as others did, with Cicero—'the beautiful union of talents, virtues and graces, that distinguished the character of the illustrious Roman orator, to which his own bore in its leading traits a marked resemblance'.

Back in London James wrote to Lady Holland: 'I know nothing of projects or arrangements . . . I have shown myself every day in the House of Commons. Direct solicitation would probably do no more for me, and I am too old to be supple jointed.'

He would have been better advised to imitate another candidate for office. James wrote to Fanny Allen:

> Brougham has in the last 18 days shown his strength and his lunacy. He had a dreadful *scene* with Lord Grey, the exact object of which I could not make

out. But after an altercation so violent, and such language of disregard towards the new ministers in the H of C last night I received a note from Lady Holland closing with these words, as I shall mark them. Brougham is chancellor!!! Brougham's possession of the Great Seal has, I am told by Dr Holland, produced the most intense alarm among lawyers and doctors. With him he brings rashness and odium, but without him in either house there could not have been a fortnight's administration. Lord Melbourne, a lazy and singular man, will be a bad secretary in the home department.

By this time Mackintosh knew he had been passed over for high office. Yet on 23 November he made one of his most impassioned speeches in the Commons in defence of the mercurial Brougham. John Wilson Croker attacked the new lord chancellor, claiming he had been heard to say he would not join the administration, and had then gone to the House of Lords although he was due to bring in a motion for parliamentary reform in the lower House. Croker said he thought until a satisfactory explanation was produced 'the character of the noble and learned Lord would be under a cloud'. Sir James stigmatised this attack as irregular and disorderly, violating the rules of the Commons, and declared any honourable and fair-dealing man must be aware nothing could be more improper. He complained Croker's insinuations and imputations were made in the absence of ministers in a position to explain Brougham's appointment.

If the protagonists had been younger this furious onslaught might have had serious consequences, for Croker was not unversed in the etiquette of the duel. He had a hand in the exchange of insults that led to the death of Mackintosh's friend John Scott nine years before.

In the new government James was again allocated the insignificant post of member of the board of control, although this time the appointment was immediate, and so was the £1,500 salary. He confessed in private: 'It is mortifying at my age and after 20 years in Parliament to be only an underling.' Even the money was little consolation, since he would have to attend the House more regularly than in the past, which meant taking a house in central London. Diarist Greville commented: 'If he had not been a man "whom no sense of wrongs could move to vengeance" he would have flung the India Board in Lord Grey's face when he was insulted with the offer of it.'

Once more Mackintosh's friends failed him. The principal list of ministers was drawn up one evening at Lansdowne House, where the marquis and his noble friends Holland, Russell and Durham helped Lord Grey in his deliberations. All figured prominently in the government. Lord Holland assured Sir James that Grey had wanted to do more for him, and begged him to accept the post 'for the good and credit of the government'. Lord Grey had the grace to apologise for not seeing the underling in person, pleading he had been 'overwhelmed by the numberless affairs pressing upon me . . . As it is I really could do no more than I have done.' His words would have carried more weight if the chosen ministers had included fewer of his own relatives.

The prime minister was confident Mackintosh would not turn against his party at the moment there was a chance of carrying the reforms he had supported for so long; if Brougham had been treated so shabbily he would have had ministers cowering from the lash of his tongue. In fact Grey despised Sir James. According to W MacCullagh Torrens, in his memoirs of Viscount Melbourne, Lord Lansdowne admitted Grey 'thought him a time-server, and rather a flatterer. He did not do him justice, and avowedly did not like him.' The Highlander, probably through the humbleness of his early life, was too deferential to his aristocratic friends, but what probably damaged him more in their eyes was his unfailing courtesy to political opponents, and willingness to praise the talents of men who differed from him. After all, many were his relatives and friends.

Some years later Brougham said in a letter to Macvey Napier: 'Lord Grey & Co never could bear him. Observe, I was no friend at all of his. Holland and Lansdowne were his sworn friends, and they treated him as they always do their friends.' This was written after the lord chancellor had himself quarrelled with his colleagues. But what he said was true, for Creevey told his stepdaughter in January 1831 Grey had been 'in fits of laughing' over dinner in mixed company because *John Bull* newspaper attacked 'Jemmy Mackintosh without mercy for taking a place at the India Board which I, Mr Creevey, moved to abolish as useless, and for which motion, he, Jemmy, himself voted'.

Apart from cabinet-making, Lord Grey had difficulties awarding places and pensions to the many minor claimants on the government, since the Whigs had been active in whittling these down when in opposition. Creevey said Lord Sefton told him Grey was almost crying when he talked 'of the difficulty and misery of depriving so many people of their subsistence'. Perhaps Mackintosh derived satisfaction in adding to his problems by pressing the claims of John Turnbull. He reported to Cresselly: 'Lord Grey has promptly recommended the husband of my poor third daughter to the secretary of the treasury to find a place for the poor man.' He became a minor official in the West Indies. To the lord chancellor, now Lord Brougham and Vaux, went a request for Robert James Mackintosh to received a commissionership of bankrupts as soon as he qualified as a barrister. This was the sinecure his father had hoped to receive more than thirty years before.

The appointment of James to a government post meant facing a by-election for his Knaresborough seat, entailing a winter journey to encounter voters already restless with the feeling parliamentary reform was at hand. He informed Lady Holland from Yorkshire:

> There being two vacancies these produced two separate writs and two distinct elections, at the first of which I was unanimously chosen with universal applause, our opponents declaring that they could not and would not oppose me and that they believed I should have been the choice of the people of Knaresborough. I was then declared by the returning officer to be duly elected. Lord Waterpark and Mr Entwistle a vulgar ignorant Manchester Tory purseproud but not naturally foolish were nominated. The multitude raised an uproar against Lord Waterpark who spoke with spirit and presence of mind. He forced them to hear him. He won the great majority of those whom we believe to be voters.

As usual, the family's change of residence, to 14 Great Cumberland Street, caused financial strains. On 6 February 1831 Mackintosh wrote to a former colleague at the board of the Colombian agricultural association, Isaac Goldsmid:

> I have no reason but what I have heard of you for asking a favour from you which I am obliged to preface by a disclosure rendered less mortifying by my opinion of your delicacy and liberality.
> My necessary removal to London has subjected me to expenses too large to be paid out of my ordinary income and which the produce of my literary labour will not anable me for some time to defray.
> A loan of three hundred pounds for about six months would set me entirely at ease and I could answer for refunding the sum with equal punctuality and thankfulness

In addition to being a successful gold bullion dealer Goldsmid was a reformer, interested in improving prison conditions, and a co-founder of the University of London. He collaborated with Robert Grant over Jewish emancipation, and later became a baronet.

Grey's administration was another uneasy Ministry of all the Talents, ranging from radicals to temporisers. His cabinet would have benefited from the skill in uniting warring factions Mackintosh had shown in the past. But all of them, and even some opponents, were aware the rising passion in the country for parliamentary reform, if thwarted, could spill over into violence if not revolution. For the earl himself it was the culmination of a struggle in which he first engaged in the 1790s. For Mackintosh's young friend, Lord John Russell, it was the start of a long political career as he shepherded the complicated Reform Bill through the Commons, with sweeping changes in the qualification for voters, and the disfranchisement of rotten boroughs in favour of cities without MPs.

Macaulay, too, grasped the chance to establish himself as a parliamentarian. Speaking for the Bill in March 1831 he became so heated he was glad to refresh himself with oranges provided by Sir James. At that time the Scot confined himself to a few remarks in supporting a petition for reform. He said he thought he had lived long enough when he saw a Bill introduced into the House 'so conducive to the maintenance of the rights and liberties of the people, so calculated to preserve and consecrate the authority of the laws, and so essential to secure the stability of the Throne and preserve the purity of Parliament'.

In the second reading debate on Lord John's Bill James found many familiar faces opposed to reform, including Sir Robert Inglis, Sir John Malcolm, and Sir Charles Forbes, the former Bombay merchant. One speaker noted the Duke of Devonshire's pocket borough of Knaresborough would still return two members under the new arrangements. When the Ayes and Noes were counted at three o'clock on the morning of 23 March the second reading passed with a majority of one. Mackintosh's long devotion to duty, his struggle to attend the Commons in spite of ill-health, had not been in vain. Never in his time had the House been more crowded, the vote being 302 for and 301 against. Many battles lay ahead, including a general election and a narrowly-averted constitutional crisis over the obstinacy of the Lords. But from that night reform became inevitable.

This had an invigorating effect on James. His niece, Elizabeth Wedgwood, wrote to her aunt Jessie Sismondi from Great Cumberland Street on 27 March:

> It has been a most interesting time to be at headquarters, and very pleasant quarters they are. Sir James, in spite of being up almost every night till near four o'clock, looks quite a different man from what he was last year, and says himself he has not felt so well for six years.

Political turmoil was not allowed to banish his pleasure in playing host. Elizabeth described 'a grand dinner' with Fanny Mackintosh as hostess attended by Bishop Copleston, Sir Thomas Denman, the new attorney-general, Jeffrey, who was now lord advocate, Lord Nugent, the widowed Lady Gifford, and Marianne Thornton. Among those who called after dinner was Wordsworth, and Mackintosh took the opportunity to make the peace between the poet and Jeffrey, who had attacked the Lakeland poet in a famous *Edinburgh Review* article many years before.

According to Elizabeth:

> They immediately began talking, and Sir James came very proudly to tell us what he had done, and to fetch us to see them; and Mr Wordsworth

looked very happy and complacent, Mr Lockhart said it was the best thing he ever saw done. The two enemies liked one another's company so much, that when the rest of the party broke up past eleven, they remained talking together with Sir James, discussing poets, orators, and novelists, till one o'clock.

Although Mackintosh and Lockhart, husband of Sir Walter Scott's eldest daughter and now living in London as editor of *The Quarterly Review*, remained political opponents, they mixed socially. Writing to Fanny Allen her brother-in-law told her he had escorted Sophia Lockhart down to the House of Commons:

> Mrs Lockhart gives a very bad account of Sir Walter, who has suffered much from giddiness occasioned, as he says, by his alarm of revolution. I rather suspect the giddiness to be the cause of the fear, and I should hope more for him from a seton, than from a majority against reform. She is a very pleasing little woman—she delighted me with the naivety with which, as we went down together, she owned how much she liked her father and her husband.

A seton was a rather odd treatment in which a skein of cotton was sewn through the skin as a counter-irritant to whatever ailed the patient.

He also told Fanny: 'The frosts of reform and the tempests of revolution have killed the whole spring crop of novels. Nothing readable has appeared. I mean readable even by so voracious a *novelophagist* as I am.'

In April the government were defeated on the committee stage of the Reform Bill, causing a general election at which they received overwhelming support. Mackintosh again travelled to Knaresborough, where his fatigue was increased by dining with some fifty supporters. He wrote to Lady Holland on 4 May:

> I am told by some that there is no doubt of my having one of the Knaresborough seats after the Reformation. But it is hard to foresee the movements of the popular mind for a year or two which in these times may be equal to as many centuries in times of quiet. It would I suppose be best for me to retire and I am disposed to wish that I had done so in November.

A month later he commented: 'I had no idea how unpleasant a parliamentary life that of a subaltern placeman is.'

As the reinforced Whigs assembled to renew the reform debate, Macaulay saw a good deal of his fellow-historian. Of a dinner at Sir George Philips on 9 June, Thomas reported to his sister Hannah: 'Mackintosh was very agreeable; and, as usually happens when I meet him, I learned something from him.' Perhaps his most valuable inheritance from Sir James was the realisation politics was a mistress whose favours could not be shared permanently with literature. Macaulay remained aware through life of the parallels between their two careers, from common admiration of Addison to the hours they dissipated in the Holland House circle. Above all he was haunted by Mackintosh's failure to write his great history of the Revolution and after—when he died he left a fragment which had only just reached the point at which King James II abdicated in 1688.

His voluminous notes were passed to Macaulay, whose own five-volume work became a classic, of literature if not of history. But it fell well short of its target, for in the introduction he told readers: 'I purpose to write the history of England from the accession of King James the Second down to a time which is within the memory of men still living.' He had reached 1701 when he died, which was the limit of the material gathered by his predecessor. Macaulay expressed warm appreciation of this valuable research, but he did not do so until four-fifths of the way through his first volume, and then only in a modest footnote.

When the younger man came to write in *The Edinburgh Review* of his friend's fragment he underlined Mackintosh's fairness, even finding some extenuation for Judge Jeffrey's ferocity because he was a sick man at the time of the Bloody Assizes. Macaulay drew a delightful contrast between the author and that other contemporary historian, Hallam:

> He was singularly mild, calm, and impartial, in his judgments of men and of parties. Almost all the distinguished writers who have treated of English history are advocates. Mr Hallam and Sir James Mackintosh alone are entitled to be called judges. But the extreme austerity of Mr Hallam takes away something from the pleasure of reading his learned, eloquent and judicious writings. He is a judge, but a hanging judge. His black cap is in constant requisition . . . Sir James, perhaps, erred a little on the other side. He liked a maiden assize, and came away with white gloves, after sitting in judgment on batches of the most notorious offenders . . . He had a quick eye for the redeeming parts of a character, and a large toleration for the infirmities of men exposed to strong temptations.

As Lord John's Reform Bill again reached its second reading in the Commons on 4 July, Mackintosh added his voice to the debate. Two very different men recorded their impressions of the scene. Radical John Hobhouse wrote: 'He spoke two hours, and spoke very well indeed—rather "caviare to the general", but sound and profound.' Henry Lytton Bulwer, just elected to Parliament, found him 'gaunt and ungainly, his accent Scotch, his voice monotonous', while his gestures consisted of 'the regular and graceless vibrations of two long arms'. but he added: 'The speech itself was remarkable. Overflowing with thought and knowledge, containing sound general principles . . . undisfigured by the violence of party spirit.'

It was too learned and too long—Macaulay said he spoke to empty benches. But he went to the heart of the matter when he reminded Tory opponents their hero Pitt believed the state of the representation should be changed with changed circumstances, and underlined the dangers of revolution if they refused to grasp the nettle of reform:

> We are now called upon to pay the arrears of a hundred and sixty years of an unreformed representation. The immediate settlement of this constitutional balance is now difficult;—it may not be without danger; but it is become necessary that we may avoid ruin. It may soon be impossible to save us by that, or by any other means.

He quoted Cicero's *De Legibus* in favour of making accessions to popular power, a quotation turned against him by Sir Robert Peel who, having had two nights to prepare his speech, remarked the Roman had also warned against 'the haste in which changes of form of government are sometimes determined on'. The second reading was carried by 367 votes to 231. The long process of pushing the Bill through its committee stage, and bullying the Lords into accepting it, continued.

Writing from the Commons on 15 July 1831 James told Fanny Allen: 'We have been several nights in a committee on the Bill but we have made scarcely any progress.' Sitting one night for six hours gave him so severe a headache he was obliged to pair on the following three evenings, after putting in an appearance at the House. He sent a note to Lady Holland that he had to attend almost every division, although he passed most of the time reading novels in a room adjoining the chamber. He could not supply her with the gossip she demanded of her correspondents: 'I know nothing out of the H of C. Any news from the world without would be very acceptable. At present the House is too provokingly occupied with its own business to do its duty as a club room.'

He seemed conscious time was running out for both of them when an ailing Sir Walter Scott visited London on his way to the Mediterranean in October. Lockhart, in his biography of his father-in-law, mentioned the frequency with which Sir James 'that master of every social charm and grace' called to see his fellow-Scot:

> Sir James's kind assiduity was the more welcome that his appearance banished the politics of the hour, on which his old friend's thoughts were too apt to brood. Their conversation, wherever it might begin, was sure to fasten ere long on Lochaber.

Another visitor to London was his favourite sister-in-law. Fanny reported to Jessie from Great Cumberland Street: 'I think Mackintosh misses poor Kitty often in his house, and the recollections of her perversenesses do not strike him now.'

The end of 1831 saw one last change of residence, this time to 15 Langham Place. The move came at an awkward time for Fanny Mackintosh. Her mother's death did not remove all obstacles to her courtship by Hensleigh Wedgwood. Mary Rich took upon herself the role of reproving chaperon to her 31-year-old stepsister. Hensleigh wrote to his beloved: 'She is not your mother and why should she interfere between you and me?'

Mackintosh himself was unhappy at the thought of losing his daughter, although disclaiming any wish to influence her choice of husband. Hensleigh wrote him complaining 'Mrs Rich seems to grudge me every minute I spend in Fanny's company and keeps such a watch over me as is quite intolerable.' He added diplomatically: 'If ever I am able to marry Fanny I should not wish to take her away from you if things could be managed otherwise.' Caution was required, since he had little income of his own and was relying on help from Sir James in obtaining a public post.

No appeal from a spirited young man ever went unheeded by Mackintosh. Hensleigh reported to his father 'he has behaved like an angel', writing off to Lord Lansdowne, Lord Brougham, Denman and others. Nevertheless it was not until late in 1831 that a place, a police magistracy, became available and enabled the couple to marry.

The wedding, in January 1832, had elements of farce. Two days before Hensleigh was ordered to bed with a bilious fever, and sent word for Fanny to buy the ring. Then it was discovered that as newcomers to the district they could not be married at All Souls, Langham Place. Frances Wedgwood, the groom's sister, said in a letter to another brother: 'Hensleigh went to the Clerk of All Souls who seemed to think there would be no difficulty in H's swearing that they had lived 15 days at Langham though they had only lived 5, however H chose to have a conscience and would not do it.' The wedding was rearranged for St Andrew's, Holborn.

Lady Holland promised to send a dress of white poplin, but it did not arrive in time and the bride borrowed the dress Frances was wearing. Robert Mackintosh almost missed his sister's wedding, being away from his Oxford quarters when her letter arrived. There was confusion at the church, well attended by the many Miss Thorntons and Inglises, because the carriage sent to fetch Hensleigh was delayed. However when the ceremony proceeded, 'Hensleigh and Fanny behaved with decorum and they neither of them had their spectacles on,' Frances wrote, but she complained Dr William Dealtry, the rector from Clapham, 'made the service very long by reading the tiresome exhortations at the end'. Perhaps this was why the bride's father asked Frances to stuff a new novel in his pocket before they set out for the church. After a breakfast for more than forty people the couple set off for Hastings in Sir James's carriage. They were to make their home with him.

The Reform Bill was still passing through the Commons, requiring frequent attendance from the subaltern placeman. Mrs Katharine Thomson, meeting him, found he was deathly pale but declared:

> Never did I see him more cheerful. An early friend of his family, a Scottish Lady of condition, upwards of eighty, sat at his hospitable board, and recalled to him the days of Adam Smith, whom Sir James remembered, and spoke of the childhood of Harry Brougham, Frank Horner and James Mackintosh, as if they were but young men still, and she—already stepping into her grave—in her prime.

The last recorded speech by Sir James was delivered in the Commons on 9 February 1832, on a subject which had interested him for several years, the disputed succession to the Portuguese throne. The Queen of that country expressed her appreciation by the gift of a valuable diamond snuff-box. But his views were attacked in an open letter, running to some 300 pages, from William Walton, who had travelled on the Iberian Peninsula and in Latin America, and whose father had represented Spain as consul in Liverpool. He also accused the knight of having been 'once so instrumental in inoculating the public with the South American loan, mining and colonizing mania'. According to Walton, Mackintosh's speeches in support of independence for the former colonies, and newspaper backing for it, were largely to blame for the subsequent upheavals in those countries and the loss of £30m by British investors. It was about this time his victim was heard to exclaim that he should like to have lived in quieter times.

Late in February Mackintosh suffered a mishap while eating, a chicken bone lodged in his throat and it was days before doctors discovered what had happened and removed the bone. Soon afterwards the Sismondis, who were visiting England, called on him before returning to Switzerland with Fanny Allen. Her pen had lost none of its point. Writing to Elizabeth Wedgwood she said she had twice accompanied Mrs Rich to hear Edward Irving preach 'and I am come out of my experiences more unbelieving than I was before—indeed I think I had a little belief'.

James continued to do his duty, such as it was, at the board of control, now headed by his cousin Charles Grant, son of the man who had been

12 and 13 (above) Relief bust of Sir James with four other worthies on a wall of what was formerly the India Office, in the quadrangle of the Foreign and Commonwealth Office: (below) an enlarged portion showing the relief bust of Sir James. Photographed by permission of the Foreign and Commonwealth Office.

14 The second of the two memorials to Sir James in London is the monument in Whigs' Corner, Westminster Abbey, by William Theed, Jnr, with that of fellow-MP George Tierney in the background. The inscription reads: To the memory of Sir James Mackintosh Jurist, Philosopher, Historian, Statesman From his youth a generous advocate of the oppressed Honoured in manhood as a Judge, learned, wise and merciful: Studious in mature age as a legislator To moderate the rigour of harsh laws and to broaden the foundations of national freedom This Monument was erected by friends of all parties and of all ranks who admired his writings delighted in his society and loved him for himself: and when a generation had passed away after his death The inscription was added by those survivors who still looked back to him with affectionate veneration.

Photographed by permission of the Dean and Chapter of Westminster Abbey.

his overlord when he was recorder of Bombay. He served on the board's judicial committee. He also continued to write dutifully to Lady Holland, telling her he had been ill again:

> I have suffered so acutely that it cost me a violent effort to go through a wearisome conversation with Sir E H Earl and Sir A Johnston on Indian appeals which have been referred to them by Grant. E is a gentleman of mild manners. J is the most abominable of bores. I do not venture out and am invisible to visitors so that I have no news.

Nevertheless he was still reading steadily, and had some comment to make on a newly-published life of Dr William Cullen, the venerable professor against whom Dr John Brown rebelled in Edinburgh in the 1780s. Current affairs did not escape notice, including an attack on Sir Francis Palgrave's work in trying to bring some order to the Public Records, a parliamentary enterprise which had Mackintosh's strong support: 'I am sorry for the plot against poor Palgrave and for his folly in a scuffle with a clerk—scandalously misrepresented in the *Globe* and the *Times* . . .

'I write in pain.'

A pencil note on the letter runs 'This is his last letter to me E V Holland'. He had been frail for so long that few who saw him realised that, at sixty-six, he was slipping away from life, lacking the stamina to overcome the after-effects of the damage done by the chicken bone. One who did was his daughter Fanny, who noted:

> He spoke habitually more of his family and friends, of his children and grandchildren, than from the nature and variety of his occupatiosn he had often opportunities of indulging in.
>
> But the two most remarkable changes which I observed in him at this period were regarding politics and his own health, both of which had for many years naturally engaged a large share of his attention—the one from inclination, the other from a long course of delicate health; he now spoke rarely upon either . . .
>
> Though he suffered constant pain, he did not look to medical assistance with much anxiety or hope. He took the medicines offered to him, but he had lost all interest in them. Nor did he as formerly watch for the arrival of Dr Darling, though he entertained a very high opinion of his skill, and felt much indebted to him for his unwearied attention to him during a period of many years.

Pious daughters sometimes indulge in wishful thinking when describing the good end made by parents. But there was the ring of truth about the account left by Fanny, who was a sensible woman of some maturity:

He would speak of God with more reverence and awe than I have almost ever met with. His voice fell—his whole person seemed to bow down, as if conscious of a superior presence . . . Our Lord Jesus Christ was very frequently the subject of his thoughts; he seemed often perplexed and unable to comprehend much of his history. He once said to me, 'It is a great mystery to me—I cannot understand it.'

James died in his home at Langham Place at a quarter to six on 30 May. He was buried five days later in the Hampstead grave that held his infant son, the first Robert, and his daughter Elizabeth. Other members of the family were to follow including a baby grandson, the child of Fanny and Hensleigh. The mother whose fervent wish was to lie with Elizabeth had been buried at Chene. Sir James and Lady Mackintosh were parted in death as so often in life.

His other memorial was a bust among the politicians in Westminster Abbey. A high-powered committee was formed to arrange a suitable epitaph, but seems to have fallen under the spell of the departed arch-procrastinator. A quarter of a century later Lord Lansdowne wrote to Lord John Russell he was

> in possession of the balance of the subscription, which Sir R Inglis when he found himself dying committed to my charge whilst you had undertaken to write the inscription. Should anything happen to me, not very improbable at my age, I should appear to have kept the money which is at Coutts in my name and done nothing with or concerning it
>
> Most I am sorry to say of the committee have died, whilst you were composing or supposed to be composing the epitaph, and if you cannot prevail upon yourself to put your shoulder to the wheel, which with you I am persuaded need only be the work of an hour, my only recourse will be the first time I am again in London, to seek out the survivors of the committee, submit a very short epitaph of my own to them, and thus acquit them as well as myself.

Eventually an Erskine grandson wrote it.

Mackintosh did not see the Reform Bill become law on 7 June 1832. But it seemed fitting that in the picture by S W Reynolds entitled 'The Reform Bill Receiving the King's assent by Royal Commission' he was included, standing with his friends Macaulay, Jeffrey, and Charles Grant.

The dead knight's affairs were soon settled. Although his effects were sworn at between £8,000 and £9,000 when administration of the 1826 will was granted, debts and expenses left only £863 to be shared by his five children. He lived on in the memory of friends. Eight years after his death Lady Holland told a visitor when she felt lonely she went into her library and imagined 'Romilly on that chair, Mackintosh here, Horner there'. Of the many tributes paid over the years, three might have pleased him best:

In looks and character, he was like Cicero (the Duc de Broglie).
Few men have had so many intimate friends (Andrew Preston Peabody,
editor *North American Review*).
He *was* a good man (Bookbinder Macdonald).

Mackintosh's works are no longer widely read. His varied talents are
displayed to more advantage in the two-volume 1,000 pages of *Memoirs*,
including extracts from letters, journals, speeches and lectures, edited by
his son 150 years ago. These were less afflicted by filial reticence than
most contemporary biographies. But William Erskine, who assisted
Robert, and deplored the burning of some manuscripts his father-in-law
had carefully boxed up, wrote despairingly, 'Who can give to others who
did not know him an idea of his diversified powers?' Croker said of the
book: 'This is, though not a good *Life* of this eminent man, a most
interesting and entertaining collection of Mackintoshiana.'

When Fanny Allen received it she wrote to a friend:

> I cannot tell you what pleasure it gives me, to read a little of these memoirs.
> When I am dressing for dinner the book is on my table, and I am going
> over it now for the second time. I cheat myself thus—and it seems to me as
> if I had spent half an hour in M's company.

It is clear Mackintosh married the wrong Miss Allen. Fanny might
have managed him better. She would certainly have loved him more.

Selected Bibliography

PUBLISHED WORKS OF SIR JAMES MACKINTOSH

Arguments Concerning the Constitutional Right of Parliament to Appoint a Regent (1788)
Vindiciae Gallicae: A Defence of the French Revolution and its English admirers against the accusations of the Right Hon. Edmund Burke, including some strictures on the late production of Mons de Calonne (1791)
A Letter to the Right Honourable William Pitt (1792)
A Letter from Earl Moira to Colonel McMahon (1798)
A Discourse on the Study of the Law of Nature and Nations (1799)
The Trial of Jean Peltier for Libel against Napoleon Buonaparte (1803, it contains Mackintosh's speech for the defence)
Proceedings at a General Meeting of the Loyal North Britons (1803, includes his speech to the meeting)
Plan of a Comparative Vocabulary of Indian Languages (1806)
Dissertation on the Progress of Ethical Philosophy (1830)
The Life of Sir Thomas More (1830)
The History of England (3 vols 1830–32)
History of the Revolution in England in 1688, prefaced by a notice of the Life, Writings and Speeches of Sir James Mackintosh (by William Bayley Wallace, 1834)
Memoirs, edited by his son, Robert James Mackintosh (2 vols 1835)
Inaugural Addresses, ed J B Hay (1839) includes his Inaugural Address and Parting Address as Rector of the University of Glasgow
Speeches, 1787–1831 (1840)
Miscellaneous Works, ed Robert James Mackintosh (3 vols 1846)
Disputatio Physiologica inauguratio de actione musculari (1787)
Royal Medical Society Paper No XVIII on Intermittent Fever

Mackintosh was a prolific journalist. From 1795–1800 he contributed to *The Monthly Review*, the principal articles being those on William Bradford, Edmund Burke, Richard Payne Knight, Edward Gibbon, William Roscoe, D O'Bryen, Thomas Erskine, George Moore and Robert Hall. From 1812 to 1826 he was an *Edinburgh Reviewer*; several of his contributions were reprinted in the *Miscellaneous Works*. For the *British Critic* in January 1801 he reviewed *L'Homme des Champs* by M. L'Abbé Delille, and for *The Foreign Quarterly Review* (November 1829) he wrote an account of Jeremy Bentham's works and his translator, Etienne Dumont.

Mackintosh's *Character of C J Fox*, originally published by the *Bombay Courier*, was reprinted in Dr Samuel Parr's *Characters of the late Charles James Fox*, while his *Character of Canning* was reprinted in *The Gentleman's Magazine* in May 1835. Before he became Recorder of Bombay he wrote much for *The Morning Chronicle*, *The Morning Post* and other newspapers; after his return he was an occasional contributor to the first. But, apart from those mentioned in the text of this book, few of his articles can be identified with certainty

UNPUBLISHED WORKS

Some Account of Holland House by Sir J Mackintosh & others (Holland House Papers, BL Add Ms 51656/7)
Revision of the System of Police founded on a Report framed by the late Recorder Sir James Mackintosh (East India Company Bombay Public Letters Collection F/4/384 9794 16 Jany 1813)

MANUSCRIPT SOURCES

The Political Ideas and Activities of Sir James Mackintosh (1765–1832): *a study in Whiggism between 1789 and 1832*, Jane L Rendall. Unpublished PhD Thesis Univ of London, 1972

There are several substantial collections of manuscripts relating to Mackintosh and his family, two of them still in private hands as I write. Others are in the British Library (mainly in the Holland House Papers), the University of Keele (Wedgwood Archives), the National Library of Scotland, Scottish Record Office (principally GD 128/48 series), the National Register of Archives (Scotland) (Blair Adam Papers), and the India Office Section of the British Library.

Smaller collections, sometimes consisting of only one letter, can be found in the University of Durham (The Earl Grey Papers), Yale University, the D M S Watson Library of University College, Princeton University, John Murray Archives, the National Library of Wales, *The Times* Archives, the Bodleian Library, Cambridge University Library, Hereford Record Office, Christ Church Library, Oxford (Hallam Papers), Huntington Library, California, while there are references to Mackintosh in the Longman archives held at Reading University, in the Horner Papers at the British Library of Political and Economic Science, and the manuscript notes by Simon Fraser Mackintosh entitled *A Collection of Historical Sketches and Anecdotes . . . relating to the Mackintoshes and Clan Chattan* (Scottish Record Office).

BOOKS (Classified by subject rather than author)

General Works

British History in the Nineteenth Century, George Macaulay Trevelyan (1922)
The Political History of England Vol XI 1801 to 1837, the Hon George C Brodrick and J K Fotheringham (1906)
English Historical Documents Vol XI ed A Aspinall and E Anthony Smith (1959)
The History of Parliament: The House of Commons 1754–1790 Vol III, ed Sir Lewis Namier and John Brooke (1964); and 1790–1820 Vol IV, ed R G Thorne (Secker & Warburg, 1986)
Parliamentary Representation 1832: England and Wales, J Holladay Philbin (1965)
English Literature 1815–1832, Ian Jack (Vol X Oxford History of English Literature, 1963)

British Literary Magazines: The Romantic Age, ed Alvin Sullivan (Greenwood Press, 1983)
A History of Philosophy, Vol VIII Bentham to Russell, Rev Father Frederick Copleston, S J (1966)
The London Daily Press 1772–1792, Lucyle T Werkmeister (1963)
A Newspaper History of England 1792–1793, Lucyle T Werkmeister
Politics and the Press c1780–1850, A Aspinall (1949)
Biographical Dictionary of Modern British Radicals, Vol I, ed Joseph O Baylen and Norbert J Grossman (Harvester Press/Humanities Press, 1979)
Reforms and Reformers of England, Henry Brewster Stanton (1853)
The Age of Reform, Sir Ernest Llewellyn Woodward (1938)
The Passing of the Great Reform Bill, Sir James Ramsay Montagu Butler (1914)
The English Jacobins: Reformers in late Eighteenth Century England Carl B Cone (1968)
Utopia and Revolution, Melvin J Lasky (1976)
The Whigs in Opposition 1815–1830, Austin Mitchell (1967)
His Majesty's Opposition 1714–1830, Archibald S Foord (1964)
That Sunny Dome: A Portrait of Regency Britain, Donald A Low (1977)
A Complete Collection of State Trials, Vols 25 and 27, Thomas Jones Howell (1818 and 1820)
Cases of Controverted Elections in the Second Parliament of the United Kingdom, Robert Henry Peckwell (1805)

Mainly Biographical

The Sexagenarian; or the Recollections of a Literary Life, Rev William Beloe (1817)
The Works of Jeremy Bentham, Vol X, ed John Bowring (1843)
City of Gold: The Biography of Bombay, Gillian Tindall (Temple Smith, 1982)
Glimpses of Old Bombay and Western India, James Douglas (1900)
Henry Brougham 1778–1868: His Public Career, Robert Stewart (Bodley Head, 1986)
Byron's Letters and Journals, ed Leslie A Marchand, Vols III–V (1974–1976)
Literary Reminiscences of Thomas Campbell, Vol II, *Yesterday and Today*, Vol II, and *Personal Reminiscences of Eminent Men*, Vol II, Cyrus Redding (1860–1867)
Canning: Politician and Statesman, Peter Dixon (1976)
Castlereagh, Ione Leigh (1951)
Rural Rides, Vol I, William Cobbett, ed G D H and Margaret Cole (1930)
Memorials of his Time, Henry Cockburn (1856)
The Collected Works of Samuel Taylor Coleridge, Vol I, eds Lewis Patton and Peter Mann (1971), and Vol III, ed David V Erdman (Routledge & Kegan Paul/Princeton University Press; 1978)
Collected Letters of Samuel Taylor Coleridge, Vol I, ed Earl Leslie Griggs (1956)
The Notebooks of Samuel Taylor Coleridge, Vols II and III, ed Kathleen Coburn (1957 and 1973)
Samuel Taylor Coleridge: A Bondage of Opium, Molly Lefebure (1974)
Omniana or horae otiosores, Robert Southey and Samuel Taylor Coleridge (1812)
Creevey's Life and Times, ed John Gore (1934)
An Essay on Medical Economy, Dr George Darling (1814)
The Autobiography of Charles Darwin, ed Nora Barlow (1958)
Stags and Serpents: The Story of the House of Cavendish and the Dukes of Devonshire, John Pearson (Macmillan, 1983)
Letters to 'Ivy' from the first Earl of Dudley, ed S H Romilly (1905)
A Memoir of Maria Edgeworth, Mrs Frances Anne Edgeworth (1867)
The Letters of Ralph Waldo Emerson, ed Ralph L Rusk (1939)

Charles James Fox, John W Derry (1972)

Fox, Christopher Hobhouse (1934)

The Gazetteer 1735–1797, Robert L Haig (1960)

The Siege of Gibraltar, T H McGuffie (1965)

The Letters of King George IV 1812–1830, ed A Aspinall

Memoirs of George IV, Robert Huish (1831)

A Fantasy of Reason: The Life and Thought of William Godwin, Don Locke (Routledge & Kegan Paul 1980)

The Life of William Godwin, Ford K Brown (1926)

St Leon, William Godwin (1799)

Personal Memoirs, Vol I, Pryse Lockhart Gordon (1830)

Letters on India, Maria Graham (1814)

Maria, Lady Callcott, Rosamund Brunel Gotch (1937)

Extracts from the Diary of a Lover of Literature, Thomas Green (1810)

The Greville Memoirs, ed Henry Reeve (1875)

Some Account of the Life and Opinions of Charles, second Earl Grey, Lieut-Col Charles Grey (1861)

Reminiscences of the Reverend Robert Hall, John Greene (1832)

The Spirit of the Age, William Hazlitt (1825)

On the Present State of Parliamentary Eloquence, William Hazlitt (1820)

Recollections of a Long Life, Lord Broughton (John Cam Hobouse), ed Lady Dorchester (1910)

The Holland House Circle, Lloyd Sanders (1908)

The Home of the Hollands, the Earl of Ilchester (1937)

The Sovereign Lady: A Life of Elizabeth Vassall, third Lady Holland, Sonia Keppel (1974)

The Journal of Elizabeth Lady Holland, Vol I, *Elizabeth, Lady Holland to her Son 1821–1845* and *The Journal of the Hon Henry Edward Fox*, all edited by the Earl of Ilchester (1908, 1946 and 1923)

Further Memoirs of the Whig Party 1807–1821, Henry Richard Vassall, Third Lord Holland, ed Lord Stavordale (1905)

Memoirs of John Horne Tooke, Alexander Stephens (1813)

Memoirs and Correspondence of Francis Horner MP, ed L Horner (1843)

Young Charles Lamb 1775–1802, Winifred F Courtney (New York University Press/ Macmillan, 1982)

The Letters of Thomas Babington Macaulay, Vols I, II and VI, ed Thomas Pinney (1974)

Thomas Babington Macaulay: The Shaping of the Historian, John Clive (1973)

A History of the Clan MacGillivray, Robert McGillivray and George B MacGillivray (1973)

The Clan Mackintosh, Jean M Dunlop (1960)

The Mackintoshes and Clan Chattan, A M Mackintosh (1903)

An Account of the Confederation of Clan Chattan, C Fraser-Mackintosh (1898)

The Mackintosh Muniments 1442–1820, ed Henry Paton (1903)

Antiquarian Notes (first and second series 1865 & 1897); and *Letters of Two Centuries Chiefly Connected with Inverness and the Highlands from 1616 to 1815* (1890), Charles Fraser-Mackintosh of Drummond

A Fragment on Mackintosh, James Mill (1835)

Memoirs of William Lamb, Second Viscount Melbourne, W MacCullagh Torrens (1980)

Memoirs, Journal and Correspondence of Thomas Moore, ed Lord John Russell (1853–1856)

History of Nairnshire, George Bain (1928)

Selections from the Correspondence of the late Macvey Napier, edited by his son, Macvey Napier (1879)

By the Banks of the Ness, Mairi A MacDonald (Paul Harris, 1982)

Dr Parr: A Portrait of the Whig Dr Johnson, Warren Derry (1966)

Memoirs of Rev Samuel Parr, Rev William Field (1828)

The Works of Samuel Parr, Vol I, John Johnstone (1828)

Mr Secretary Peel, Norman Gash (1961)

Sir Robert Ker Porter's Caracas Diary, ed Walter Dupouy (1966)

Baghdad in Bygone Days, Constance M Alexander (1928) (In all but name this is a biography of Claudius James Rich and his wife)

The Italian Journal of Samuel Rogers, ed J R Hale (1956)

Recollections of the Table Talk of Samuel Rogers, ed Morchard Bishop (Oliver Stonor, 1952)

The Early Life of Samuel Rogers, P W Clayden (1887)

Diary, Reminiscences and Correspondence of Henry Crabb Robinson, Vol II, ed Thomas Sadler (1869)

Valiant Crusade: The History of the RSPCA, Arthur W Moss (1961)

Memoranda of a Residence at the Court of London (2nd series), Richard Rush (1845)

The Life of Lord John Russell, Sir Spencer Walpole (1889)

Opium and the Romantic Imagination, Alethea Hayter (1968)

The Later Correspondence of Lord John Russell, Vol I, ed G P Gooch (1925)

Collections and Recollections by One who has kept a Diary, G W E Russell (1899)

The Journal of Sir Walter Scott, ed W E K Anderson (1972)

Memoirs of the Life of Sir Walter Scott, John Gibson Lockhart (1837, 1838)

The Letters of Sir Walter Scott, Vol I and III, ed H J C Grierson (1932)

The Letters of Sydney Smith, ed N C Smith (1953)

Sydney Smith, Alan S Bell (Clarendon Press, Oxford, 1980)

The Smith of Smiths, Hesketh Pearson (1934)

The Spencers of Althorp, Georgina Battiscombe (Constable 1984)

Madame de Staël, Margaret Leland Goldsmith (1938)

Letters from the Lake Poets, ed Mary Stuart (1889)

A Memoir of the Life and Writings of the late William Taylor of Norwich, ed J W Robberds (1843)

Memoir of Thomas Thomson, Advocate, Cosmo Innes (1854)

Marion Thornton: A Domestic Biography, E M Forster (1956)

Life, Letters and Journals of George Ticknor, Vol I, ed George S Hillard (1876)

Notes and Materials for the History of University College, W P Ker (1898)

A Letter addressed to Sir James Mackintosh on his Motion respecting the Affairs of Portugal, William Walton (1829)

The Wedgwood Circle 1730–1897, Barbara and Hensleigh Wedgwood (Studio Vista, 1980)

The Value of a Maimed Life: Extracts from the Manuscript Notes of Thomas Wedgwood, selected by Margaret Olivia Tremayne (1912)

Tom Wedgwood: The First Photographer, R B Litchfield (1903)

A Group of Englishmen . . . being the records of the Younger Wedgwoods, Eliza Meteyard (1871)

Emma Darwin: A Century of Letters, edited by her daughter Henrietta Litchfield (1915)

Memoirs and Correspondence of the most noble Richard Marquess Wellesley, Vol II, Robert R Pearce (1846)

The 'Pope' of Holland House: Selections from the Correspondence of John Wishaw, ed Lady Seymour (1906)

The Love Letters of William and Mary Wordsworth, ed Beth Darlington (Chatto and Windus, 1982)

The Letters of William and Dorothy Wordsworth: The Middle Years, Part I, arranged and edited by the late Ernest de Selincourt; revd Mary Moorman (1969)

ARTICLES AND MISCELLANEOUS PUBLICATIONS

The Athenaeum, 18 March 1828, pp 249–50, 'Sketches of Contemporary Authors—Mackintosh' (attributed to John Sterling)

Blackwood's Magazine, May 1819, pp 197–9. 'A few Remarks on the New Whig Guide' (attributed to John Wilson); July 1823, pp 93–8, 'Vindiciae Gallicae', John Gibson Lockhart

The British Museum Quarterly, Vol XXVII, 1963/64, pp 18–21, 'The Rich Manuscripts', J R Fawcett Thompson

The Charles Lamb Bulletin, October 1977, pp 73–92, 'New Lamb Texts from the Albion', Winifred F Courtney

Clan Chattan Journal (passim)

The Edinburgh Review, July 1835, pp 265–322; October 1835 pp 205–255 (articles on Mackintosh by, respectively, Lord Macaulay, and Lord Jeffrey)

Eighteenth Century Studies, Vol 7, 1973/4 pp 193–206, 'James Mackintosh, Burke and the Cause of Reform', William Christian

English Historical Review, Oct 1935, pp 620–38, 'The Leadership of the Whig Party in the House of Commons', Michael Roberts: July 1926, pp 389–411, 'English Party organization in the Early Nineteenth Century', A Aspinall

Fraser's Magazine, Vol 65, 1862, pp 595–602, 'Editors and Newspaper and Periodical writers of the Last Generation', by an old apprentice of the Law (A V Kirwan)

The Gentleman's Magazine November 1887, pp 472–87, 'Coleridge Among the Journalists', H R Fox-Bourne

The Law Magazine, August 1832, pp 163–73, 'Recollections of Sir James Mackintosh', by an old pupil

The Metropolitan, May–August 1832, p 219, 'The Life and Writings of Sir James Mackintosh', Thomas Campbell

The National Library of Wales Journal, Vol XVII, 1971–72, pp 136–60, 217–37, 321–42, 'A Pembrokeshire County Family in the Eighteenth Century', Elizabeth Inglis-Jones

New Monthly Magazine, July 1832, pp 42–9, 'The Illustrious Dead: Sir James Mackintosh' (attributed to Henry Bulwer)

North American Review, October 1832, pp 433–72, 'Sir James Mackintosh', A H Everett; October 1845, pp 483–5, '*The Critics*', Edwin P Whipple; April 1848, pp 261–80, 'Sir James Mackintosh', Andrew P Peabody

Notes and Queries, 6 January 1855, p 8, 'School and College Fees Eighty Years Since', R Carruthers; 4 May 1895, pp 354–5, 'Tomb of Sir James Mackintosh', John T Page

Parliamentary Affairs Vols XIV and XV (1961/2) Series of eight articles on 'The Old House of Commons and its Members', A Aspinall

Promoter Benefit Company prospectus

Public Characters of 1806, pp 208–59, 'Sir James Mackintosh'

The Quarterly Review, July 1835, pp 250–94, 'review of Mackintosh's *Memoirs*', J W Croker; October 1915, pp 540–54, 'Allens, Wedgwoods and Darwins', Mrs Humphry Ward

Renaissance and Modern Studies (university of Nottingham) 21, pp 106–18, James Mackintosh: Vindiciae Gallicae', James T Boulton

The Royal Engineers Journal, April 1912, pp 245–62, 'A Lady's Experiences in the Great Siege of Gibraltar', Diary of Mrs Green

Tait's Magazine, May 1834, pp247–58, Thomas De Quincey

The Times Literary Supplement, 9 April 1970, p 388, 'An unpublished Letter on the *Edinburgh Review*', A S Bell

Transactions of the Gaelic Society of Inverness, Vol XIX 5 December 1894, pp 107–10 'Minor Highland Families', No VII, 'The Mackintoshes of Kellachie', Charles Fraser-Mackintosh

Transactions of the Royal Historical Society, Fifth Series, Vol 8 (1958) 'Dr Joseph Priestley, John Wilkinson and the French Revolutionists', Dr W H Chaloner

Outline of Mackintosh's Career

1765	Birth at Aldourie
1775	To school at Fortrose
1778	Declares himself a Whig
1780	Death of mother in Gibraltar. At Aberdeen University, where he begins to study Cicero
1782	Falls in love with Miss Scott
1784	Goes to Edinburgh to study medicine and lead a life of dissipation. Elected to the Speculative Society and speaks against the Slave Trade.
1785	Attends Brae Lochaber with Clan Chief
1787	Qualifies as a doctor
1788	Settles in London. Death of father makes him Mackintosh of Kyllachy and he turns his hand to journalism. His first political pamphlet on behalf of the future Prince Regent
1789	Marries Catharine Stuart. Tour of Low Countries and birth of daughter Mary
1790	Back in London. Becomes Foreign editor of *The Oracle*. Commences law studies
1791	Publication of *Vindiciae Gallicae* wins admiration of leading Whigs. Meets Dr Parr
1792	Attacks William Pitt in pamphlet. Birth of second daughter Maitland. Friendship with George Canning begins. Accepts honorary citizenship of Republican France
1793	Shelters Joseph Gerrald, later transported on sedition charges
1794	Birth and death of first son
1795	Called to the Bar. Birth of third daughter Kitty
1796	Visits Burke, who completes his disillusionment with French Revolution
1797	Death of first wife
1798	Coleridge seeks his aid over money and play. Second marriage to Catherine Allen brings him into the Wedgwood Circle. Offer of partnership in *The Morning Post* from Daniel Stuart. Foundation of The King of Clubs
1799	Lectures on the Law of Nature and Nations and quarrels with Godwin. First visit to Holland House
1800	Denounces French Revolution. Scurrilous attacks on him by Coleridge, later echoed by Charles Lamb. Birth of favourite daughter Fanny
1801	Friendship with Sydney Smith begins

1802   Birth of second son who also dies in infancy. Meets Napoleon in Paris

1803   Defence of Peltier and attack on Napoleon. Birth of last daughter Elizabeth. Knighted on appointment as Recorder of Bombay

1804   Takes up duties in India and embarks on reformation of police, penal laws and prisons. Founds Bombay Literary Society

1805   His stand against corruption upsets local establishment

1806   Birth of Robert James, an heir who would outlive Mackintosh. Takes additional post of judge of a court of vice-admiralty in Bombay

1808   Suffers first severe illness. Daughter Mary marries Claudius James Rich

1809   Meets Maria Graham. Maitland Mackintosh marries William Erskine

1810   Lady Mackintosh returns to England

1811   Resigns as Recorder and sails home. Kitty Mackintosh becomes Lady Wiseman

1812   Rejects overtures to become government supporter from Tory prime minister and the Prince Regent

1813   Becomes a leading Whig spokesman as MP for Nairn, and an Edinburgh Reviewer. Friendship with Byron and Mme de Staël

1814   Joins The Club founded by Johnson. Champions freedom for Poland. Visits Paris, where Wellington consults him over Slave Trade, and goes on to Switzerland

1815   Powerful attack on government policy towards America

1816   Receives honorary doctorate from Oxford

1818   Becomes part-time professor at Haileybury East India College

1819   MP for Knaresborough which he represents until his death. Succeeds Sir Samuel Romilly as leading advocate of law reform and carries Commons vote to reduce capital punishment. Visit from George Ticknor

1821   Joins Dr Waugh in appeal for John Scott's widow

1822   Meets Washington Irving. Receives honorary doctorate from Harvard University

1823   Election as Rector of Glasgow University in opposition to Sir Walter Scott. Death of daughter Elizabeth. Scandal of Lady Wiseman's elopement

1824   Co-founder of the Athenaeum. Backs independence for Latin American colonies and foresees Panama Canal. Helps found RSPCA. Attends coronation of French King

1825   Presses Commons to consider Irish grievances

1826   Makes his will. Loses money in Colombian investment scheme and other ventures

1827   Becomes privy councillor. Impresses Charles Darwin. Last of many visits to Althorp

1828   Presents petition over proposals for uniting Canada

1829   Publishes *Dissertation on the Progress of Ethical Philosophy*

1830   Death of Lady Mackintosh. Publication of *History of England* begins

1831   Takes part in famous Reform Bill debates and becomes friendly with Macaulay. Brings about reconciliation of Wordsworth and Francis Jeffrey. Urges case for Coleridge to receive pension

1832   Marriage of daughter Fanny. His last letter to Lady Holland. Death. Burial at Hampstead

Index